WITH

**Books are to be returned on or before
the last date below.**

Books are to be returned on or before
the last date below.

**7-DAY
LOAN**

23 APR 1999

2 4 MAY 1999

1 6 FEB 2000

1 4 SEP 2001

2 MAR 2004

1998

6

1998

LIBREX —

3 1111 00599 1110

Transforming Socialist Economies

STUDIES OF COMMUNISM IN TRANSITION

Series Editor: Ronald J. Hill

*Professor of Soviet Government
and Fellow of Trinity College
Dublin, Eire*

Studies of Communism in Transition is an important series which applies academic analysis and clarity of thought to the recent traumatic events in eastern and central Europe. As many of the preconceptions of the last half century are cast aside, newly independent and autonomous sovereign states are being forced to address long-term, organic problems which had been suppressed by, or appeased within, the Communist system of rule.

The series is edited under the sponsorship of Lorton House, an independent charitable association which exists to advance education in and promote the academic study of communism and related political concepts.

Transforming Socialist Economies

The Case of Poland and Czechoslovakia

Martin Myant

*Reader in the Department of
Economics and Management,
University of Paisley,
Scotland*

Edward Elgar

Published by
Edward Elgar Publishing Limited
Gower House
Croft Road
Aldershot
Hants GU11 3HR
England

Edward Elgar Publishing Company
Old Post Road
Brookfield
Vermont 05036
USA

A CIP catalogue record for this book is available from the British Library

ISBN 1 85278 786 4

Printed and Bound in Great Britain by
Hartnolls Limited, Bodmin, Cornwall.

Contents

Tables

Acknowledgements

This book would have been impossible without help and encouragement from a large number of individuals. My colleagues at the University of Paisley enabled me to rearrange teaching and other responsibilities to allow for a four-month leave of absence during which I could start to write up the finished work. Visits to Czechoslovakia in 1989, 1990 and 1991 were arranged through the British Academy as were visits to Hungary in 1990 and Poland in 1991. A small grant from the Nuffield Foundation financed trips to Poland in 1990 and 1991.

I benefited from discussions with many people in those countries including research workers, academics, government officials, government ministers and businessmen. I am especially grateful for the hospitality of many friends at Czechoslovakia's federal Ministry of Finance, at the Economics Institute and the Institute of Forecasting of the Czechoslovak Academy of Sciences, at the High School of Economics in Prague, at the Economics Institute of the Slovak Academy of Sciences, at the Economics Institute of the Polish and Hungarian Academies of Sciences and at Warsaw University.

Invaluable technical assistence was provided by Peter Wilson, Michelle Page and Linda McLean. Alistair Young and Ronald Hill both made many helpful comments on an earlier version. Needless to say, any remaining mistakes are entirely the responsibility of the author.

Abbreviations

BS	*Biuletyn Statystyczny*, Statistical Bulletin, Polish statistical monthly.
CMEA	Council for Mutual Economic Assistance.
ČSKOS	Československá konfederace odborových svazů, Czechoslovak Confederation of Trade Unions.
GDP	Gross Domestic Product.
GN	*Gospodarka Narodowa*, National Economy, Polish economic monthly.
GW	*Gazeta Wyborcza*, Election Newspaper, Polish daily.
HN	*Hospodářské noviny*, Economic Newspaper, Czechoslovak economic weekly and government daily from 1991.
LD	*Lidová demokracie*, Peoples' Democracy, Czech daily.
LN	*Lidové noviny*, Peoples' Newspaper, Czech daily.
NH	*Národní hospodářství*, National Economy, Czechoslovak economic monthly.
NMP	Net Material Product.
OPZZ	Ogólnopolskie Porozumienie Związków Zawodowych, All-Polish Alliance of Trade Unions.
RP	*Rudé právo*, Red Truth, Czech daily.
SP	*Statistické přehledy*, Statistical Survey, Czechoslovak statistical monthly.
SS	*Svobodné slovo*, Free Word, Czech daily.
TS	*Tygodnik Solidarność*, Solidarity Weekly, Polish weekly.

ŻG   *Życie Gospodarcze*, Economic Life, Polish economic weekly.

ŻW   *Życie Warszawy*, Warsaw Life, Polish daily.

Introduction

The countries of East Central Europe are currently in the middle of a unique attempt to transform their centrally-planned economies into modern market systems. The aim is to achieve the kind of capitalism that already exists in the wealthy countries of Western Europe. It is seen by political leaders in Poland and Czechoslovakia as a key element in a more general transformation to bring their societies back into the mainstream of European culture. Governments in these two countries have chosen to head for their economic objective in a rapid and simple way, starting with price and exchange rate liberalisation, a sharply deflationary macroeconomic policy and speedy privatisation.

It is too early to say for certain where these societies are heading, but three points seem undeniable. The first is that economic performance has been far worse than expected not only by supporters but also by many critics of the chosen strategy. Rather than leading rapidly towards modern market economies, policies have contributed to depressions which, unless official statistics are quite extraordinarily inaccurate, are of unprecedented depth. The second point is that there is no certainty of an early recovery. There are some signs of a return to growth, but they are not yet convincing evidence of a clear trend and it will be at least several years before the 1989 levels of national income have been restored. The third point is that economic disappointments have had a strong influence on political developments. A return to the past with the reelection of Communist-dominated governments is very unlikely but, rather than the anticipated stability around new democratic institutions, political life is characterised by paralysis and division.

This book aims to trace and explain how Poland and Czechoslovakia have been led into their current difficulties. It divides into four parts with the final, brief concluding section aiming to summarise some of the possible general lessons.

1

The first part covers the heritage left from central planning. Chapter 1 shows the increasingly disappointing economic performance and creeping stagnation of the years up to 1989. This is explained by factors inherent in the economic system which was substantially different both from a market system and from the textbook model of how central planning should operate. Chapter 2 covers largely unsuccessful attempts to improve performance by various kinds of reforms. The attitudes of political leaders varied over the decades but, by the late 1980s, 'reform' had become the universal objective and even claim to legitimacy of almost all Eastern European leaderships.

It cannot be said for certain that reform could never have been successful. Things might have been very different in a different political climate, without the limitations on democracy stemming from the effective monopoly of power for one hierarchically organised ruling party. Nevertheless, reform attempts spanned more than 30 years, albeit with clear breaks and reversals on various occasions. The common failure of so many attempts, based on several different conceptions, inevitably encouraged the view that searching for a 'third way', based neither on central planning nor on Western European capitalism, was ultimately a waste of effort.

The socialist framework, meaning the overwhelming predominace of state ownership and a commitment to stability and security for the population, increasingly appeared as the most fundamental barrier to an improvement in performance. By 1989 the only reason for restricting ideas for changing the economic system within the framework of reform to socialism was that nothing more radical was likely to find acceptance from the political authorities. After the overthrow of Communist power a completely new framework could be adopted, the basis for which is outlined in Chapter 2. The term 'reform' has itself been rejected in favour of 'transformation' by many advocates of radical change. Somewhat surprisingly, this is less clearly the case in Czechoslovakia where the federal government's major economic policy document of September 1990 still carried the term 'reform' in its title.

The second and third parts of the book cover the development and effects of this new strategy in Poland and Czechoslovakia respectively. The two parts cannot follow identical structures, because the effects of and links between different policies were somewhat different between the two. In Poland there was a richer history of earlier reform attempts, the most recent of which are covered in Chapter 3. The key element of policy in the first stage of the economic transformation, which became known as the Balcerowicz programme and is covered in Chapter 4, was then agreed after minimal public discussion.

In Czechoslovakia there was less of a recent history of reform, as indicated in Chapter 7, but more of a delay between the ending of Communist power and the start of serious economic change. Chapter 8 covers this interlude during which a number of opposing ideas on economic strategy could be clarified. It has no direct parallel in Polish experience while Chapter 9 covers similar ground in the Czechoslovak case to Chapter 4.

Chapters 5 and 10 cover broadly similar issues in the two countries, concentrating on the effects of the so-called 'shock therapy' on agriculture, manufacturing and some other sectors of the economy. However, in the Czechoslovak case there was a more obvious willingness from the three governments — the Czech, Slovak and federal levels all had some powers over major policy decisions — to accept the need for policy modifications. Chapter 6, covering the Polish attempts to find a way out of depression is therefore less clearly linked to developments in individual sectors. Ideas for an alternative to permanent depression centred on the ultimately fruitless effort to 'accelerate' privatisation. In Czechoslovakia there were more visible attempts at pragmatic corrections to policies for individual sectors. Privatisation there, as covered in Chapter 11, took place within a different policy context leading to more consistency and a far greater degree of success in achieving policy objectives. The roots of this and other differences between the experiences of the two countries are taken up in the final, concluding chapter.

Part I

Reforming the Socialist Economy

1. The Failure of Planning

The Performance of the System

The usual starting point for a discussion of economic performance is the growth in national income. There are well-known reservations to using this as the only measure, not least because higher output need not always mean greater welfare for society. There are also problems with comparisons across systems. The standard Eastern Europe measure has been Net Material Product which measures the value of physical outputs minus physical inputs in the 'productive' sector. It differs from Gross Domestic Product primarily by taking account of 'non-productive' activities, such as public services, only in so far as they consume outputs from the productive sector, and by including a deduction for depreciation on fixed assets. GDP is usually more than 20 per cent higher than NMP, but the growth rate of the latter has generally been slightly higher. However, due to the greater variability of activity levels in 'productive' activities, it is significantly lower during depressions.

With these reservations in mind, Table 1.1 would appear to indicate generally rapid growth in the 1950s, as new industries were built up and labour flowed out of agriculture, but a subsequent long-run tendency to decline. The two countries differ slightly, but growth performance can be divided into roughly the same periods (Myant, 1989a, and Jezierski and Petz, 1988). Czechoslovakia suffered depression in the early 1960s, but then recovered and continued to grow through the next decade. The reasonable success of the 1970s was accompanied by favourable terms for the import of Soviet raw materials and a gradual increase in hard currency debt which reached $1.4 billion in 1975 and $6.8 billion in 1980. The depression at the start of the 1980s and relative stagnation over that decade followed attempts first to pay off that debt and then to keep it under control. By

the end of 1989 it had reached $7.9 billion, with debt service payments
equivalent to 25 per cent of hard currency exports. Against this
background, it is reasonable to refer to a downward trend in the
system's ability to generate economic growth.

*Table 1.1 Average annual per capita rates of growth in Net Material
Product in Poland and Czechoslovakia 1948-1989*

	Poland	Czechoslovakia
1948-53	12.4	8.5
1954-60	5.5	6.0
1961-65	4.9	1.2
1965-70	5.2	6.6
1971-78	7.0	4.4
1979-82	−7.4	1.1
1983-89	3.1	2.1

Source: Calculated from GUS and FSÚ, various issues.

Poland experienced the same rapid expansion in the 1950s, less of
an interruption in the early 1960s and a renewed acceleration in the
1970s. This latter phase was based on borrowing to buy technology,
but much of the investment was misdirected and the country was left
crippled by an enormous debt burden. From a level of $1.1 billion in
1970, gross debt reached $25.1 billion in 1980 with a debt service ratio
of 101 per cent (Myant, 1982, Chapter 4). This was the immediate
cause of the depression from 1978 to 1982. Growth rates for the rest
of the 1980s must be judged remarkably unimpressive. The NMP per
capita level of 1978 was never regained and debt even continued to
grow, reaching $40 billion in 1989. Set in this context, Polish
experience too is consistent with a hypothesis of steadily declining
performance.

Even these figures, however, allow for too optimistic a conclusion.
Recent comparisons of national income levels suggest that Poland and
Czechoslovakia did substantially worse than would be implied by

official statistics. Thus estimates suggested that Poland's economy was more productive than Spain's in 1950 and, if official figures are to be believed, it enjoyed higher average growth rates over the following decades. Nevertheless, the World Bank's International Comparison Project showed Spanish GDP per capita in 1985 to be 87 per cent above the Polish level (Łaski and Zięba, 1989). Czechoslovakia has yet to take part in such a major international comparative study, but available evidence points in the same direction. GDP per head had fallen to maybe 55 per cent of the Austrian level by the mid-1980s while the gap was possibly around 10 per cent in 1960 (Šujan, 1990, and Havlík, 1992). The implication, in both cases, could be a reduction of annual growth rates by around two percentage points.

The main source of inaccuracy in the official figures lies in hidden inflation. The system of central planning gave rewards for achieving output targets measured sometimes in physical, but more usually in value terms. Lower levels in the hierarchy therefore had an incentive to exaggerate output. This may have led on occasion to deliberate falsification of results. More generally, it led to efforts to win agreement for price increases. This was typically a matter for negotiation with a central authority with enterprises claiming the right to a price rise on the basis of an alleged improvement in product quality. The sectors in which this was most easily achieved were those with the least homogeneous products, and especially the investment goods sector in which almost every product may be unique.

An ambitious attempt to recalculate Czechoslovak growth rates by taking account of this and several other distortions reveals an average GDP per capita growth rate of around 2 per cent for the 1961 to 1988 period, with effective stagnation after 1976 (Nachtigal, 1991). Increases in personal consumption seem to have been exaggerated only slightly, but the error for investment was substantial. This has enormous significance in reinforcing doubts about a long-standing assumption that centrally-planned economies were driven to high levels of investment. Thus a recalculation of its share in NMP in 1988, using 1961 prices and correcting for hidden inflation in all sectors, could suggest a figure in the 5-12 per cent range, compared with 27 per cent in 1961. 1988 prices suggest a figure of 32 per cent.

This picture of increasingly stagnant and by European standards backward economies is reinforced by three further aspects of performance. The first is the low level of international competitiveness. Most exports were, in fact, not even directed into the most competitive markets. The Czechoslovak economy was reoriented in the early 1950s towards selling to the Soviet Union: around a third of NMP was exported in the 1980s, with 80 per cent of that going to socialist economies. For the larger Polish economy, only a quarter of NMP was exported, and around 40 per cent of that went to socialist economies.

Despite this apparent difference between the two, neither country could claim many successes in exporting to advanced capitalist countries apart from raw materials and other basic products, such as steel and timber. Those manufactured goods that were sold typically found a place at the bottom end of Western markets, with prices per kilogram between one-third and two-thirds of the competitive level (Myant, 1989a, pp.230-5, and 1989b, pp.3-4). Only a very few traditional industries stood up well, such as Czechoslovak crystal and isolated segments of the engineering industry.

A second aspect is the evidence of structural stagnation. The 1950s saw the rapid build-up of the most basic industries, such as mining, energy and metallurgy. The less industrialised Polish economy continued with this trend for somewhat longer. Employment in most sectors of Czechoslovak industry, however, shows near constancy from the end of the 1950s. The only substantial growth is in chemicals and engineering, while no classified sectors show significant decline. Indeed, employment in much of light industry was roughly unchanging from as far back as 1950, reflecting a low level of investment in either expansion or modernisation. The fuel, energy and metallurgy sectors accounted for 17 per cent of industrial employment in 1960 and 16 per cent in 1989. The Polish picture is different primarily because total employment grew more rapidly, but the sectoral structure displays much of the same stability. Fuel, energy and metallurgy accounted for 21 per cent of employment in 1989, against 23 per cent in 1960, and light industry was neglected very much as in Czechoslovakia (Jezierski and Petz, 1988, p.300).

This contrasts with the relatively rapid structural transformations in advanced market economies. Eastern Europe has been left with a strong bias towards those sectors which were no longer the driving force for growth in the most advanced countries by the 1970s. A particularly striking comparison is energy consumption per capita.

While household consumption was low by international standards, the level for the Czechoslovak economy as a whole in 1987 was 12 per cent above West Germany's, while Poland was only 15 per cent behind the latter, despite the substantial gap in per capita GDPs. Behind these figures lies a relatively large energy sector servicing a relatively large energy-consuming, materials-processing industry — producing steel, cement, aluminium and other basic products — which is itself inefficient by world standards.

Not only is this structure symptomatic of a relatively backward economy, it also has strictly limited potential for three reasons. First, these are sectors in which newly industrialised countries, with very low wages, are exacerbating already fierce international competition. Secondly, growth depends on exhaustible reserves of raw materials, and both Poland and Czechoslovakia can foresee the end of their traditional domestic energy sources. Thirdly, owing to the declining quality of domestically mined coal, growth has taken a form that has been highly damaging to the environment. In the mid-1980s pollution of the atmosphere per capita with sulphur in Czechoslovakia and Poland was respectively 4.8 and 2.7 times the West German level (GUS, 1990, pp.534-5).

The third disappointing aspect of performance is the low level of consumption of modern consumer goods. The indicator of car ownership per household, for example, shows Poland at under a third and Czechoslovakia around 55 per cent of the West German level in 1988. The gap in reality was much wider owing to the lower original quality and greater average age of the Eastern Europeans' vehicles. The most flattering comparison can be derived from figures on food consumption. Czechoslovakia's annual average meat consumption per head was 91 kg in 1988. The Austrian figure was 90 kg. For Poland the figure was 68 kg, not too far behind Spain's 83 kg.

The overall assessment, however, must be negative. Only three reservations can be added. The first is that growth was faster than in the inter-war period (Teichová, 1988, and Jezierski and Petz, 1988). This may once have been politically important, but is of little relevance today. The second is that the system of central planning did bring certain social benefits in the form of greater equality and social security (Kalecki, 1964, and Krejčí, 1972). The latter refers in particular to the absence of open unemployment while the former has been clearly demonstrated for both countries and helped consolidate the regimes for many years. These factors, however, have also rather lost significance with a generation that is more impressed by the gap in living standards in relation to Western Europe. The third reservation relates to performance when compared with countries outside Europe. Set in that context Poland and Czechoslovakia have not done too badly. In the words of the long-standing former dissident Karol Modzelewski (1991, p.1), socialism 'brought Poland neither into the First nor into the Third World'. It was somewhat better endowed than developing countries at the end of the 1940s and that remains its position today.

In political terms, however, none of this is as important as the broken promises of prosperity leaving a yawning gap in living standards and technology with neighbouring Western European countries. Indeed, the failure of the economy to satisfy aspirations for high consumption has been cited as one of the major causes of political instability in Poland from at least as far back as the 1960s (Jezierski and Petz, 1988, pp.325-6). It could further have contributed to the choice of an ultimately disastrous growth strategy in the 1970s (Myant, 1982) and has been named as a major factor in the economic crisis at the end of that decade (Pajestka, 1981). Frustration over living standards was never so apparent among Czechoslovaks who could see themselves as better off than other Eastern Europeans, with the exception of East Germans, and who had less contact with advanced capitalist countries. Nevertheless, by the end of the 1980s economic failure relative to Western Europe had become a factor that undermined the credibility of Communist power and contributed decisively to its collapse. It had by then become so general and so complete that it could not be explained away by individual policy mistakes.

The Objectives of Planning

There are numerous descriptive accounts of how central planning worked which can help explain its disappointing results (eg Nove, 1991, and Ellman, 1989). The philosophy behind the system was meant to be the Marxist view that conscious, which in practice meant centralised, control over economic processes would lead to a more just and more efficient system than allowed for by the 'anarchy' or 'spontaneous division of labour' of the market.

The accepted ideology provided no clear blueprint for a system of central planning, but it did shut out certain alternatives, by encouraging the view that market relations were irrelevant or counterproductive, and gave a strong bias towards seeking solutions by further centralisation. Against this background the system of central planning evolved as a series of pragmatic steps around three broad objectives.

The first was the desire to maintain balance at both the micro- and macro- levels. For individual productive inputs this could be done by rationing and central allocation, by instructions to enterprises to increase output of particular products and by directing investment and resources to overcoming those shortages that caused particular problems. Planning in this context amounted to a series of corrections to past plans so as to bring into balance the multitude of supply and demand relationships.

The means for achieving balance at the macro- level also required the centre actively imposing limits and constraints on individual enterprises. Wage control systems, for example, typically working by constraining the wage bill of each unit in the economy, were one of the means for controlling aggregate consumer demand. These and other limits could not be the same for every enterprise. Some obviously needed a higher wage bill, more energy or more hard currency. However, once each enterprise is given individualised treatment, the central authorities have to decide between competing demands. As, in reality, different units in the economy clearly do have conflicting interests, this inevitably creates scope for haggling and bargaining between different levels in the hierarchy. The point is taken up in detail later.

The second objective of central planning relates to a range of social policy aims. The bottom line was the desire to prevent major public outbursts of discontent. More generally, there was a desire to give people the feeling of the greatest possible stability and security. This, seen as the great benefit of socialism, led to some fairly obvious objectives, such as the avoidance of open unemployment and an attempt to ensure a steady rise in living standards. There were also some more specific and arbitrary objectives, such as a desire in Poland to maintain a set relationship between agricultural and industrial earnings. Frequently, however, the only effective instruments for ensuring these social objectives involved selective intervention in the activities of individual enterprises. Thus redundancies could be avoided by subsidising continued production. Although obviously welcome to the subsidised enterprise, this was one of the factors creating the perceived need for a highly progressive profits tax: social policy, it has frequently been argued, was pursued by the centre protecting the inefficient at the expense of the efficient. The dangers of this were not evident from the most traditional Marxist perspective, which saw no conflict between social objectives and efficiency.

A further means towards the chosen social policy objectives was to distort the pattern of prices away from what would have been derived in a functioning market system. Indeed, many consumer goods prices, including many foods, housing and domestic energy and children's clothing, were held down to way below the level for profitable production. Retail prices were calculated with individualised and highly variable rates of turnover tax such that prices as received by producers bore no necessary relationship to prices paid by consumers. The system could then only function on the basis of a complex system of subsidisation and central control.

The Polish authorities' nervousness about food price rises was so great that subsidies several times reached 10 per cent of the state budget. Food, however, was an exception both on account of its political sensitivity and because production was, to varying degrees, outside the state sector and therefore outside the scope of administrative directives. More typically, prices below the cost of production were not balanced by state subsidies and the resulting losses had to be covered by cross-subsidisation within the producing enterprise. This obviously required accompanying central directives to ensure continued production of unprofitable goods.

The third and final objective of central planning was to give a strategic direction to the economy. The Hungarian economist János Kornai (1990a, p.132) has suggested that the term planning could be given two meanings. A coherent process of setting targets and assigning instruments to achieve them, compatible with this third objective, he judges as the only activity worthy to be called planning. The rest, as discussed above, should be put under the heading of 'direct bureaucratic control'. The argument has considerable validity, but the sad truth is that what Kornai reasonably regards as genuine planning lost its significance over the years. It seemed to be successful during the rapid build up of heavy industry in the early 1950s, but is far less apparent in the later years of structural stagnation. Even Poland's investment boom of the early 1970s, dependent very much on the build up of foreign debt, appeared rather as expansion across all sectors.

This failure of strategic planning used often to be explained in terms of an 'overload' theory. The central planners were so busy balancing supply and demand of so many individual items, so it was suggested, that they could not keep track of long-term objectives. Overload certainly was a persistent problem, making a coherent system of 'direct bureaucratic control' practically unattainable, but it is not a convincing explanation for the failure over the years of central planners to influence long-term trends. If overload were the central problem, then separate bodies that were created to formulate long-term plans should have alleviated the difficulty long ago.

The important point must be that priority was given to objectives that conflicted with and therefore disrupted longer-term plans. Thus ideas for structural change invariably encountered fierce opposition from managements and groups of employees in non-favoured sectors. The conflict here was with the aim of maintaining security and social stability. Investment plans were also disrupted by the demands of short-term balance with scarce resources going to overcoming specific shortages as they arose.

The primacy of these short-term policy objectives was also the main factor shaping the institutional structure of centralised planning. At its apex was a single directing centre. In constitutional terms this was the government operating through a supreme central planning body. In practice, of course, the party leadership represented a higher authority, but its apparatus at lower levels was required to do no more than help in the implementation of instructions passed down through government bodies.

The centre worked out national plans, tried to achieve balance and passed instructions down a hierarchy of ministries, covering branches of the economy, associations of enterprises, individual enterprises and then plants and workshops. Other institutions helped in this process. A unified banking system ensured that credits were granted in line with plan targets. Financial policy, in harmony with centralised price setting, ensured that lower levels were constrained in the resources they actually used. Nominally, then, money did exist. It was, however, substantially different from the money that plays so crucial a role in a market economy because enterprises had access to it only when allowed by the centre and only for precisely defined purposes.

A further help to the centre was a much higher level of concentration than is found anywhere in Western Europe. In Poland the average employment in state-owned industrial enterprises was 1,069 in 1989: there were also smaller cooperative and private firms accounting for a quarter of industrial employment. In Czechoslovak industrial enterprises, however, the average employment level was 2,950 in 1960 and 3,155 in 1989 while only one per cent were in enterprises employing under 500. This was frequently justified in terms of the need for economies of scale in production, or in innovation or research and development. In reality, however, such uniformity of organisational size stemmed from the desire of central authorities to lighten their burden by decentralising some powers. The precise coordination of production could be devolved to lower levels while the priorities of broad balance and social policy were run from the centre. Large units could also resolve the problem of the need to subsidise enterprises which, thanks to centrally-determined prices, were making 'planned' losses. Such firms could be incorporated into a larger, financially viable whole.

How Planning Really Worked

By the time central planning had collapsed, a considerable body of research had been undertaken on how the system really functioned. It was by then quite clear that central planning, in the sense of a central body genuinely able to take and enforce all or most of the important decisions, was largely a myth.

Attention had shifted towards analysing a bargaining process between levels in the hierarchy whereby operational — usually one-year — plans were formulated. It was realised from very early on that enterprises were able to influence the plan formulation process by distorting the information they provided to the central authorities. The question was whether their monopoly of information on their own input needs and output potential did not mean that plan instructions were really written by those who were meant to receive them. In other words, lower levels in the hierarchy, rather than the apparently omnipotent centre, could be the real source of decisions. This shift towards seeing the central actor in the plan formulation process as the enterprises, which is particularly prominent in Kornai's writings, can only be accepted with a very severe proviso. As will be argued, for all their power, enterprises operated within a very specific environment.

There is therefore little to be gained by trying to analyse enterprise behaviour around a simple maximand, analogous to the profit maximisation assumed for simple theories of a market economy. The enterprise was radically different as it was constrained by the centre's power within the hierarchy. The key to understanding its motivation is to distinguish two overlapping spheres of activity, bargaining over resources and targets and then production after targets have been set.

The principal objectives within the bargaining sphere were a soft plan target and the maximum allocation of inputs. The objective in the sphere of production was to fulfil the agreed plan target. There was no incentive to reach any level of output, sales or profit that was not defined from the sphere of bargaining. Output maximisation, for example, was quickly found to be counterproductive as it amounted to an invitation to the centre to impose a harder target for the next planning period. Production in one period was therefore itself one of the elements in bargaining over targets for the next period.

The degree to which an enterprise could satisfy its objectives within the bargaining process depended on its ability to wield influence up the hierarchy. The next level, the association or combine, generally played a double game. It had an interest in its subordinate bodies being given attainable plans and therefore supported demands for more resources and easier targets. However, it also had to allocate scarce resources between its subordinates and could therefore reject what it saw as excessively soft plans. The same logic applied up the hierarchy at least to the ministry level.

Individual enterprises therefore had a strong incentive, and often plenty of opportunity, to form coalitions, to lobby and to seek the promotion of their protégés up the hierarchy. They could thereby gain control of the relevant part of their environment for satisfying their own objectives. To this end they could enlist the help of parallel hierarchies, such as local government, party organisations, trade unions or any other legally existing bodies.

In general the information reaching the centre during the plan formulation phase was highly distorted. When aggregated it inevitably showed a substantial excess of demand for inputs over their supply. It was only at the centre, at the level of the supreme planning body, that there was any incentive to ensure global balance. Even its ability, however, was limited, partly because of the complexity of the task and partly because of the desire from the political leadership to increase living standards and to claim a rapid growth rate by yielding to demands from below for investment.

In the early days of central planning, attempts were frequently made to impose very tough targets on lower levels. Experience, however, soon taught that widespread failure to achieve enterprise plans led to imbalances and breakdowns throughout the economy. In other cases enterprises seemed to become immune to hectoring from above and simply ignored impossible targets. There was very little in practice that could be done, even within a highly repressive political system, to force such recalcitrant managers to achieve the impossible (Myant, 1989a, and Goldmann, 1985, pp.65-6).

The central planners therefore had a strong tendency to accept the information received from enterprises as the basis for plan formulation. They did, in the interests of achieving balance, frequently change targets during implementation or impose tougher targets on some enterprises from the start. This, of course, was the main factor encouraging enterprises to conceal capacity and to bargain for excessive resources. Nevertheless, in view of the practical obstacles to differentiating between individual enterprises, they preferred to correct information received from below only by assuming that all outputs could be slightly higher and all inputs slightly lower. The end result was that instructions tended to be written by those who received them, but only in the sense that they gave the desired security and attainable targets to the great bulk of enterprises. There were, however, major obstacles to an enterprise winning approval for a plan which would allow it to gain substantial extra resources for expansion. Indeed, there was no mechanism at all encouraging enterprises to set themselves long-term objectives in the production sphere.

Plan formulation was therefore a highly conservative process. Planning tended to be 'from the achieved level', with targets set slightly above those of the previous period for enterprises that achieved their targets. Those that failed had to take some short-term penalties, but might have earned the reward of an easier target in future. As the centre learned to set more realistic targets, so the planners increasingly lost any ambitions to impose significant structural changes.

This account points to the need for a careful interpretation of the place of plan targets within the economic system. They cannot be seen as the essential determinant of output. That was more likely to be determined in any one year on the basis of the previous year's result with a small addition to reflect the general expectation of a slight improvement in productivity. The target had more relevance as a determinant of incomes and bonuses within the enterprise as these varied with the degree of plan fulfilment. Perhaps the most striking evidence for this is that plan targets were frequently changed during the course of a year, often in response to claims from enterprises that changed circumstances had made the original target impossible.

Nominally, incomes were not determined by collective bargaining, but were set by centrally-determined scales. In practice there was scope for substantial variation. There is therefore some analogy between the plan formulation process under central planning and collective wage bargaining in market economies. The former generally involved only a narrow group around the director, but top enterprise managements frequently used arguments against tough targets, or to justify conceal-ing output potential, along the lines that the director felt responsible for the incomes and conditions of the whole work collective.

This had important implications for relationships within the enterprise. The best way for management to minimise conflicts was to be successful in bargaining with higher levels. Opinion poll evidence in Poland even suggested that employees saw management as the best representative of their own interests (Kozek, 1989, p.122). That does not mean that there was a great deal of democracy in workplaces: plenty of evidence indicates firmly to the contrary. It could be partly a complaint at the inadequacy of politically manipulated trade unions. The poll result is, however, fully consistent with the logic of the system of central planning which tended to create a harmony of interests within enterprise collectives and, to a lesser extent, within whole sectors.

Who Wins the Bargaining Game?

This account raises the question of which enterprises were more successful than others in the bargaining process. Evidence from Poland, where an annual survey of the performance of the 500 biggest industrial enterprises was published in the management journal *Zarządzanie* from 1984 onwards, leaves little doubt that a fairly stable structure of unequal power did take shape favouring the biggest. This can be seen by relative levels of wages and other benefits which were dependent on the ability to win approval for soft targets. There were random variations between individual enterprises, maybe suggesting that some were more successful than others in extending their influence up the hierarchy. Less comprehensive Czechoslovak evidence (eg Kolanda, 1984) also suggests that success tended to be associated with organisational size, which is obviously likely to confer political influence, and definitely not with economic performance.

Various attempts have been made to explore the relative power of enterprises in more depth. One interesting argument, with possible implications for the means of transition to a market economy, is that something approaching market relationships existed even under traditional centralised planning. As one author put it 'it is a very specific kind of market, organisationally monopolised, forcibly cartelised, operating with poor and restricted coordination, but it nevertheless is a market' (Mlčoch, 1990, p.925). The core of the argument is the observation that success in fulfilling plan targets depended to a great extent on success in 'horizontal' contacts with other enterprises and that means that familiar market concepts such as monopoly power could be important.

It is true that, in purely numerical terms, horizontal links appeared to be more important than vertical ones. They were, however, far less important in creating and shaping institutional and organisational structures (Hrnčíř, 1990). Whenever major conflicts arose, the resolution was at least partly dependent on the ability to influence higher levels in the hierarchy.

The subtleties of enterprise strength can be amplified around three examples (Mlčoch, 1990). The first relates to bargaining over prices in general. The argument needs to be clarified with a brief explanation of the system of 'wholesale' and retail prices. The former, paid to producers, were completely separated from the latter by the system of positive and negative turnover taxes. Wholesale prices were traditionally fixed over periods of several years. This price stability, it was hoped, could make financial planning easier. Unfortunately, cost structures changed gradually over time, so that prices increasingly deviated from their cost plus base. There were therefore periodic revisions of all wholesale prices. Experience taught, however, that profits rose slightly more than intended during price revisions. There were also wide variations between sectors, suggesting that the most powerful were able to manipulate the process in their own favour.

A second example relates to bargaining over prices in the specific situations arising from product innovations. Traditionally these were used as an opportunity to ask for a price rise from the central authorities. That, however, could lead to conflict with the interests of purchasing enterprises while provoking aspirations for a share in the benefits from component suppliers. The former tried to argue that the innovation was of trivial significance while the latter claimed that it depended on improved inputs. Again, the issue was decided up the hierarchy. With the exception of the very sensitive case of food, the least resistance to price rises was likely to come for goods going to final consumers only. Indeed, the centre could actually welcome the opportunity to implement 'hidden' price rises, based on bogus or insignificant innovations, that helped reduce real aggregate consumer demand while inflating economic growth indicators.

The third example relates to the tendency for enterprises nearer to the start of the production chain to receive favoured treatment. The logic of planning led to priority for basic industries which provided key inputs to other sectors. Thus the energy sector could expect better treatment than consumer goods or social services. Shortages in the former threatened plan targets for all sectors, and hence the overall economic growth targets that were a major objective for the political leaders, while shortages from the latter caused problems only for consumers.

The favoured position of basic industries was reflected in job security, relatively high wages and a high share in investment. Customers, having experienced shortages or erratic supplies, could have been won to join a coalition supporting this. They would, however, have logically been opposed to any scope for raw material suppliers to exploit monopoly power through the market. Thus they would have favoured central rather than market allocation and opposed high raw material prices. The outcome in practice was typically high investment but low prices requiring substantial state subsidisation of basic industries: it can be seen as a compromise which could keep happy all those directly concerned (Józefiak, 1984, pp.131-2).

The basic industries and the prices of their products were therefore the furthest removed from any logic of the market. Near the other extreme were consumer goods producers which had far less administrative constraint on price increases. There may even have been cases of competition between state enterprises, although only over sales of current output. The short-term nature of planning horizons made it extremely unlikely that there could be competition relating to investment, innovation and the long-term development of new products. An equilibrium for the whole system could therefore be conceived in which equilibrium wholesale prices would refer not to a level derived from the market, but to a level reflecting the relative strengths of different enterprises and sectors in terms of their ability to influence the central decision makers. Similarly, equilibrium levels of investment would reflect lobbying power and the extent to which a sector's position in the production process helped in the organisation of a coalition.

Was it a Shortage Economy?

The preceding analysis suggests that central planning was so different from a market economy that it has to be interpreted with the help of substantially different concepts. A major, but not fully satisfactory alternative derives from the 'economics of shortage', worked out by

Kornai as an extension of his outstanding descriptive work on the failures of planning. He aimed to explain the most visible forms of shortage, the queues for consumer goods and the persistent delays in investment projects, and even elevated 'shortage' to the status of a principal analytical category for explaining the system's behaviour as a whole.

Some familiar terms need to be defined carefully. Kornai (1980) argued that shortage was the 'normal' state for the system, continually generated by forces inherent within the method of bureaucratic control. He therefore regarded the equilibrium condition as one that embodied shortage. The term 'disequilibrium' was, however, still typically used in the narrowly economic sense of an imbalance between supply and demand.

The starting point for Kornai's analysis is an assumed enterprise objective of maximum size. This, he suggested, could partly reflect the 'noble' motive of believing one's own sphere of activity to be extremely worthwhile. It could also partly reflect a natural predilection of top managers towards power, prestige, high salary and the other benefits of controlling a large organisation. There is an obvious analogy here with the economic theories of bureaucracy associated with Downs (1967) and Niskanen (1971).

Having set this objective, Kornai then argued that enterprises faced a 'soft budget constraint', meaning that they were accustomed to expect subsidisation, credits or some other form of financial help should difficulties arise. The scope for this was not unlimited — asking for financial help from a higher level was not completely reliable or painless — and that meant that there was some sort of budget constraint. It was, however, vague and flexible, depending on the political influence of the enterprise in question. Enterprises therefore had an 'almost insatiable' demand for inputs, and especially for investment spending (Kornai, 1980, p.195). A firm in a capitalist system, on the other hand, could be expected to undertake careful assessment before committing itself to spending. It would shy away from projects that might threaten to lead to losses because it encounters a 'hard' budget constraint as expressed most clearly in the ultimate penalty of bankruptcy.

It is fairly simple to argue from these starting points that the system should have been characterised by persistent and general shortage.

Thus it is assumed that approval was granted for a total volume of investment beyond the economy's capacity. Employment and wages rose in the investment goods and construction sectors spreading disequilibrium to the consumer goods sector. If the resulting shortages were covered by imports, this led to external imbalance. If imports were constrained, then there was either a rise in consumer goods prices or, if that too was forbidden by central controls, shortages and queues. Shortage thereby became a persistent feature of the whole system.

Moreover, in Kornai's view, it was the key factor governing the behaviour of the units in the economy. Thus the tendency at all levels was to hoard inputs that might become scarce. This applied both to producers and to consumers. The latter acquired the habit of buying whatever was available, even if not needed immediately, in case it should not be available later. Shortage thereby created more shortage. It also meant that producers could sell practically anything they produced, with no incentive to care about innovation or product quality. Shortage could therefore often be 'the cause and inefficiency the effect' (Kornai, 1982, p.96).

Despite the quality of his empirical work, Kornai's theoretical position can be challenged. It is heavily dependent on his assumption that enterprises have long-term objectives in the production sphere, and that they can impose their will at least in the main on the central planners. Both of these are questionable. If managers aimed for status and power, that need not imply expansion of the productive capacity of their current workplace. They could have had easier options in promotion to another enterprise or up the existing hierarchy. Moreover, the best way to expand an existing enterprise was usually by merger. There were times when management careers were built by advocating ambitious and unrealistic investment plans. That was the case in Poland in the 1970s, but at that time the policy from the top was for high investment and rapid growth.

It was, of course, always very difficult for the centre to maintain aggregate balance between the supply of and demand for resources, but the outcome depended at least in part on the preferences and decisions of the top leadership. At one time Kornai tended to downplay these political factors, arguing that systemic causes alone were a 'sufficient' condition for generalised shortage. He thereby evaded the question of which factors really were the most important in causing the alleged disequilibria. In later accounts (e.g. 1990a, p.130) he was more prepared to accept that 'investment hunger' was due both to the desire for growth from top policy makers and planners and to the soft budget constraints at lower levels. He also accepted that excess household demand could be controlled by macroeconomic management. With an effective wage control system, he accepted, high investment need not lead to excess demand for consumer goods.

This points towards an alternative view in which inefficiency was derived not from persistent excess demand but from rigidities, inflexibilities and the short time horizon imposed by the plan bargaining process. Supply for individual products adapted slowly to demand because enterprises had no need to be responsive. Even if their goods could not be sold, experience taught that they could receive help from a higher level in the form of a revised plan target. Enterprises therefore had no inherent motivation to respond to customer demands, nor any particular ambitions for growth and expansion. The concept of the soft budget constraint therefore appears as no more than an analogy to a concept relevant to a normal market system. It does not provide the best explanation for enterprise behaviour under the very different system of central planning.

In this alternative view, then, shortage is not 'the' cause of inefficiency. It is, however, an important phenomenon with major implications for the working of the system causing, as Kornai argues, tendencies towards hoarding and panic buying. The issue is important because a possible policy implication of Kornai's arguments is that the starting point for improving the system's performance could be a cut in aggregate demand to eliminate shortage. It is a view that has played a role in Eastern Europe but, when put in such a simple form, it must be judged untenable.

Doubts about the details of Kornai's analysis are reinforced by the weakness of empirical evidence for persistent macro-disequilibrium in the investment and consumer goods markets. In both cases the situation differs enormously between countries, suggesting no simple link to the system, and has been the subject of considerable controversy. In relation to investment, there quite obviously is excess demand during the bargaining process, when enterprises submit their requests for resources. The real question is whether excess demand is carried over from the bargaining into the production sphere.

There is a widespread assumption that the answer was positive in all centrally-planned economies in most periods. This could then explain the undeniable phenomena of excessive delays in investment projects and the scattering of investment resources over large numbers of projects. Costs and the necessary time for completion were deliberately understated in enterprise proposals, it is argued. The central authorities, presumably because they lacked the technical or political strength to make realistic assessments for themselves, approved a greater volume of investment than the economy could deliver.

There are reservations to this account. Available figures make it impossible to give a conclusive demonstration of excessive investment, apart from certain clearly defined periods when it was encouraged from the centre. The phenomena of investment scatter and slow completion times are largely explicable in terms of poor organisation, the inflexibility of the planning system and the nature of incentives to certain enterprises (Myant, 1989a). It is quite possible that the system should be criticised for under- rather than over-investment, especially in view of the recalculation of national income estimates to take account of hidden inflation. These are much easier to reconcile with a view of enterprises lacking any long-term ambitions, than with Kornai's notion of a drive towards growth and investment.

In fact, the nature and structure of investment is relatively easy to explain as an *effect* of shortage, in the sense of poor allocation and low flexibility leading to shortages of specific goods. Investment was directed towards, as Kornai (1980, pp.230-3) described it, 'putting out fires', in other words to overcoming those existing bottlenecks that were causing the greatest immediate concern at the centre, without regard to long-term investment plans. This implies that considerable support from outside an enterprise was needed before investment would be approved. It is therefore difficult to accept that enterprises were able to impose on the centre a persistent state of chronic over-investment.

It is also unclear whether problems with investment spilled over into more general disequilibrium. The limiting factors were the wage control system and the commitment to a balanced budget. In so far as these were effective, it should have been possible to maintain aggregate equilibrium on the consumer goods market. There can be little serious doubt that these equilibrating mechanisms broke down over long periods in Poland, most notably in the late 1970s and early 1980s and again at the end of the 1980s. The reason, however, was a political and social climate in which wage demands could not be resisted, although the problem was exacerbated by the nature of reform attempts discussed in Chapter 3. Expressed in terms of the objectives of central planning, the aim of aggregate balance came into conflict with the popular aspiration for a higher living standard than balance would permit. For the Czechoslovak case, however, evidence of persistent disequilibrium on the consumer goods market as a whole is far from conclusive (Myant, 1989a, pp.214-18).

This, it can be repeated, is quite compatible with shortages of specific goods, which follow from the lack of adaptability of the system. Even if they are balanced by surpluses of other goods, this can still have a profound effect on consumer behaviour. Faced with irregularity of supply, consumers develop the habit of buying whatever is available, thereby creating shortages. In Czechoslovakia, however, this appears to have been a periodic phenomenon, with waves of panic buying clearing stocks of previously unsaleable goods.

From Bargaining to Stagnation

An account of how the system functions centring on bargaining between levels can provide a satisfactory explanation for technological and structural stagnation. It has long been argued that the system of plan targets created a minimal incentive to innovate within the enterprise. Any success in achieving higher productivity was penalised with a higher plan target. Any failure to cope with disruption, leading to a temporary drop in output, risked penalties for failing to reach plan targets. This was a particularly serious problem as a successful innovation frequently depended on changes in inputs from a number of other enterprises. They may have had no interest in changing from a product range that had served well for plan fulfilment in the past.

The result, then, was a highly inflexible system in which the strongest incentive was to keep doing the same as in the past. Each enterprise tried to minimise its dependence on others by producing as many of its components as possible and by keeping as far as it could to existing patterns of contact with other enterprises. One study of innovation in Poland actually reached the conclusion that there was no incentive to change inherent within the system (Krajewski, 1985). Pressures had to come from outside, for example from foreign customers insisting on a higher technical level for a product, or from the utilisation of a foreign licence forcing improvements from component suppliers. In Czechoslovakia it was often suggested before 1989 that Western restrictions on the sale of advanced technology were probably irrelevant because nobody seemed interested in introducing innovations anyway (Myant, 1989a, pp.240-7). Licences from the most promising post-war innovations, in textile machinery and contact lenses, were sold to Western firms because of lack of domestic productive capacity. In reality that means that domestic producers were happy to reach plan targets with existing product ranges.

All of this sits very uneasily alongside a view of the enterprise striving with an 'almost insatiable' appetite for ever more investment. It is more compatible with an enterprise that is both constrained and protected within the system to so great an extent that it has effectively no long-term objectives. Indeed, the unchanging list of names of the large industrial enterprises in Poland and Czechoslovakia suggest that, once established, an enterprise was effectively indestructible.

It is clear from all this that the enterprise in a centrally-planned system differed substantially from the large corporation in a market system. The former was likely to be big, producing an unchanging product and making as many of the necessary components as possible. There was no logic in diversifying into new product ranges, or in contracting out component production to specialist firms. There was, on the contrary, every reason for diversifying into component production so as to achieve the maximum of autarky and hence security.

The enterprise was likely to be a monopoly, in the sense of being the sole producer of its product. This was the most advantageous for the enterprise and simplified the tasks of central planners. Where there were several manufacturers of similar products the background was usually a political deadlock with all insisting on retaining their separate identities. They generally operated as a cartel for sales purposes, but in other respects, such as technology and innovation, worked independently. A notorious example is the Czechoslovak goods vehicle industry. Three enterprises manufactured lorries from substantially different design conceptions and each had enough political strength to prevent a merger which could have brought the benefits of economies of scale.

In one sense then, the socialist enterprise was more secure than the firm under capitalism, as it could hope for permanent protection against competition. However, it lacked genuine financial autonomy, suffering confiscation of funds not spent in a given period and was permanently answerable to a higher authority for how financial resources were allocated. It could not, for example, build up funds over a period of time or raise finance externally with which to further its own objectives. All success therefore depended ultimately on the ability to influence higher levels in the hierarchy. It is, of course, far from unknown for large capitalist corporations to foster and exploit links in the political hierarchy. That, however, is only one means to further their objectives and is usually less important than market-oriented activities.

2. The Limits of Reform

Many attempts were made over the years prior to the collapse of Communist power to improve on the system's performance by introducing 'reforms', meaning changes in the system of management while still retaining the essence of the existing structures. The Communist Party's effective monopoly of power was not challenged and neither was the socialist essence of the system, in terms of state ownership, broad state direction of the economy and the continuation of the past social objectives. The most substantial examples prior to the 1980s included reform attempts in Czechoslovakia in the late 1960s, in Poland after 1956 and again to a lesser extent in the early 1970s. More ambitious still were the development of the self-management model in Yugoslavia, especially after 1965, and Hungary's New Economic Mechanism starting in 1968.

This past experience provided part of the background to the thinking that dominated policy making after the ending of Communist power. Above all, it encouraged the conclusion that past failures were due to continual, and politically unavoidable, attempts to constrain reform to partial adjustments to the existing socialist system. The alternative, waiting to emerge in the new political climate, was to start from the clear aim of a full market economy. The market, however, was inevitably understood on the basis of the highly abstract orthodox economic theories in which it appears as a self-regulating system coordinated purely through price mechanisms. This may be a very helpful abstraction for analysing aspects of behaviour in an existing market economy but, as the latter part of this chapters shows, it carries real dangers when used as the main basis for policies aimed at creating a new system from scratch.

Pragmatic Decentralisation

Most reform attempts at least up to the 1980s can be characterised in the terminology of the Polish economist Cezary Józefiak (1984, p.135) as aiming for a 'pragmatically decentralised' model within which 'the central authorities decided to limit the extent of their economic administration'. The assumption was that socialism was still essentially a superior system, but that disappointing results had been caused by over-centralisation and excessive bureaucratisation. The aim was therefore to create an alternative with more emphasis on horizontal links, fewer central commands and more incentive for enterprises to respond to customers' demands.

Central allocation was therefore reduced and quantity and volume targets replaced where possible by the profit indicator. Planning, however, was not abandoned in total. Indeed, the usual hope was that 'real' planning, as opposed to bureaucratic allocation, could begin once the centre had rid itself of the burden of balancing supply and demand relationships throughout the economy. In the usual terminology, the aim was to 'combine' the plan with the market, or to use 'market instruments' to achieve the plan's objectives. Moreover, central controls continued especially over investment, or at least over major investment projects. Price liberalisation was very limited, foreign trade liberalisation minimal and enterprises, remaining part of a state hierarchy, lacked the financial independence of a privately-owned firm: the centre still had the power to intervene in their affairs whenever it liked. This, then, was not a real market system.

Despite ambitious hopes that a new system would quickly emerge and show its superiority, these changes were invariably either reversed or effectively incorporated within the logic of the old system. Quantity targets reappeared, partial relaxation of prices was reversed, limits were reimposed on wage bills and on the use of scarce inputs. Even in Hungary, where profit was meant to become a stimulus to greater efficiency, a complex system of penalties and bonuses emerged that left an enterprise's final financial position totally independent of its economic performance (Kornai, 1990a). Lobbying power was still the determinant of success. Indeed, even the abandonment of one-year operational plans was met by the emergence of 'informal' commands whereby, for example, an enterprise facing the shortage of an input could ask the central authorities to 'persuade' a supplier to increase deliveries. This reversal was obviously the result of decisions taken by top party leaders who controlled policy making. They, however, were not usually unequivocal opponents of all reform and were often willing to try ideas that they had been assured by expert economists would enable them to claim credit for a better economic performance. They were, however, notoriously nervous lest economic reform should encourage ideas for political change. Thus Poland's post-1956 reform was kept within firm limits (Kozek, 1989, p.86). The Czechoslovak authorities in the early and mid-1960s at first allowed reformers to work out their ideas, but then set limits to what they would tolerate. After the political changes following the Soviet invasion of 1968 they moved to total hostility. In Hungary in the late 1960s and early 1970s, party leader János Kádár is frequently cited as a supporter of reform, but he too had to accept limits. Above all, he was constrained by the Soviet insistence that there could be no full alternative 'model' of socialism (Berend, 1990, p.207).

The leadership's ambivalence typically showed itself as problems arose during implementation. Steps towards the market quickly produced conflict with the traditional objectives of equilibrium and social stability. Relaxation of central controls inevitably led to more visible inflationary pressures, new inequalities and even the threat of unemployment. Inequalities could appear particularly arbitrary as the old system left enterprises and sectors in widely varying financial starting positions depending on the age and efficiency of assets acquired under central planning and on the still arbitrary price system. This did not matter under a system in which the centre had the power to reallocate funds at will. It suddenly became a major problem when enterprises were expected to become financially independent.

The centre could have chosen to ignore these social problems and conflicts and press ahead with reform. That, however, would have conflicted with its continuing basic objectives derived from its socialist ideology. It was therefore likely to intervene in the interests of social and economic stability. The most effective means to achieve that was to use the existing machinery with essentially traditional methods. Direct controls were reimposed, or maintained, on prices, enterprise wage bills and investment. Scarce goods were subject again to central allocation. Profits were confiscated from some enterprises and subsidies paid to others. Thus the reforms were reversed.

This choice was reinforced by pressures from further down the hierarchy where officials had the job of administering and checking on activities in enterprises. Most of their tasks were highly specialised, geared towards the short-term policy objectives of equilibrium and social stability, and would have become largely pointless within any other system, as would the whole structure of central bodies and ministries. Not surprisingly, survey evidence has generally shown views from ministry officials to be very conservative on economic reform (Masłyk-Musiał and Pańków, 1990).

Pressures for reversal also came from managements, backed by employees, in those enterprises that had been successful under central planning in winning the favour of higher levels. Within the prevailing political atmosphere, in which nobody could openly challenge policies approved by the top leadership, this could not be expressed as opposition to reform in general. The point was rather that these enterprises continued to behave 'in the old way', pressing the centre to help them overcome problems that were caused by changes to the rules or by other external factors. Even in the less favoured sectors, such as the light and consumer goods industries, managements were reluctant to embrace a fully decentralised system which could weaken their position in the face of monopoly suppliers.

As important as this veiled opposition from enterprises was a lack of any idea as to how their behaviour should change within a competitive market system. Many enjoyed effectively monopoly positions and might therefore anyway have continued with much of their old complacency. Many others, especially in the food and consumer goods industries and in some service sectors, could have been in a position to compete with each other.

However, the evidence both from experience and from opinion surveys confirms that reforms had a minimal impact on how managements understood their role across all sectors. They sought out the safety of existing rules, contracts and franchising agreements. They had become used over the years to frequent changes in rules − this volatility being one of the characteristic features of the bargaining game under central planning − and had generally learnt not to treat them as permanent. Reform attempts were therefore often dismissed as just another episode in the inconsistency and incompetence of higher levels.

This inaction was carried through into relationships inside enterprises. Opinion surveys confirmed that workers in Poland frequently approved in general of the idea of economic reform, but they did not see it as a process requiring sacrifices, greater work effort or even new initiatives from employees. Instead, they viewed it as a means to overcome their own immediate problems, such as consumer goods shortages outside the enterprise and poor wages and conditions in the workplace. They certainly did not expect changes that would lead to greater conflicts (Kozek, 1989, pp.110 and 131). Such expectations were a further constraint on management, encouraging recourse to the standard conflict resolution device of seeking outside help. The political leadership was also unprepared for the possibility of sharper conflicts so that workers' expectations and attitudes could have been a further factor encouraging a return towards central controls.

'Pragmatic decentralisation', it seems, was too narrowly conceived to bring significant changes to the system. It seems reasonable to conclude that serious change would be possible only with a new political structure and an acceptance that the forms of stability and security regarded as the gains of socialism would have to be abandoned. Not surprisingly, that was a view that found little public expression prior to 1989. There were, however, frequent proposals for taking reform further so as to overcome the barriers that had been encountered.

The most frequent starting point saw the key in the strengthening of enterprise independence. Units failed to change their behaviour and start competing, it was suggested, because directors were still appointed by, and ultimately answerable to higher levels. They therefore naturally accepted orders from ministry officials who, as in the past, divided up and allocated tasks. The solution was therefore to abolish much of the hierarchy between enterprises and the central planning body.

In practice progress was remarkably slow. In Hungary in 1956 it was suggested for the first time that all branch ministries, which controlled industrial enterprises, should be abolished and replaced by a single ministry of industry with advisory powers only. In 1981 the objective was achieved. In Poland the aim after 1981 was for a progressive reduction in the number of ministries. Caution reflected both scepticism at all levels over the usefulness of the full reform model and a continuing concern with the 'social problem' of the several thousand ministry officials (Gliński et al., 1989, p.56). Not surprisingly, as the administrative hierarchy was adjusted only slowly, officials were able to live up to the normal bureaucratic tradition of creating work for themselves which meant returning to or continuing with the same activities as before.

Moreover, a new economic system needs to be specified as more than just decentralisation from the existing centralised planning. It was also necessary to specify how and by whom directors would be appointed, how they would be controlled and what objectives they would be set. The danger otherwise was that excessive state control would be replaced by no control at all.

The Self-Management Option

One frequently suggested step towards overcoming the barriers to reform, although one that was hardly ever considered compatible with socialism by the Czechoslovak authorities, was the introduction of self-management. The original inspiration had little to do with the details of economic reform. Workers' or employees' councils were formed at various times in Eastern Europe, including Poland and Czechoslovakia at the end of World War II, largely as organisations of political power. Lacking a clearly defined role in the system of economic management, their position was quickly eroded as managers and technical specialists asserted their authority (Kozak, 1989, and Myant, 1981). Employee councils emerged in Czechoslovakia again in 1968 but were suppressed in 1969: their existence was too brief for their role within the system of management to be clarified. Polish experience is more substantial and complex, but the idea of self-management was developed the furthest in Yugoslavia.

Its origins were, again, political relating primarily to Tito's effort in the 1950s to create a credible alternative to the Soviet model which was condemned for its 'concentration of all functions − economic, political, cultural and others into one centre' and for its dependence on an 'immense bureaucratic apparatus' (Kavčič, 1972, p.24).

Set within the context of an attempt to advance economic reform, this could have been a means to free enterprises from the bureaucratic hierarchy, as management could become answerable to elected representatives of employees. It might also have at least partly offset working-class doubts over the social consequences of reform by granting the compensation of greater power in workplaces. Advocates often hoped that workers would become enthusiastic supporters, helping to mobilise enough pressure to break obstruction and conservatism throughout the existing apparatus.

Indeed, the advocates of self-management presented grandiose hopes of transcending the 'pragmatism' of the existing authorities while claiming to base themselves on 'a different socio-economic doctrine of socialism' (Józefiak, 1984, p.142). In fact, self-management has had a firm place in practically all branches of socialist thought with the possible exception of Marxism. It could be seen as an alternative to the 'bureaucratic' model, but the basis was still a collective institution, the self-managing enterprise, rather than the individual as in pure market theories. There was therefore an apparently happy coincidence between the needs of overcoming barriers to economic reform and a development of socialist ideology. Nevertheless, there are a number of grounds for doubting whether self-management, if understood as the totality rather than just as a part of the system, could ever function satisfactorily.

One of the most widely discussed problems relates to the textbook theory of the labour-managed firm. Attempts have been made to confirm predictions of 'perverse' behaviour, leading to unemployment and a poorly functioning labour market, in Yugoslav experience (Estrin, 1983). The model, however, is highly abstract while the phenomena observed are broadly explicable as the result of conscious government policy decisions (Mihailović, 1981).

At a less abstract level, the self-management option can be criticised for failing to provide a convincing solution to all the obstacles encountered to 'pragmatic decentralisation'. It is, for example, unclear whether it can be reconciled with the traditional policy objectives of stability, equality and security. Neither is it clear how a fully self-managing system could overcome all the inflexibilities of traditional central planning: in particular, mechanisms would have to be specified for the creation, merger and dissolution of enterprises.

Other critics, basing themselves on property rights theory, have argued that employees could be expected to use their power to pay out all available funds in wages or even sell the firm's assets for their own gain (Chiplin et al., 1977). This difficulty could be overcome by requiring all employees also to be owners with a financial stake in the enterprise. State-owned firms would thereby be converted into share-owning cooperatives. This, however, could appear perversely to restrict labour mobility as new recruits would have to buy shares. Successful firms, presumably with higher share prices, would find it harder to recruit labour, and hence also to raise capital, thereby restricting their expansion. The conclusion must be that self-management cannot be viable without substantial accompanying constraints on employees' powers and hence on enterprise autonomy.

Empirical evidence from Poland, and even more clearly from Yugoslavia, adds to the doubts derived from theoretical considerations. In the latter case, official rhetoric came to portray self-management as the guiding principle for the whole economic system. Its core was a network of elected employee councils with powers which for a short period included the hiring and firing of enterprise directors. At other times this responsibility was shared with various state bodies. The experience has been studied in considerable detail, and the general conclusion seems to be that true self-management was never as important as claimed.

Indeed, overall Yugoslav economic performance seems remarkably similar to that of others in Eastern Europe. Rapid growth in the 1950s and 1960s — average annual rates for GNP were 8.2 per cent for 1952-62 and 6.5 per cent for 1963-73 — gave way to slower progress in the 1970s and ultimate stagnation in the 1980s. This final phase was precipitated by a debt crisis following high levels of borrowing in the 1970s. Without these credits effective stagnation could have set in around the start of the latter decade (Mencinger, 1992). By the end of the 1980s, Yugoslav governments were following the general Eastern European trend of abandoning socialism and Marxism and seeking means for a transition to a full market system. The final catastrophic breakup of the federation seemed to confirm the ultimate demise of the idea of self-management.

Moreover, considerable evidence over all time periods suggests a relatively small direct influence for employee representatives (Obradović and Dunn, 1978) who generally did little more than agree to proposals from management. They could face ridicule if they argued, often abstained in votes and even willingly ceded powers to 'business boards' made up only of executives (Drezga, 1983, and Comisso, 1979). Far from behaving as if subordinated to employees' organs, managements typically regarded the representative bodies as a useful channel for passing on information about decisions and for gaining wider acceptance among employees.

There is no consistent evidence of employee representatives setting an enterprise's strategic objectives, but there is evidence of a latent, and sometimes open, conflict over the nature of self-management and over the short-term objectives of the enterprise. Within this, the employees' representatives often sided with management. They were, however, liable to be embarrassed by accusations of becoming 'yes-men' (Drezga, 1983, p.271), and frequently recognised the need to express employees' views if the institution of self-management was to command any interest and support.

The conflict was often presented in very general terms as if employees were fighting against bureaucracy. From the employees' side came accusations that the director was 'an autocrat, a despot' and 'a pathological obstacle to the development of self-management' (Šifter, 1978, pp.14-15). More specifically, employees often assumed that workers' self-management should give to the worker the right to 'decide over what he has produced'. Indeed, whenever the conflict took concrete shape it centred on the shares of enterprise revenue to be used for wages, as favoured by employees (Granick, 1975, and Prašnikar, 1983-4), as opposed to investment, as favoured by management (Kamušić, 1970, and Farkas, 1975). Workers, then, did not seek a full management role, but they did try to influence the issues that most directly and tangibly affected living standards. The issues of wages and housing were frequently raised by employee representatives on self-management bodies. They were also regularly raised at general meetings of employees, even though the agenda was set by the political activists from the party and trade union organisations in conjunction with the management.

There was, then, no single, simple, unifying objective for the self-managed enterprise. Different groups tried to use the institution to achieve their own, sometimes conflicting objectives. In general, and despite various attempts by the political leadership to breathe life into their cherished ideal of self-management, the director enjoyed the most power (Kavčič, 1972, p.77).

The most extreme version of self-management, based on the notion of 'associated labour' as codified in the 1974 constitution, aimed to decentralise power into the most basic economic units possible. Enterprises were to be broken up into single activity units, sometimes with as few as 20 employees, which were then to be coordinated by a complex system of 'self-management agreements'. This model could never have worked in full. It was impracticable both for its denial of the role of professional management — in marketing, innovation, personnel policy and other areas — and for its organisational complexity. If the task of replacing the market by central coordination was impossible, then there could be little chance of coordinating all units by voluntary agreements. In the early 1980s there were 80,000 of these basic organisations. Half had no plan of medium-term development while little credibility could be attached to those plans that did exist. If they were genuinely formulated 'from below', then there is no reason to suppose that they were in harmony with each other (Mihailović, 1981, p.220).

In reality it seems that power typically remained with the existing enterprise structures and the economy functioned on the basis of 'informal centralisation'. New institutions were created to regulate relationships, implicitly contradicting the philosophy of the reform, while the ruling League of Communists acted as an 'institutional glue' holding together an otherwise anarchic system (Tyson, 1980). In the words of the Yugoslav economist Kosta Mihailović (1981, p.218), the country had 'neither a market nor a planned economy'. The market had very limited institutional recognition and its effectiveness as a disciplining force was consistently attenuated by legal regulations and central intervention which reflected a continuing partial commitment to the traditional social aims of socialism.

Thus a constitutional guarantee of the right to work did not eliminate unemployment — levels were high especially in the less developed parts of the federation — but made redundancies practically impossible in state-owned enterprises. Minimum wage rules, and the power of many employees to insist on substantially higher levels, meant that many enterprises actually had wage bills greater than their revenue and yet continued in operation (Sirc, 1979, p.159, and Dyker, 1990, p.70). Bankruptcy was an empty threat, thanks largely to political interventions aimed at warding off workers' protests. There was therefore no powerful punishment for enterprises that failed.

Planning was also limited amounting, especially after 1965, to the setting and enforcing of broad structural objectives through the allocation of investment credits. There was no detailed central balancing of resources and demands in an effort to seek broad equilibrium. Within this system, resources went to the sectors and enterprises with the most political influence. Informal pressures stepped in where formal controls or mechanisms were inadequate, leaving enormous scope for nepotism and favouritism. Contacts through party organisations, through government bodies and through banks were the key to gaining funds.

There are clear similarities here with the formally-planned economies of Eastern Europe, and Kornai (1990a, p.35) has suggested that the Yugoslav system exhibited 'all the attributes of a rather soft budget constraint'. In fact, it was probably a better example than the formally-centrally-planned economies of Eastern Europe. There was persistent disequilibrium shown in high inflation, averaging around 17 per cent in the 1970s, and in continual balance of payments deficits: exports in some years paid for barely half the imports. These imbalances stemmed from a system that maintained some commitment to the traditional social aims of socialism, but had abandoned those powers of intervention in the internal affairs of enterprises that helped towards balance at the macro-level under traditional central planning. As elsewhere in Eastern Europe, disequilibrium cannot be attributed entirely to enterprise behaviour, as high investment was often encouraged by government policies, or demanded by local government bodies as much as by existing enterprises. There are also clear differences in the softness of the budget constraint across sectors, as revealed by research on the pattern of wage distribution and investment finance (Korošić, 1983) which indicated the nature of an approximate hierarchy.

Self-financing covered on average around a third of investment costs, but the figure varied enormously between enterprises and sectors while wages were more uniform. The most favoured enterprises could afford high wages and needed below average, if not minimal, credits to finance their investment thanks to high prices earned from weakly restrained monopoly power. In these firms internal conflict was low as pay was high enough for employees not to demand a greater share of the enterprises' total revenue: an 'unwritten rule' warned them against 'excessive' earnings.

Slightly less favoured sectors could finance high wages, but needed above-average levels of credit, often never repaid, for investment. In these cases the limiting factors were competitive markets and strong pressure on wages to keep up a relative position won at some time in the past. The conflict between the two possible objectives of the enterprise was resolved as political influence gave access to outside help softening the budget constraint. This need not always have conflicted with economic rationality as these enterprises were frequently oriented towards highly competitive export markets, and may have been forced to keep up wages so as to retain labour.

A third group, typically labour-intensive activities such as internal trade or the textile industry, accepted below-average wages, and enjoyed a high level of self-financing of investment. Prices were constrained by strong domestic, and sometimes external competition, but pressure for higher wages was evidently containable. The least favoured, or 'neglected', sectors had to endure low wages and low investment. The most striking example of this was the railways which, thanks to subdivision between the republics in the federation, lacked significant political influence at the crucial federal level (Korošić, 1983, pp.85 and 91-2). Throughout, then, the decisive factor was the power of the enterprises, expressed more frequently than elsewhere in Eastern Europe through the market but often still through the familiar mechanism of political favouritism.

Within this context, the Yugoslav theory of a self-managed economy was either irrelevant or harmful in that its proclamation as a panacea stifled any effort to confront the need to develop a genuine market system, or to exercise firm central control. One example cannot completely prove that failure is inevitable, but there is no evidence that self-management could have been more successful within a different political context, for example without the dominating and frequently repressive role of the League of Communists. The available evidence rather suggests that the spontaneous preference among employees was for a trade union organisation giving a strong voice in the workplace, protection in the detailed organisation of work and a national voice on major issues that directly affected living standards, such as housing policy.

From Self-Management to Socialisation

Unlike Yugoslavia self-management as a general concept has been favoured in Poland in certain periods only and has never been elevated to the status of a supreme economic mechanism. Its emergence and development is tied very closely to the notion of general democratisation within a broadly socialist framework. Thus workers' councils reemerged in 1956, amid the political and social turmoil of the time, but were soon reincorporated into a centralised system of management (Myant, 1982, Chapter 3, and Jarosz, 1988). Representative bodies within the enterprise did little more than support management initiatives while their only role outside was usually to support the director in bargaining with higher levels.

A self-management movement gained strength again after the massive strike wave of 1980 had led to the recognition of the Solidarity union. There were, however, two opposing conceptions. The Solidarity view, accepted by its National Coordinating Commission in July 1981, was for self-management as a framework for eliminating the power of the *nomenklatura*, the top management personnel who were appointed only after approval from the party apparatus. The idea was to by-pass in total the existing state apparatus, removing the whole sphere of economic decisions from party control.

The government's opposing conception saw self-management as a means to incorporate discontent and to weaken the new, independent trade unions. Indeed, Solidarity was very suspicious of the idea until a rather sudden conversion in the summer of 1981. The two broad perspectives both contributed to new compromise laws on self-management and on the state enterprise passed in September 1981. Any notion of giving full ownership rights to employees, thereby destroying the economic power of the state machine, was firmly rejected. Enterprises were still to be state owned, but they were to be given financial independence with employee representatives acquiring the power to appoint the director. An exception was made for 1,300 enterprises in basic and defence-related industries judged to be of 'fundamental importance to the economy' in which employees were limited to the right of veto over a government body's appointment. For all enterprises, however, the laws left ambiguities in the relationship between the director and self-management bodies such that the centre could still claim the right of arbitrary intervention.

After the introduction of martial law in December 1981 self-management bodies were suspended. Their right to appoint and dismiss the director was removed and they were often allowed to revive their activities only if they renounced further powers (Jarosz, 1988, p.105). Thus the whole Polish experience, at all times, could strengthen the view that self-management was part of a struggle against political authoritarianism and bureaucratic power.

Nevertheless, neither research on councils' activities nor surveys of employees' attitudes support hopes that self-management could become part of a successful model of the economy. Opinion polls consistently showed support for the idea in general terms, but no clear conception of what it was to achieve (Jarosz, 1988). Moreover, in 1956 and 1981 when self-management had genuine mass popularity, workers' councils emerged around general discontent over the state of the economy and over low wages. Support fell away in the later 1950s when the councils failed to bring tangible material benefits (Kozek, 1989). Despite attempts by some Polish researchers to suggest that reform could be based upon self-management (E.Balcerowicz, 1990), there was little sign of representative bodies struggling to extend their role within the management structure generally.

Nevertheless, at its first congress in September 1981 Solidarity extended the idea into the notion of a 'self-managing republic'. Employee control in workplaces was to be supplemented by greater autonomy for communities and a democratically elected parliament. Even the ruling party spoke of the need for democratisation, consultation and participation although, of course, that did not extend to the abdication from its monopoly of power. Moreover, the introduction of martial law in December 1981 quite clearly contradicted any rhetoric about creating genuinely democratic conditions.

Nevertheless, a number of Polish economists developed from this basis the notion of the 'socialisation' of the economy (Błaszczyk, 1983) which was to some degree incorporated into official reform proposals of the 1980s. The basis was to be the reinforcement of enterprise independence by the strengthening of self-management, supplemented by the 'socialisation of central planning'. This meant the participation of representatives of social organisations in deciding on the aims of a strategic plan, in choosing between alternatives and in overseeing the final implementation.

Alongside rhetoric about a further development of socialism, this was carefully justified in terms of the past experience of 'pragmatic decentralisation'. The democratisation of political life was seen both as a means of easing transition — providing a form of compensation for a population reluctant to accept material sacrifices — and as the basis for a better system of planning.

The assumption was that past failures were due to secrecy in the formulation process. A government backed by a popular mandate, and allowing the open expression of conflicting views and interests could, it was suggested, resist sectoral pressures more effectively. There are obviously grounds for scepticism. Polish experience of the early 1980s, when independent trade unions joined in debates over economic policy, showed that discussion over the broadest of policy issues could lead to deadlock. The far more complex and technical discussion of the precise allocation of resources need have fared no better. As with self-management, democracy might be an important part of an economic system but could hardly be the defining characteristic on its own. The great unanswered question related to the place for market relations and the price mechanism. Indeed, the emphasis throughout the 1980s shifted rather towards what Kornai described as 'radical' reform in which past failures were related to the absence of genuine market prices.

The collapse of Communist power in 1989 radically transformed the context for ideas on economic reform. There were, however, broadly two alternative routes. The first was to continue with a pragmatic evolution of past ideas, only without the constraints of Marxist ideology and the need to keep to the traditional aims of socialism. That would have meant gradually and pragmatically reinventing elements of a market system. As Chapter 3 shows, that process was to some extent under way in Poland by the late 1980s, but without very encouraging results.

The second alternative was to start from an abstract theory of a market and then try to put it into practice. A key role was played by the neo-liberal and property rights schools which were attractive partly because of their simplicity and intelligibility, partly because they seemed to be so clearly opposed to Marxism and partly because of the power of the critique of socialism that they could generate. Orthodox neo-classical economics *assumes* private property and allocation through the price mechanism, but Hayek *argued* for them and made predictions of what could happen in their absence. His ideas were bound to ring a bell with those who had observed the failures of central planning.

Hayek and the Market

Hayek's famous critique of socialism (1935) is based on the argument that rational allocation is a practical impossibility in the absence of market-determined prices. He predicted that an attempt at full central planning would lead to misallocation, with some sectors overgrown and others under-developed. In fact, rather than misallocation, central planning has led more directly into stagnation. Nevertheless, the absence of a rational price system has clearly been a barrier both to efficiency and to reform. It is the only mechanism that seems capable of replacing the dependence on political pressures in allocation decisions which, as argued in Chapter 1, has been the main cause of structural stagnation. Experience would therefore seem to confirm Hayek's conclusion that market-determined prices are a fundamental precondition for a functioning market system.

For the price mechanism to work, Hayek argued, there had to be private ownership. He saw the two inextricably linked in a world made up of isolated individuals (1949, p.17), each using '*his* particular knowledge and skill for furthering the aims for which *he* cares' within a clearly defined 'sphere of responsibility'. This view blended well with the property rights approach which proclaims the importance of clearly defining ownership. Although that could be compatible with state ownership, the usual assumption is that private property should be preferred.

This could appear to overcome three identifiable problems from the experience of central planning. The first is the barrier to reform relating to the lack of enterprise independence: this can be overcome by clearly defining ownership as ownership by identifiable individuals. The second is the inefficiency of units in the economy as demonstrated, for example, by the lack of interest in cutting inputs: this again can be countered if clearly defined private owners have a direct interest in ensuring that their assets are used to yield the highest possible income. The third problem is the alleged soft budget constraint: this could again be eliminated if identifiable owners were concerned to ensure that only potentially profitable investments were undertaken.

It may be legitimate to conclude from neo-liberal and property rights theories that a functioning price system and clearly defined ownership, although it is not yet justified to jump to the conclusion that that must always be private, are essential parts of an efficient economic system. Hayek and others went further, effectively assuming that these two elements are all that is needed for a market system. Thus Hayek (1944, pp.27 and 69) was prepared to tolerate some minimal interventionist acts, and he distanced himself verbally from 'a dogmatic *laissez-faire* attitude', but he never attempted to give any principles for judging when intervention might be positively beneficial. All his substantive comments were devoted to condemning specific forms of intervention. Indeed, he defiantly defined 'exploitation' to mean going against the logic of the market to alleviate its social consequences.

If there is a conflict between the market, which should in theory embody efficiency, and social justice, then Hayek sided decisively with the former. The trouble is that the price mechanism is not always a reliable guide to the prospects of a firm or sector across all time periods. Neither does it necessarily ensure the fastest and most effective adjustment to changed circumstances. There have been many cases of state intervention supporting inefficiency in market economies, but the history of capitalist economies is also full of cases of state intervention preventing unnecessary social hardship while also improving productive efficiency.

The weaknesses in Hayek's approach, as it relates specifically to a strategy for transition to the market, can be summarised around three issues. The first, and least substantial, relates to Paretian welfare economics, as outlined in standard basic textbooks. Within this, 'traditional' market failures — such as monopolies, externalities and public goods — are analysed around a static equilibrium framework. It is assumed that an equilibrium is reached but that, in terms of the desirable criterion of an abstract, perfectly competitive economy with everyone paying the full social cost for resources they use, it is not the most desirable equilibrium. Hayek was not very concerned with this, because he argued for the market primarily as the means to move towards an equilibrium. Prices to him, as outlined below, are primarily imparters of information to which actors in an economic system react. Comparisons of equilibria, he observed, assumed this process to take place automatically and thereby missed the most important role of the price mechanism.

Nevertheless, by implicitly treating the desirability of the equilibrium as an irrelevant question, Hayek dodged an important issue and left himself with no criterion for judging whether or not the free market would always provide the most desirable outcome. Rejecting Hayek's view could have policy implications for a transition strategy justifying, for example, the speedy preparation of interventionist policies on energy, the environment and transport. These are areas where the impact of market failures is often substantial.

The second line of criticism relates to Hayek's view of the price mechanism itself. His wonder at its operation is displayed in his well-known parable of the reactions to the scarcity of a raw material. Thanks to the market, the price will rise. Then 'without perhaps more than a handful of people knowing the cause, tens of thousands of people ... are made to use the material or its products more sparingly' (1949, p.87). This example, however, is less convincing than Hayek would have us believe. It picks on one area, raw materials, where 'auction' prices, meaning prices that change very rapidly so as to keep demand in line with supply, are more likely to prevail than, for example, in manufacturing industry.

Even for raw materials, however, reactions to the price change depend crucially on the assessment of further information. Thus if the change is judged to be a mere temporary fluctuation — and that can only be assessed on the basis of an understanding of its causes — then it may be ignored by the users of the raw material. Depending on their assessment of future trends, they may alternatively find means of reducing its consumption, either temporarily or permanently. Similarly, producers of the raw material may decide on major new investment, but only after assessing the cause and hence permanence of the shortage.

The implication is that price signals alone are inadequate because they relate to one particular point in time only. A modern firm, however, takes decisions that must relate to a number of different time periods. It has to adopt forms of behaviour appropriate to a longer time horizon and requires more subtlety than just blind responses to every price change. The point can be illustrated with reference to the role and significance of prices in two important sectors of the economy.

The first is agriculture, characterised in advanced countries by substantial state intervention aimed at limiting the notorious price instability which would otherwise cause sudden and unpredictable fluctuations in farmers' incomes. This intervention cannot be explained away as an economically irrational concession to a political lobby. In fact, the strength of the political pressure is a reflection of the inappropriateness of the price mechanism on its own due to the disjunction in time between signals and appropriate responses.

Agricultural products are homogeneous and the optimal scale of production is small relative to the size of the market: there are therefore large numbers of producers unable to control the price or the total quantity produced. Moreover, the production cycle is long making instantaneous adjustments to changes in price or demand impossible. The significance of this is very clear in the recent experiences of agricultural enterprises in Poland and Czechoslovakia where allowing free reign to the price mechanism quickly threatened to produce economic instability and social catastrophe with no certainty of a desirable outcome at any point in the future.

The place of the price mechanism is slightly different in manufacturing industry. Although an absolute distinction is dangerous — there are undoubtedly shades of grey in between — non-auction prices tend to prevail. Firms are not compelled to vary product prices in response to every short-term variation in supply and demand and have very good reasons for not doing so (Okun, 1981). In particular, customer loyalty and goodwill could be squandered by taking every opportunity to raise prices in times of high demand. Similarly, the benefits in terms of winning new customers from a drop in price in harder times are often very doubtful.

Generally, then, price is set on the basis of longer-term consider-ations of what the market, made up of stable and regular customers, will bear. The firm is more likely to react to immediate demand variations by altering output and may even prefer to absorb, for a time at least, the impact of price changes (Kaldor, 1985). Thus, despite Hayek's beliefs, prices are often not crucial for maintaining short-run coordination between economic units.

Nevertheless, there is a crucial distinction between prices in market and in centrally-planned economies. The former, despite considerable stability over significant time periods and a range of well-known distortions, are ultimately derived from the market. They are part of the data given to firms from the outside rather than being an element that firms themselves can control. Although, for reasons already explained, prices *cannot* be the only consideration in every decision taken, they are one crucial element in practically all important decisions that relate to the use of resources. Precisely because they are derived as part of a market process that is broadly competitive, they give an approximate indication of the 'socially necessary' inputs required for the production of the good and therefore mean that calculations can be 'rational' in the wider social sense of the allocation of resources. The market environment also means that, with survival and prosperity dependent on financial success, price signals must in the end be taken seriously: firms therefore have to act on the basis of their 'rational' calculations. Hayek was right that a price mechanism is essential, but he exaggerated what it can achieve.

Hayek and the Firm

The third and most important line of criticism of Hayek's approach, and also of the property rights school, is that it cannot explain the growth and prominence of the large companies that dominate modern capitalist economies. Indeed, if all relationships could be satisfactorily mediated through the price mechanism, then larger organisations based on internal authority would seem to be unnecessary. Hayek largely ignored the theory of the firm. Others, from a property rights perspective, have tried to construct a notion of a firm as 'a collection of contracts that govern the operations of multiple resource owners' (Barzel, 1989, p.56). Thus the firm is explained in terms of individuals, motivated by their own direct self-interest, entering into market-like relationships with each other. The boundaries of the firm are therefore not necessarily particularly significant. The question is rather one of permanence of contractual relations (Alchian and Woodward, 1988).

This fails to relate to the modern large corporation for three main reasons. The first is that it sits uneasily alongside the time horizon of modern business. Major companies today can hope for a life expectancy greater than that of their employees, or of individual shareholders. Their existence is more permanent than is implied by their reduction to a 'nexus of contracts', the formulation suggested by Alchian and Demsetz (1972). The second reason is that large firms today are typically not controlled directly by owners. Decision-making power has passed to professional managers. The third is that the theory does not match up with firms' varied and complex internal life: this point is taken up later.

One response to the evidence of a separation between ownership and control has been to ignore or deny it. Thus Mises (1949, pp.304 and 704) continued to insist that there must be an 'entrepreneur' carrying the 'burden' of financial risk and taking the major decisions. Mere managers have to be checked very closely by the owners who alone are 'under the incentive to preserve their property and make profits' (Mises, 1936, pp.138-41). This is the most logical position for those totally convinced of 'the productivity-enhancing role of the having of *private* wealth' (Demsetz, 1988, p.230). It is, however, untenable in the face of a mass of empirical evidence.

It is true that top managers often own some shares. In sociological terms there need be no major distinction between the two groups with top management appearing as 'the leading echelon of the property-owning class' (Baran and Sweezy, 1966, p.46). Nevertheless, there is a significant difference in their relationships to the individual firm. The owner has the more transient relationship, being able to sell shares at any time. Career managers are more likely to be tied to the long-term prosperity of the firm which has given them their power, status and wealth.

Indeed it has been powerfully argued by Chandler (1977 and 1990), on the basis of his massive studies of US and other large corporations, that firms in the technology and 'management' intensive sectors of modern manufacturing are successful only when they eliminate major owners from decision making. Only then can professional management teams operate free from arbitrary and unhelpful interventions. Some other international comparisons point to a very varied picture with loose control from owners and stock markets, as in Japan, possibly enabling managements to establish a longer-term perspective: in some other East Asian societies close involvement by owners seems to be no obvious disadvantage.

Nevertheless, the very existence of a large joint stock company does depend on limiting to a certain degree the rights of owners. The point was investigated thoroughly in the classic study of US business by Berle and Means (1968), first published in 1932. They were observing a situation in which a whole body of law had developed recognising, defining and regulating the existence of the corporation as a distinct entity. It could buy, sell, own, enter into contracts, sue or be sued, all in its own right. Nominally, it was owned by shareholders, but their powers were actually heavily constrained by further legal regulations.

This might at first seem surprising as it could imply that the state has intervened to weaken the power of owners. In practice, however, laws to prevent some kinds of shareholder interventions are essential to prevent a group of owners — it could even be a majority — from using the company's assets in their own interests and against those of other shareholders. They could, for example, launder funds into another firm. Instead, laws were developed making clear that management had to represent the interests of *all* shareholders, and even creditors too, and this was possible only if individual shareholders themselves were prevented from intervening in specific deals. It seemed to Berle and Means (1968, pp.64, 245 and 119) that the notion of 'active' owner-ship was a thing of the past. The shareholder was 'a passive agent' and had become 'simply a supplier of capital on terms less definite than those customarily given or demanded by bondholders'. Managers were thereby left with 'almost absolute power' with the law being the best protection against its abuse.

With its legal integrity thus protected, the firm becomes a perm-anent institution rather than just a 'nexus of contracts'. This enables it to develop an internal life in which, in Chandler's terminology, the 'invisible hand' can be replaced by the 'visible hand' wherever hierarchical organisation is more effective. Employment practices can be adapted, in the interests of creating stable and loyal work collectives. The firm may incur some cost in less prosperous times by retaining employees and maintaining wage levels at the expense of profits. It thereby replaces the 'invisible hand' with what Okun (1981) dubbed the 'invisible handshake'. Thus the internal organisation of the firm can be a form of protection against pressures from the market obviating the necessity to respond immediately to every price signal.

One possible conclusion from these criticisms of neo-liberal and property rights theories is that there is no powerful case for private ownership. The separation of ownership from control has been used by such diverse writers as Schumpeter (1953) and Engels (1969) to support the view that owners serve no socially useful function. It would, however, be wrong to follow the classical Marxist line. Although both prices and ownership play a less dominant role than is ascribed to them in neo-liberal theory, that does not mean that modern capitalism is like a planned economy but with continuing formal private ownership.

The increased scope for the 'visible hand' and the protection offered for employees in the internal organisation of firms are a response to a competitive market environment. Moreover, that protection is conditional on market success rather than being an absolute guarantee and this has important implications for individuals' behaviour. Thus, for example, employees who are offered greater security of employment know that they will lose their jobs if, and probably before, the firm closes. It is only in these circumstances that the 'invisible handshake', with its offer of greater security, can encourage commitment and initiative from employees.

This provides a powerful argument for competition between firms but, as is often argued from the British experience of privatisation (Vickers and Yarrow, 1988), the case for private ownership is less overwhelming. If Berle and Means were right to argue that the most important control on private sector managers operates through the legal system, then it should be possible to formulate rules for firms under state ownership that would lead to similar behaviour and hence enterprise performance. Indeed, empirical studies on Western European nationalised industries do not give any clear answers as to their relative efficiency and certainly suggest no gap comparable to that between overall performance in Eastern and Western Europe. There is certainly nothing in the experiences of state ownership, privatisation or industrial policy in Western Europe that could support hopes that the sudden transfer to private ownership of inexperienced and technologically backward state enterprises will lead to a dramatic improvement in performance.

Nevertheless, four arguments can be put in favour of private ownership as an ultimate objective for large-scale industry. The first is the clarification of a firm's independent existence without which neither genuine competition nor a long time horizon are possible. One of the major problems in British nationalised industries has been frequent arbitrary intervention disrupting business plans in the interest of short-term government policy objectives of political pressures (NEDO, 1976). Guidelines can be constructed to rule this out, but the temptations for politicians to intervene are strong.

The second argument relates to the flexibility of the joint stock company in the raising of finance on terms advantageous to a firm with a long time horizon that wants freedom from continual checks on its short-term results. It could even be said that it helps to overcome the obstacle to expansion which would be imposed by a very hard budget constraint. It is true that very little share dealing is concerned with new issues, but a developed and functioning capital market does provide an element of flexibility absent under central planning.

The third argument relates to the flexibility in organisational structures allowed by stock markets with the takeover and merger mechanisms. The value of this is often questioned because substantial evidence on share prices and takeovers has not confirmed that the process works in the interests of economic rationality. Moreover, there are many cases where state intervention, or even ownership, has been the driving force for rationalisation within sectors.

Nevertheless, there clearly are differences from central planning, where rationalisation largely ended with the first phase of reorganisation after Communist takeovers. Moreover, no mechanism emerged for bringing new managerial expertise into enterprises, for integrating across frontiers or for tying enterprises into long-term relationships with each other as can be helped by mutual share ownership. Part of the difference is simply the confirmation of enterprise independence, such that employees may ultimately recognise the pointlessness of resisting rationalisation, reorganisation and sometimes takeover when the alternative could be bankruptcy and closure. Nevertheless, even confirming legal independence under a form of state ownership could hardly achieve the multifarious forms of flexibility made possible by the institutional structure of stock markets and private owners.

The fourth and most tentative advantage is the possible disciplining effect of private owners. Three possible mechanisms for controlling management involve shareholders removing the directors, share prices falling so that expansion by new issues is effectively ruled out and low share prices facilitating hostile takeover. It has, however, been argued that stock market control may be too arbitrary and too strong in the UK and USA, discouraging firms from taking an adequately long-term view. In Japan and Germany shareholders' powers are much weaker and hostile takeovers are largely unknown. These differences, however, are less significant than the enormous gap with practices under centrally-planned systems which failed to evolve a means of controlling the behaviour of economic units without depriving them of the necessary degree of autonomy. The great merit of dispersed share ownership is that control tends to operate through institutional mechanisms that simply confirm the commonality of interests between management and owners rather than by detailed interventions.

From Theory to Strategy

Neo-liberal ideas had a powerful impact on the architects of post-1989 economic policy. There were, however, two broad obstacles to using the theory directly to formulate a strategy and this meant that policy emerged out of a continual conflict with a more pragmatic approach. The first obstacle relates to practical difficulties. The need would seem to be for the fastest possible price liberalisation and privatisation, but the former was considered certain to lead into inflation while the latter was not possible by orthodox means in view of the low level of personal savings. In practice, the solution was to use a highly restrictive monetary and demand-management policy in an effort to prevent inflation and also to simulate the pressure on enterprises that it was thought would result from private ownership.

There was considerable uncertainty over the next step with some believing for a long time that privatisation could be achieved in a single, sweeping measure: they gradually had to moderate their hopes. One alternative was put by Kornai in *The Road to a Free Economy*, a book titled as a conscious tribute to Hayek's famous condemnation of state intervention in the economy in almost any form, *The Road to Serfdom*.

Kornai envisaged the development of 'a new middle class', composed of 'industrious, thrifty entrepreneurs who want to move upward in society' who would be the creators of new firms. He trusted that their businesses would grow eventually into 'large-size or even mammoth' firms. Thus, it would appear, new growth was to begin very much as it might have done in an early stage of capitalism. The existing state enterprises, however, were dismissed as effectively unreformable and nothing very explicit was said about their future.

This was a consistent position, also put by others in slightly different forms, and it had considerable influence. Nevertheless, when spelled out, it seemed to rely on a questionable view of the nature of a modern economy. Kornai, in fact, did not consider the implications of the evolution into 'corporate' capitalism and saw 'impersonalised' property as an aspect of current advanced economies that should not be followed. He developed on Hayek's inaccurate view (1960, p.28) to claim that major innovations have largely been the result of the work of 'identifiable enterprising individuals or groups who financed the whole process from their own pocket' (Kornai, 1990b, p.75). The truth is nearer to Schumpeter's view that a key factor in innovation and business development was the availability of outside finance, through credit and share issues, which effectively softened the short-run budget constraint. Even Schumpeter, with his individual entrepreneurship as the 'pivot on which everything turns' (1954, p.555), probably overstates 'the personal element'. Chandler's studies rather suggest a close link between innovation and expert collective management.

A more immediately serious problem relates to the future of state enterprises. Within a neo-liberal world, allowing unprofitable enterprises to collapse and work collectives to disperse could be expected to lead to an almost instantaneous and highly beneficial reallocation of capital and labour to those with the gift of entrepreneurial ability. Such hopes are totally naive. Perhaps even more significantly, there was simply no chance of them gaining widespread acceptance. Neo-liberal ideology could therefore never be the sole foundation for policy making. It could, however, become a barrier to the formulation of new rules for the management of existing state enterprises and to active state intervention in trying to solve their problems. By ruling out the most realistic next steps, it helped contribute to a paralysis of policy making in the state sector.

The second broad obstacle to basing a strategy on neo-liberal ideology relates to the logic of the theory itself. Hayek's praise for the price system (1949, p.8) was as a mechanism that could bring 'order into human affairs' *not* from 'deliberate design' but as 'the unforeseen result of individual actions'. He directly counterposed it to the Marxist view that society should be shaped and coordinated by a conscious will. That, he believed, could never work. Unfortunately, creating a full market system, without returning first to scratch, would seem inevitably to require a gigantic act of social engineering. Even a strategy of the slowest possible, 'spontaneous' evolution would hardly be free of this criticism as it would mean considerable continuity from the structures created under central planning. Without starting from scratch all over again, there is simply no way to repeat anything that could remotely approximate to the gradual process whereby modern capitalism evolved. This issue was to reemerge in later conflicts as even staunch followers of Hayek, once in positions of governmental power, began to behave exactly as their theories predicted and started to engage in a little social engineering themselves.

PART II

Economic Transformation in Poland

3. The Legacy of the 1980s

The Commitment to Reform

Poland's economic situation at the end of the 1980s could, in many respects, already be described as catastrophic. Net material product in 1988 was still 1 per cent below the level in 1978, the last year before the economic crisis of the early 1980s, and declined again in 1989. Personal consumption was up by a marginally more satisfying 12 per cent, but that was only 3.5 per cent in per capita terms and was at the expense of an extremely low level of investment. The decade had seen no restructuring towards modern sectors of industry and there was no new basis for growth (Myant, 1989b). Hard currency debt, reaching $40 bn in 1989, was equal to five times the convertible currency exports in that year. With little chance that it could ever be repaid, this was still a crippling constraint on any hopes of recovery. By forcing a continuing drive towards exports, it contributed to an increase in shortages of various kinds of consumer goods, which had fallen for a time after a peak in 1981.

Economic policy in the 1980s in Poland was dominated by a verbal commitment to continue with the ideas developed and approved in the 1980-81 period when the Solidarity union enjoyed a legal existence. It was accepted that the economy was in deep crisis, that recovery depended on a more radical economic reform than had ever been implemented before and that economic reform and political democratisation were closely interrelated. In practice, however, commitment to democracy was contradicted by acts of political repression, including the banning of Solidarity after the imposition of martial law on 13 December 1981. There was some political relaxation in later years, but the authorities could never win genuine public trust. Without this they could not win acceptance for cutting demand as a precondition both for maintaining macroeconomic equilibrium and for reducing the burden of foreign debt.

Moreover, reform efforts were persistently stunted by their dependence on the political priorities of those in power and were never based on a systematic assessment of barriers or shortcomings in previous efforts. This was reflected in three persistent characteristics. The first was that the position of the top party leaders could not be questioned: they were not prepared to countenance the suggestion that they could be the principal barrier. The second was that actual proposals were derived from a compromise between political forces, and in particular a compromise with those who were essentially opposed to reform. The most radical advocates typically pushed for following the Hungarian example. The inadequacies of that model have already been discussed in Chapter 2, but even the proposals based on it were themselves consistently watered down in later discussion (Karpiński, 1986, Chapter 10). The third consequence was a continuation of political taboos linked to the leadership's ideological position: reform was definitely to be restricted within the socialist framework.

It was no longer possible to maintain the commitment to continually rising living standards but, until almost the end of the decade, there was no serious discussion of ownership relations. More generally, restrictions on open discussion made it impossible to develop a coherent vision of what the reform was really aimed at. The leadership was certainly committed to 'radical' measures, wanted to see them implemented quickly and hoped that that would yield positive results. The nature of the economic system that they would lead to was, however, never very clear.

One widely-held view is that, although reforms were implemented inconsistently, half-heartedly and often at a superficial level only, changes did lead to the creation of, at least, a 'hybrid' system (Mujżel, 1990). This, it should be added, was not a reference to the coexistence of a private sector with nationalised enterprises, a point which is touched on below. The emphasis was consistently on reforms within the state sector alone. It seems, however, that within this 'hybrid' the elements that dominated in determining the system's performance and behaviour were ones familiar from the old system. The point can be explored first with a discussion of the changes implemented which can then be related back to some of the more general points considered in Chapter 2.

Among the significant changes were a reorganisation of central organs with a reduction in the number of ministries and in their total employment. The scope of the central allocation system was reduced and a degree of price liberalisation introduced. Indeed, 55 per cent of prices were nominally freed which was a greater proportion than in Hungary at the time. In practice, however, these measures did not fundamentally alter enterprise behaviour largely because, as in previous reforms, the factors determining enterprise prosperity remained unchanged. Thus the central level retained considerable power which it could justify in terms of the short-term policy objective of keeping a check on open inflation: even after the use of the armed forces to crush independent trade unions the authorities were still cautious of imposing uncompensated increases in the prices of basic goods that they still controlled.

They also reintroduced a range of implicit and explicit limits on prices such that enterprises continued largely with the old cost-plus principle. Higher prices risked censure from the centre for making monopoly profits and this could lead to the imposition of direct controls, the simple confiscation in tax of any profit judged to be excessive, or the loss of some other beneficence. Lower prices obviously risked financial difficulties. There was, of course, no problem with the market absorbing price increases as enterprises typically enjoyed monopoly positions within conditions of shortage. The means of implicit price control in turn ensured that full equilibrium could never be restored on consumer goods markets.

Under these circumstances, it would have made little difference if the centre had controlled all prices directly. The effect was the same as it could control enterprises' ability to go beyond the cost-plus principle. It could therefore still decide on the allocation of resources by, for example, tolerating price increases when it wanted to allow investment in a particular enterprise. The fact that nominally only 20 per cent of investment costs were decided centrally or that the state budget accounted for only 47 per cent of the value of national income in 1986 — compared with over 70 per cent in Czechoslovakia — therefore need not be crucial.

As in the reformed Hungarian system the centre retained considerable further discretionary power through variable tax and subsidy rates and the continued central allocation of raw materials and foreign exchange, reflecting persistent shortages of these categories. Despite a commitment to achieving currency convertibility, the exchange rate was set at a level that left around 30 per cent of exports to both trading blocks unprofitable. A lower exchange rate would have solved that problem at the expense of higher input costs and hence domestic inflation. The general conclusion of those implementing reform was that they failed in the fundamental aim of breaking the traditional system of allocation. It was with 'considerable surprise' that they noticed the continuation of bargaining between levels in the hierarchy (Karpiński, 1986, p.314).

The Weaknesses of the 'Second Stage'

This failure of reform to bring significant changes was becoming increasingly clear by the mid-1980s. At the ruling party's Tenth Congress in 1986 the decision was taken to implement a 'second stage' of the reform around the slogan of the 'acceleration' of changes. In essence the intention was to put into practice those measures decided on before, in terms of enterprise independence, but still not implemented. The key was to be the speedy achievement of market equilibrium, by means of price increases. This would free the way for the elimination of the central controls or implicit constraints and of the central allocation of vital inputs.

Two novelties were added to this fairly traditional reform package. The first was an attempt to win popular consent for what it was recognised would be, at least temporarily, painful measures. This implied a recognition that the failure to restore equilibrium in the past stemmed at least in part from the failure of the authorities to win popular trust. The promise this time was of two to three years of hardship before prosperity. Thus all should be going well by the end of 1990: the justification for this timescale was never explained but it was the same as promises made in the first reform proposal from 1981.

The belief evidently was that at the end of that brief period a new system would have emerged leading to renewed growth.

The hope of winning public acceptance culminated in a referendum in November 1987 on the questions of radical economic reform and an unspecified form of political democratisation. The result was a disappointment. Only a 44 per cent minority of those eligible to vote supported the government's economic reform proposals, although that amounted to 66 per cent of those voting. The government concluded that it would still proceed with price increases, albeit somewhat more gradually. Later events suggested that the results of the referendum, held under conditions in which no opposition groups were allowed to campaign, greatly overestimated the willingness of the population to accept the government's strategy.

The second novelty was the relaxation of some old taboos. The question of clarifying, and possibly changing, ownership relations figured prominently in the debate over the details of the 'second stage'. In the end, the final compromise eliminated any radical new ideas in that direction. Nevertheless, the aim was accepted of creating equal conditions for state-owned, cooperative and private firms, the latter accounting for nearly 20 per cent of Net Material Product. The private sector had previously been tolerated, but subjected to various forms of discrimination. Conditions were also eased for joint ventures with foreign participation, although majority foreign ownership was still permitted only for those of Polish origin. A further novelty was the activation of a law on financing state enterprises, originally passed in November 1985, to allow scope for the creation of new firms under the joint ownership of state enterprises and other bodies, including private individuals. The way was cleared for the creation of joint stock companies which, it was hoped, would help overcome the inflexibility of the old system and give new scope for innovation and enterprise.

There were also various institutional changes which might, in another context, have been judged highly positively. The Central Planning Commission was deposed from its position of unique supremacy, renamed more innocuously the Central Planning Office, and left as an equal partner with the Ministry of Finance. The latter, through a new State Treasury, was to become the formal owner of state enterprises. The 'monobank' system, in which one monopoly bank controls all allocation of finance in line with the central planners' decisions, was abolished. Instead, as of May 1988, nine financially independent commercial banks began to operate alongside the National Bank so that there could be competition in offering credit.

Indeed, the World Bank (1988, p.5) was generally impressed. It saw the 'main fault' in the previous system in the individualised and variable interest rates and subsidies which served to 'weaken market signals'. Marek Dąbrowski (1990a, p.19), one of Poland's 'radical' reformers, was also cautiously optimistic. He likened the changes introduced under the 'second stage' to the Hungarian reforms which he still believed to have created 'undoubtedly a new variant of the system of functioning'. In his view, the results of Poland's efforts differed only by creating a system of 'much less stability', owing to continuing partial successes for attempts at recentralisation. He was impressed by the great breakthrough of allowing discussion of the need to transform ownership relations. Specific measures appeared to him as a combin-ation of good intentions and frequent sabotage by the same officials who failed to understand economic reform in the past: thus the central apparatus *was* being reduced and there *was* talk of the need for demonopolisation and deconcentration (Dąbrowski, 1990b, pp.99-101).

Nevertheless, the 'second stage' set off to a disastrous start. The fundamental problem was not in the institutional changes, but rather that it was not based on the necessary social consensus. Under these circumstances the institutional changes led to a worsening rather than an improvement in the economic situation. Problems were clear from the start when sharp price rises in January 1988, including a 140 per cent increase for food, were met with the reemergence of a strike movement. Despite opinion polls consistently showing a majority in favour of economic reform in general, the government had clearly failed to convince the industrial workers that they would have to be the first to bear substantial sacrifices.

This socio-political barrier to reform made it impossible to 'harden' the budget constraints on enterprises. A strongly anti-inflationary wage control system had been in place since 1982, with nominally punitive taxes on increases above a specified percentage. Nevertheless, enterprise managements typically responded to strikes by conceding wage increases pretty rapidly. Institutional changes were meant to have prevented this. Thus the chairman of the National Bank Władysław Baka announced a policy of 'strengthening money', meaning a tightening of credit controls. This proved ineffective because the government, unable to allow bankruptcies and unemployment and trying to hold some check on open inflation, yielded to demands for subsidies (Kołodko, 1989, pp.54-6).

Thus, instead of a single round of price rises to reach a general equilibrium, the economy was plunged into a chaotic spiral in which wage and subsidy increases fed still more price rises. The point was summarised by one critic of the government: 'inflation in Poland is not a monetary process with social consequences: on the contrary, it is a social process with monetary consequences' (Kołodko, 1990, p.71). In terms of the discussion of reform models in Chapter 2, Poland was moving close to the Yugoslav version only under conditions of possibly even more intense social conflict. Controls provided by central administrative planning had been relaxed, but no effective mechanisms had emerged to take their place. Indeed, state intervention had the effect of protecting enterprises against outside pressures thereby ensuring that no control mechanisms could emerge.

From Reform to Chaos

The failure of the 'second stage' led quickly to the reappearance of serious and general shortages of practically all manufactured consumer goods on a level as bad as in 1980-81. Although figures suggest that wages rose faster than prices, the effect of standing and moaning in queues again and relying ever more on the black market was to create the impression of a sharp fall in living standards. Indeed, the very fact that wages were rising was a factor fuelling the increase in shortages. Nevertheless, the most widespread response was pressure for more wage increases and a further strike wave started in August 1988. Over the whole year 55,000 participated, complaining primarily of falling living standards, but many non-strikers were granted wage rises too. Estimates of the inflationary overhang, the volume of forced saving built up as a result of shortages, are as always not very reliable. The sort of guess likely to have been believed by the government suggested that a reduction of effective demand of almost 40 per cent would have been required to restore market equilibrium (Lipowski, 1990).

Other estimates were of the same order, but must be treated with caution. The average level of savings registered in domestic currency was little over the average monthly income. A growth of shortage need not lead to forced saving. Other responses are 'forced substitution', meaning buying less satisfactory goods that happen to be available, and purchasing from the second economy at inflated prices, thereby absorbing the purchasing power produced by higher wages. Evidence in later years suggests that the inflationary overhang may not have been significant. Indeed, shortage encouraged panic buying and it seemed at the start of 1990 that households might be over-stocked with goods rather than purchasing power.

The shift towards the black or second economy became particularly strong as controls on foreign contacts weakened after the early 1980s until by 1986, research suggests, up to 25 per cent of personal incomes were from 'secondary' activities, with foreign trade transactions providing up to 10 per cent (Grzegorczyk, 1989). The return of rapid inflation saw a still stronger switch towards reliance on hard currency with the so-called 'dollarisation' of the economy. Convertible currency was increasingly used in internal transactions, even for some basic consumer goods, and became the most sensible form for savings at a time of rapid inflation. This itself helped further increase the black-market value of the dollar.

A subsidiary consequence of this was to make complete nonsense of any pretence that the authorities could influence the pattern of income distribution. Thus a study of 'high' incomes, meaning the top 10 per cent of earners, suggested that hardly any were dependent primarily on salaries from the state sector. Among high earners there were some farmers and private businessmen, some with specialised intellectual skills, such as a few writers, but the largest group made gains primarily from dealings that involved international travel or hard currency. Thus of one million who travelled abroad a minimum of a third could be involved in some trading thereby earning the equivalent of the average annual salary within a couple of months. They could buy and sell between different Eastern European countries, as varying price relativities and patterns of shortage combined with arbitrarily set exchange rates to make many such transactions highly profitable. They could even work, maybe illegally and on low rates of pay, in Western Europe. Overall, the true distribution of income looked at least as unequal as that of the USA. There certainly could be no pretence that it was any more just (Mieszczankowski and Pawlicki, 1989).

The onset of 'stagflation' also created serious difficulties for the state budget. It was generally slightly in deficit throughout the 1980s, with spending on average 1.4 per cent above revenues in the 1982-88 period. That, of course, is indicative of a persistent inability of the centre to maintain overall balance in the face of competing pressures from lobby groups. The situation worsened in 1988 and then 1989 saw a deficit equivalent to 11.9 per cent of revenues or 3.4 per cent of Net Material Product. This stemmed partly from a renewed attempt to hold down the price of basic goods and especially food in the shops so as to stem the wave of discontent. In the light of an escalation of other prices, including inevitably inputs to agriculture, this could only be achieved by a growing state subsidy to cover the difference between retail prices and purchase prices to farmers.

This peaked at 14.4 per cent of budget spending in 1988 and was running at an even higher level in the first half of 1989. The situation was made even more critical by a collapse in revenues from enterprises in 1989, down 9.6 per cent in real terms, with a major reduction from turnover tax which presumably also reflected the desire to suppress visible inflation. Thus the escalation of the budget deficit can be interpreted as a consequence of the failure to restore equilibrium through centrally-determined price increases. The obstacle was the impossibility of reconciling, within existing resource constraints, the competing pressures from lobbies, such as agriculture and some industrial enterprises, and from the population.

The consensus of professional economists' opinions at the end of 1987 had been to warn against the price increases of January 1988. A more gradual attempt to reach equilibrium, it was suggested, was the only way to avoid a wage-price spiral. This advice, however, might already have been too late and looked increasingly irrelevant later in the year. It was by then effectively impossible to find any economist who saw any prospect of the government's reform strategy leading to any positive outcome at all. The trouble by then was not that the reform measures had been half-hearted, leading only to a 'hybrid' system. A still stronger criticism was that 'the economy is completely decomposed' and 'in disequilibrium across the whole range' (G.Kołodko, *ŻG*, 1989, No.28, p.3).

This comment, it should be added, came from an economist who had been prominent in defending the government against criticisms from Solidarity in the early 1980s. The failure of reform attempts through the 1980s was extremely demoralising for those who had hoped that a Communist Party could still lead a reform movement. It seemed that the more determination it put into reform, so the worse the economic situation became. The familiar controls from planning had collapsed, but no market system was emerging to replace them. A familiar suggestion was that the outcome was 'a state of "nothingness" — neither plan nor market' (W.Herer, *ŻG*, 1989, No.28, p.1). It became increasingly popular to suggest that this state could not last. As one supporter of Solidarity put it, 'sooner or later' it would have to move to 'a much more stable state'. There were therefore two options: 'the contemporary capitalist economy or existing socialism, known as the planned economy' (J.Eysymontt, *ŻG*, 1989, No.18, p.7).

From the strictly economic point of view, there is no inherent reason why the system should have moved in either of these directions. It gave the outward appearance of disintegration, but this was not creating new or exceptional problems for state enterprises. Thanks to the disintegration of central controls softening budget constraints, managements were able to limit the extent to which shortages and price increases caused conflict within enterprises by yielding to wage demands. There was, then, no automatic compulsion towards change from the state-owned core of the economy. Indeed, its condition had much in common with that of state enterprises in other 'mature' centrally-planned economies. Rather than 'disintegrating' it was in a state of cosy stagnation.

While the state sector remained protected, it was being supplemented by the most rudimentary form of market, operating largely on the basis of legal, semi-legal or even fully illegal small trading. Most of this provided no serious basis for the rapid emergence of a new or rationally reformed economic system. Official figures show the trends very clearly. Thus while the 1980s saw remarkable stability in the number of enterprises and even in the sectoral structure of the state-owned part of the economy, non-agricultural private sector employment grew from 611,700 in 1980 to 1,187,900 in 1988 and 1,515,200 in 1989. By December 1989 there were even 291,250 private enterprises in industry with a total employment of 717,400. These were mostly very small and often dependent on larger state enterprises. A dynamic sector of flexible and growing firms was at best only just beginning to emerge.

A reincorporation of the unofficial into the official economy could theoretically have been achieved via a return to central planning. That, however, would have had no chance of permanence without the prior restoration of market equilibrium and price stability. The precondition for that was a government with the trust and credibility to demand considerable sacrifices. Neither need the alternative, a transition to the market, have developed spontaneously out of the existing economic system. It too required a clear political decision. That could be either for an orderly process of transition or a decision to relax controls on state enterprises to such an extent as to allow their disintegration.

A New Determination from the Government

A final twist to this picture of apparent disintegration was added by a sudden determination from the government to push ahead with reform. The stimulus was the first wave of strikes in April 1988. The response, shrouded at first in bizarre secrecy, was a new law giving immense additional powers to the centre. It was to be allowed to take any necessary steps to restore equilibrium, to push through the 'second stage', to impose its will on enterprise managements or to liquidate state enterprises, if that were 'for the good of the national economy'. The draft law was not debated at all until it reached parliament on 11 May 1988 where, despite some fierce objections, it was passed unanimously. It appeared as a sort of 'martial law' in the economic field.

The motivation behind the measure was clearly an unstated belief that the reform was facing various obstacles within enterprise managements, and possibly also from employees' councils, as their right to veto dissolution of an enterprise was to be overruled. There was therefore an implicit rejection this time of any suggestion that reforms were failing from the absence of wider participation or that they were incompatible with the existing structure of political power. It need hardly be added that the authorities initiated no open discussion and made no explicit reference to these fairly simple theoretical issues.

Solidarity as an organisation was still illegal and based its criticisms of the government on the ultimately sterile complaint that reforms should not be at the expense of living standards. Among those who were later to emerge as its leading economists two quite different lines of attack were developing in relation to these emergency powers, and indeed to the 'second stage' as a whole. One was to point to the absence of associated political change as the fundamental barrier. The other, gaining strength by the end of the decade among professional economists and pressed especially persuasively by Marek Dąbrowski (1990b, p.103), was to argue that the whole philosophy of 'imitating market solutions by the state' was fundamentally flawed. Instead, the need was to create the mechanisms and institutions through which a genuine market could operate.

This, then, was a fundamentally different argument. There was no criticism of the extent of the price changes, or of their impact on living standards. Neither was the political context given much prominence. Instead, the argument centred exclusively on the use of a non-market mechanism, meaning centrally-administered price rises, to bring about market equilibrium. In terms of the reform models set out in Chapter 2, the first of these approaches corresponds to the 'socialisation' version while the second to Kornai's 'radical' reform.

The emergency powers themselves seem to have achieved little apart from throwing the legal system into chaos and creating more uncertainty in enterprises' environment. It seems, again, that attempts to eliminate inefficient enterprises made minimal headway. The powers were used for some reorganisation and for some transfers of ownership, but nothing that created genuinely competitive market structures. Despite verbal commitments to demonopolisation and deconcentration other steps, such as a strengthening of some industrial combines, worked in the opposite direction. Thus in 1978 there were 4,428 state or cooperative enterprises, with an average of 1,039 employees. By 1987 5,617 enterprises employed on average 751 while by the end of 1989 the respective figures were 6,008 and 669. There had been some deconcentration, but hardly a transformation of the structure.

There was, however, one dramatic and bold new development relating to the Lenin shipyard in Gdańsk, the birthplace of Solidarity in 1980. Its closure had been on the cards for some years, but the issue was brought to a head after the formation of a new government under Mieczysław Rakowski in October 1988. Using the special powers and desperate to appear to be taking decisive action to speed up reform the government announced the impending closure on 31 October. On some other occasions the law was used to break strikes and it seemed to Solidarity to be self-evident that the primary motivation was political.

The economic arguments are confused and a leading Solidarity economist argued that losses could be transformed into profits by more rational price and exchange rate systems (Bugaj, 1989). Nevertheless, the adviser to the Minister of Industry could put a strong case for closure (Tomal, 1989). He maintained that a strategy of shifting towards less material and energy-intensive sectors, plus a new recognition of the need to respond to the profit criterion, meant that 'many enterprises' would have to face 'the prospect of liquidation'. Shipbuilding happened to be first with the careful estimates suggesting that capacity should be cut by 35 to 40 per cent. More than one yard could therefore expect to be closed. The decision, it was claimed, had effectively been taken under the previous Messner government, but ministers lacked the courage to carry it through at the time. It was now insisted on by Deputy Prime Minister Sekuła and Wilczek, the private entrepreneur chosen by Rakowski as Minister of Industry.

There could be a purist argument that all such changes should be left to the market, or at least should wait until prices set freely by the market could be used as a basis for calculations. In reality, as argued in Chapter 2, no current price can ever be a precise guide. Moreover, major industrial reorganisations of this kind are frequently dependent on state intervention in market economies.

After the change in government in 1989, nothing emerged to contradict the government's position. For a time it seemed that a saviour had been found in the form of Barbara Piasecka-Johnson of the US firm Johnson and Johnson. During a visit to Gdańsk she took the 'spontaneous decision' to save the yard, based on her 'unlimited faith' in 'Polish workers and engineers' (Jezierski, 1989, p.4). A letter of intent was signed on 1 June 1989 with the hope that a new firm would emerge with a 55 per cent foreign share and $100 million of new investment. In the event, the agreement failed owing to the refusal of the local Solidarity organisation to accept the wages, employment levels and working conditions demanded by the prospective US owner. The enterprise was taken out of liquidation and back into state ownership in April 1990. This satisfied demands from Solidarity organisations, but gave no guarantee that the enterprise, or shipbuilding in general, would not be a continuing drain on the state's resources.

A further important development under the Rakowski government was the growth of new joint stock companies, using the legal framework passed in 1985. Several thousand of these emerged in 1989 and 1990. The form of joint stock company with majority state ownership was actually chosen in the government's rather belated programme for economic recovery, published in July 1989, as the target to which state enterprises should be transformed. The institutional context, however, was still a very rudimentary system of company law.

It was thus extremely easy for individuals to make rapid fortunes. The key was that the director of a state enterprise could invest part of its assets into a new enterprise in which he could have a direct interest. Sometimes deals involved joint ventures with foreign firms, in which the domestic firm seemed to have made a deliberately 'bad' deal in the interests of furthering the career of its director within the new firm. Sometimes assets were sold or leased way below their real value to a new firm in which the state enterprise's director was a shareholder. Often the arrangements were complex, concealing what was really happening, and involved a number of high officials.

As a general term of disapprobation, these companies were known as *nomenklatura* companies, to indicate their origins in the old power structure. Their overall economic impact was small, but their political impact was substantial. They encouraged references to a 'pathological' form of privatisation based on the 'decay' or 'decomposition' of the Communist system and on 'giving ownership' to the *nomenklatura*. Attempts to use the law against the machinations involved finally came to an end on 6 November 1990 when the Ministry of the Interior announced that it was ending its investigations as no evidence had been found of any laws being breached.

There were, it should be added, some voices favouring this process as an essential form of 'post-Communist primitive accumulation'. Others saw its positive role in speeding up the destruction of the old system (J.Staniszkis and A.Paszyński, quoted in Kowalik, 1991, pp.260-2). There are, however, at least three reasons for firmly rejecting such opinions. The first is the dependence of the process on what all recognised to be morally reprehensible acts. Beyond a few clever deals exploiting legal loopholes, there was no real entrepreneurship involved. This was hardly the beginning of a stable, ordered market system which has to exist within a legally regulated environment.

The second reason, in a sense confirming the first, is that the new companies were hardly ever involved in production: they were typically for specific trading deals and may therefore, by breaking down existing links, have served to worsen market disequilibrium without enhancing at all prospects for future recovery. Hopes that they would allow for flexibility or the concentration of managerial and technical expertise, and hence for the exploitation of possible innovations, were simply not realised under the existing legal framework.

The third reason relates to the kind of economic transformation implied by the emergence of the *nomenklatura* companies. In the words of one commentator, it was imbued with the 'propaganda of defeat' (Kowalik, 1991, p.262). The existing economy was seen as so hopeless that it might as well be demolished, leaving a clean sheet from which to start again. It can be added that the fresh start was seen as requiring no more than private property to set the system in motion.

The disappointments of the Rakowski government had a substantial impact on measures adopted in the following years. A balanced assessment of its failures is therefore important. A parliamentary commission was even set up which overwhelmingly agreed on 26 July 1990 that Rakowski had a major personal responsibility for policies which caused 'a fundamental deepening of the crisis in the Polish economy' (Dryll, 1990d, p.3). The judgement was not completely conclusive or unanimous with some presenting the government as the last attempt to hold back the transformation, while others, such as the former Deputy Prime Minister, Ireneusz Sekuła, saw it 'opening the door to a new Poland'.

Ryszard Bugaj, one of Solidarity's most respected economists throughout the 1980s and the chairman of the commission, bent towards the former view, although he accepted that Rakowski's motives were often 'not unambiguous'. He was still unhappy about the economic motives for trying to close the Gdańsk shipyard, although Rakowski (1991) has put up a spirited defence, but accepted that it could have been partially motivated by a desire to impress Mrs Thatcher who visited Poland shortly after the decision had been announced. The real issue for Bugaj, however, was the political context. Rakowski's measures, he thought, were clearly differentiated from later government policies because 'they were not backed up by society's acceptance'. More generally, he saw the decision to close the shipyard as a proclamation 'that reform in Poland would be implemented under the protection of the police and army'.

A full assessment of even the very first months of the Rakowski government would have to acknowledge three points. The first is that its overall impact was limited. It was not able to control economic processes or reverse the 'disintegration' in the system. Even a key commitment to formulate a plan for economic consolidation proved unattainable. The second point has to be a recognition of the government's priorities. Eliminating inflation was implicitly accorded a low priority, perhaps because the task was recognised to be hopeless. Instead, efforts were concentrated on solving the country's debt problems by negotiating with foreign governments — again without any major effect — and on some reform steps. The third point is that, within this context, the attempt to close the Gdańsk shipyard and the growth of *nomenklatura* companies may deserve a more positive assessment. It may be a long time before a Polish government could boast such clear achievements in transforming the structure of existing state-owned industries. The trouble is that these measures were simply condemned and either reversed or halted. There was no scope for learning the lessons that transformation to a market economy requires as a matter of urgency a new system of company law and a means to prove that decisions on plant closures have some relationship to economic rationality.

The Round Table

In practice Rakowski's greatest contribution was his attempt to bring the opposition into a partnership via the 'Round Table' discussions between the government, Solidarity and other social organisations in February to April 1989. He had throughout his long career frequently reiterated the view that major political reforms were essential and that the old model of power had to be abandoned. It gave him a reputation as a leading reformer within the party. Generally, however, he had stepped back from giving his ideas any concrete form.

As the 'second stage' was failing, he claims to have convinced President Jaruzelski of the need for major concessions towards what was clearly recognised to be a permanent and influential opposition. By the start of 1989 he had, narrowly, won over the party's Central Committee. Buoyed by opinion polls suggesting that his 'decisive' government was commanding widespread support, he aimed to allow the relegalisation of Solidarity, to bring into the government any of the 'constructive' opposition who would join him and then to press ahead with vigorous economic reform. He hoped essentially to win in public debate with an opposition that he believed would prove internally divided and unable to produce a coherent alternative programme (Rakowski, 1991).

The key concessions at the Round Table talks were the relegalisation of Solidarity and an acceptance of free elections in 1989, albeit with a rigged result in one of the parliamentary chambers aimed to ensure continued Communist dominance (Sanford and Myant, 1991). It seems to have been assumed that Rakowski would emerge heading a more strongly placed government which might risk genuinely free elections a couple of years later. Debates about economic policy developed around this assumption. They were the stormiest and longest meetings, and produced the least agreement.

Solidarity's criticisms centred on two areas. The first was the general philosophy of reform. Discussions generally among the community of economists had succeeded in raising plenty of questions and doubts while providing few clear answers. It had, until then, been assumed that socialism and reform were compatible. The assumption was still that some sort of 'third way', neither capitalism nor traditional socialism, would emerge. It was only just beginning to be accepted that conditions for a market to operate might have to be created first by, for example, changes relating to ownership (Mikołajczyk, 1989). The central issues were therefore still the means and pace of transition, it being assumed that the aim could clarify itself in time.

Attacks on the government from Solidarity were consistent with this limitation, concentrating on the 'government's paternalistic autocratic attitude', as exemplified by the decision over the Gdańsk shipyard and the method of privatisation evading any public control or scrutiny. This was linked to an alternative notion of a reform which was to be 'ours' rather than 'theirs' (J.Osiatyński, ŻG, 1989, No.18, p.6). It was to be based on 'self-management and the market'. The government was accused of 'imposing the idea of universal managerialism' which would, as in past reforms, fail to allow genuine enterprise independence and therefore prove inconsistent with the market (Tarnowski and Bugaj, 1989, p.5).

The second area related to inflation and living standards. On the government's side the main dilemma had been over the acceptable pace of the restoration of equilibrium and hence the possible freeing of more prices. There was a strong body accepting the gradual solution, partly because of the fiasco of the second stage and partly owing to scepticism as to whether free markets were all that crucial (Mieszczankowski, 1988). Nevertheless, at the discussions their representatives pressed hard for zero indexation of wages, rapid marketisation in agriculture and full agreement on an economic programme that would put an end to inflationary pressures.

It was Solidarity that seemed to be more cautious. As an organisation it was still operating under conditions of illegality and had not formulated an agreed position. Its ideas had not changed much from the early 1980s and were still at the stage of an eclectic combination of basic trade union demands and a powerful critique of the old system based on general faith in self-management and the market. The incompatibility of these positions could hardly be accepted at that time by its spokesmen. They therefore insisted: 'we cannot accept a fall in real wages' (Tarnowski and Bugaj, 1989, p.5). They did, of course, verbally recognise the need to bring markets into equilibrium and to keep inflation within reasonable limits. They insisted, however, that measures to control inflation had to recognise certain limits to society's tolerance. One possibility was to start with price increases for some luxury goods — a concept difficult to define in terms of anything actually available — rather than food (Jeziorański and Bugaj, 1989).

The final outcome was an agreement that broadly restated the government's strategic objectives without making it clear how they could be achieved. There was a declaration favouring equality between the different forms of ownership, but no commitment to privatisation.

Self-management was given new encouragement and destruction of monopoly power promised. Prices would not be freed, the explanation for reticence being the continued existence of monopolies and the huge excess demand. The economy was to be restructured, away from fuel, energy and raw materials. It was to be opened to the world and the debt problem overcome. These were all worthy intentions. The question was whether even the first step towards them could be successfully taken. The crucial issue here was wage control as a means to ensure market equilibrium.

Tough negotiations had defeated an attempt from the OPZZ unions to insist on 100 per cent wage indexation. Their proposal was formulated in such a way that it could even have meant wage increases above the level of inflation. This union grouping, the All-Polish Alliance of Trade Unions, had thereby moved a long way from its origins as party-dominated loyal partner to the government, created in the early 1980s after the relaxation of martial law (Myant, 1989b). By the end of the decade, although never formally in opposition, they had become something of a thorn in the government's side (Kozak, 1989). Their role during the 'second stage', perhaps largely due to a perceived need at least to keep pace with any militant noises heard from the still illegal Solidarity, was to keep insisting that living standards had to be defended. Rakowski found them more negative than he thought Solidarity would be and saw the OPZZ leadership as an ally of hardliners in the party who shared its opposition to the relegalisation of Solidarity.

An 80 per cent indexation figure was finally agreed, rising to 90 per cent for the last half of 1989, with the second month of each quarter as the date for responding to results from the previous quarter. This, it was claimed from the government's side, would successfully prevent accelerating inflation (Baka, 1989). It would, however, do little to bring it down quickly. In all, this was not an economic programme that could promise speedy success for economic reform. It was, of course, never put to the test as a Solidarity-dominated government was formed following a resounding victory across all except one of the seats open to a free contest in the elections.

The Marketisation of Food

Before leaving office Rakowski took one last 'decisive' step which launched the country a little further down the road to the market. This was the 'marketisation' of food, meaning the freeing of practically all food prices and the elimination of state subsidies. It had been demanded by farmers' representatives at the Round Table. Solidarity representatives could only take an evasive position, welcoming the idea as a general principle, but seeming to welcome even more the idea that its implementation should be delayed. It was vigorously backed by Deputy Prime Minister Kazimierz Olesiak, a member of the United Peasants' Party which was a loyal partner to the ruling party nominally representing farmers' interests, and decided on at the government meeting of 29 July 1989.

Table 3.1 Economic performance in Poland in 1989

	Jan-July	Aug	Sept	Oct	Nov	Dec
All prices	8.5	39.5	34.4	54.8	22.4	17.7
Food prices	8.2	80.4	44.5	65.1	17.4	11.6
Personal expenditure	6.9	31.2	39.0	36.7	16.1	38.5
Industrial output	−2.2	0.2	13.6	−2.3	−2.7	11.7
Savings rate	15.7	22.3	21.1	15.6	24.8	8.5
State budget	140.2	94.5	135.2	105.2	106.1	97.5

The January to July data show the averages of each individual monthly figure. All figures are percentage changes on the previous month except for the savings rate, which measures saving as a proportion of personal incomes, while the state budget figure refers to the ratio of expenditure to revenues.

Source: Calculated from *BS*, various issues.

The justification included 'expert opinion' that the transition to the market had to be fast. There was said to be a threat of a collapse in agricultural output in the face of unstable and uncertain price relations and Olesiak consistently pressed the view that this had to be an absolute priority area for the government. The aim, then, was to achieve a stable market equilibrium and ensure an increase in food production. Urgency was accentuated after strong pressure from farmers led the government to increase purchase prices for agriculture, thereby throwing the budget into its massive deficit. Compensation was paid to pensioners and some others on low incomes while most wage earners were to be protected by the indexation system.

Table 3.1 shows the background in the early part of 1989 with high monthly inflation, recorded personal consumption not quite keeping pace, industrial output falling and a state budget severely in deficit. The immediate effect of marketisation was to exacerbate market instability with huge price movements, way above the level predicted, and wide variations between localities. Confusion was increased by some farmers holding back deliveries in the expectation of higher prices later. By the end of the year, however, as Table 3.1 shows, inflation was slackening, although not by enough to justify claims of stabilisation.

A partial success could be claimed with the sharp reduction in the state budget deficit following the reduction in food subsidies in July. Figures for the last five months still show a deficit of 1.4 per cent of expenditure, very much as in earlier years of the decade. The figures on wages, consumer spending and the savings rate suggest that incomes were rising rapidly enough to maintain living standards and even leave a surplus for saving. Thus the year ended with the state sector of industry going into decline, consumer prices rising more rapidly than for many years, a state budget still showing a deficit and no indication that the somewhat chaotic steps towards a market had done anything to resolve the perceived problem of an inflationary overhang from forced saving in the past.

There are some reservations about the accuracy of statistics, and particularly in relation to those for output. Official figures show a 4.2 per cent fall in the state sector of industry including a substantial drop for food production. Thus meat output dropped by 11 per cent while consumer surveys suggest slightly higher consumption per head than in 1988 and an increase in net exports. The official figures may have been becoming less reliable as more transactions by-passed the state-controlled sector. In particular, many farmers were selling more of their produce directly to customers on the streets.

There was no shortage of critics who regarded the step as a lunatic measure. Even Prime Minister Rakowski later commented (1991, p.243): 'to this day I really cannot explain why I did it'. It was argued, predictably, that it could have been done more slowly and after more thorough preparation. It contained an irrational 'social' element in the continued subsidisation of some of the cheapest foods: this need not have been any help to the poorest sections of society as there was no reason to assume that they could fight their way to the front of the queues which inevitably developed for any subsidised goods. It did not even fully satisfy farmers who claimed to have been promised from the Round Table imported animal feed, other necessary materials and an end to inflation. They still complained of 'a lack of stable conditions', without which they saw no incentive to increase production, and therefore continued to call for more government assistance on top of the marketisation (J.Ślisz, *ŻG*, 1989, No.38, p.1).

These criticisms need to be put into context. Real incomes in agriculture rose by 21.9 per cent in 1988 and by 13.6 per cent in 1989 while real output was roughly stable. Farmers therefore benefited considerably from price movements. 1989 even saw a higher use of fertiliser, one of the previously scarce inputs. There is therefore no reason to take seriously warnings of impending collapse in agriculture in late 1989.

Nevertheless, none of the other criticisms of marketisation alter the essential point that a transition to market prices for food was a necessary step and that, in view of the extent of market imbalances in Poland at the time, any such change was bound to be accompanied by a fair amount of chaos. Better preparation would certainly have been desirable, and later Czechoslovak experience indicates how the extreme price fluctuations could have been reduced. There could also have been steps towards the demonopolisation of the food processing sector which was agriculture's direct customer. Nevertheless, the general principle of marketisation was correct and, once taken, there was no real question of reversing the step. It was actually a substantial help to the incoming Solidarity-dominated government which did not have to take responsibility for the short-term chaos and could later boast of having brought hyper-inflation under control.

4. The Balcerowicz Programme

On 12 September 1989 Poland's first Solidarity-dominated government took office under the prime ministership of the Catholic intellectual Tadeusz Mazowiecki. It still contained four ministers from the old ruling party, but all but one of these were removed by July 1990 and none were left by the end of that year. Solidarity itself was effectively a loose umbrella label for a range of former opposition groupings. The union as such never regained its former mass following, recording only 2.36 million members at the end of 1989. As a political force it was divided even on the issue of whether to take governmental office.

Opinion polls initially suggested that the Mazowiecki government enjoyed enormous trust and Finance Minister Leszek Balcerowicz, the main architect of economic policy, retained considerable respect as a professional economist committed to a firm break with the Communist past. Nevertheless, polls quickly confirmed growing disillusionment over economic issues and especially over living standards. Positive support for the government's economic programme dropped from 42 per cent in March 1990 to 31 per cent by the end of the year and only 15 per cent still saw no need to modify existing policies (Śmiłowski, 1991).

This public disillusionment provided the background to intensifying divisions throughout 1990 leading to the contest between Wałęsa and Mazowiecki for the presidency in November 1990. The result, with Mazowiecki winning only 18 per cent of the vote and Wałęsa 40 per cent of a 60 per cent poll on the first ballot, indicated the depth of disillusionment with the first Solidarity government. The point was further emphasised by a 23 per cent vote for eccentric Polish-born Canadian millionaire Stanisław Tymiński.

Wałęsa won on the second ballot and, following some complex manoeuvring, a new government was formed under Jan Krzysztof Bielecki, but it never enjoyed the same trust as had Mazowiecki at the start of his term. By the time of the parliamentary elections on 27

October 1991 around 90 per cent were describing the economic situation as 'bad'. Barely over 40 per cent of those eligible turned out to vote and no political grouping emerged in a position to dominate the new parliament. The largest was Mazowiecki's Democratic Union with just over 12 per cent, but closely followed by the 'post-Communist' Union of the Democratic Left. No government could count on solid backing in a parliament fragmented between 18 groupings.

Thus, in little over two years, Poland's new democratic institutions were on the point of paralysis. The fragmentation of political life was ultimately making the taking of any decision at all a time consuming and hazardous process. This obviously had serious consequences for the making of economic policy, but it should be seen at least in part as a consequence of the effects of the chosen economic strategy. This chapter therefore aims to show how the strategy was chosen and how it led to an economic performance far below the hopes and expectations of its advocates.

A Policy is Chosen

There was never unanimity in the Solidarity camp over economic policy, but the initiative in the late summer of 1989 passed to various academic economists who had criticised past reform efforts primarily for their failure to go further in embracing market principles. They had not previously been very interested in the social context of reform or in the need for a broad consensus. After the fairly sudden decision to form the Mazowiecki government, they had to work quickly to give coherence to its economic thinking.

A major stimulus was a visit from Jeffrey Sachs of Harvard University who addressed the Senate's Economic Commission on 22 August. The Solidarity representatives listened, impressed that he claimed to have advised governments in Venezuela, Argentina and Bolivia, and were at last filled with optimism as he outlined his notion of 'a sudden, decisive jump'. He insisted, with what was to become a familiar justification for almost all subsequent policies, that 'there is no alternative'. The basic points were to be market prices, a unified and stable exchange rate, an end to subsidies, a balanced budget and an opening to foreign and domestic capital (*GW,* 23 August 1989).

His argument for speed was partly a political one derived from Latin American experiences: time, it was claimed, could allow 'demagogues' to emerge and block socially painful but allegedly necessary measures. Supporters of the notion in Poland may have shared this view but preferred to refer in public to a window of opportunity created by an international political situation that might still prove to be temporary. Sachs also argued that speed would make possible a linking of macroeconomic stabilisation with systemic changes, including the creation of a competitive environment and privatisation of state enterprises.

This would then mean, he assumed, automatic controls on inflation via firms' hard budget constraints. He was, however, somewhat contradictory on this point, even when he outlined his ideas at greater length (Lipton and Sachs, 1990), tending towards an implicit acceptance that systemic change could not be rapid. He therefore advocated substituting the free market with strong anti-inflationary measures for some time to come. The key issue here was to be wage control, in line with the standard IMF package for Latin American countries gripped by similar problems of debt and high inflation. A final point was a suggestion, which had proved particularly attractive when mentioned to the Polish MPs in August, that reduction to the burden of hard currency debt could be achieved given IMF backing which would be more likely if his kind of programme were followed.

There were some opponents, or at least sceptics, from the 'left' in relation to the Sachs plan. To varying degrees they advocated a slower process claiming that the standard IMF package would not work in the specific Polish conditions of state ownership and monopolised production. Sachs was pretty dismissive claiming to have spoken in his life to 'at least 25 Finance Ministers' of whom allegedly all claimed to be operating in exceptional and very difficult conditions.

Some other MPs, taking a more 'pro-capitalist' position differed from Sachs by advocating speedy systemic change alongside 'stabilisation'. This was the view of a group of leading pro-market Solidarity economists formed in August around Janusz Beksiak, a strong critic of the Round Table agreements from the start, and including Stefan Kurowski, Tomasz Gruszecki, Jan Winiecki and Jerzy Eysymontt.

They saw the two aspects as 'two sides to the same coin' (Gruszecki, ŻG, 1991, No.1, p.5) and were particularly firm in condemning wage control as 'an element operating against the system we are trying to create' (J.Beksiak, TS, 1989, No.26, p.5). Generally, however, the Sachs line, interpreted as speedy stabilisation with systemic change still a vague aspiration for the future, triumphed quickly.

This was taken up and developed by a group of economists around Balcerowicz. They left vague the relationship between systemic change and stabilisation, but one of Balcerowicz's closest advisers later confessed 'to having the impression' that 'the Balcerowicz team were not expecting rapid structural changes' (Gomułka, ŻG, 1991, No.1, p.5). Although Balcerowicz himself recognised the complexity of the relationship between shortage and inefficiency, he did see shortages and the soft budget constraint as major determinants of the system's weaknesses (Balcerowicz, 1989, pp.189 and 271). His closest colleague, following the logic of this position, firmly believed that a deflationary policy, replacing a sellers' with a buyers' market, would be enough to force dramatic restructuring and efficiency gains (M.Dąbrowski, TS, 1989, No.26, p.5).

When Balcerowicz introduced himself to parliament on 8 September 1989 he had to admit that the road he was proposing was full of uncertainties. He suggested, however, that the time had come 'to shut our eyes and jump into the hole, without checking either the state of the water or the depth of the drop'. The only options he saw as being between 'a short preparation' and 'no preparation at all', corresponding to a 'fast' or a 'very fast' variant. The target was to be 'a modern economy of the capitalist Western type'. That meant private ownership rather than the 'self-managed model'. The first step was to be 'stifling inflation by total price liberalisation'. He prudently avoided being too specific on the length of the transition, but suggested that the 'suffering' would last 'months and not years' (ŻG, 1989, No.38, p.6 and ŻW, 9-10 September 1989).

His strongest supporter in the government appeared to be Minister of Industry Tadeusz Syryjczyk, a private entrepreneur and free market enthusiast whose explicit guiding belief while in office was that the only good industrial policy was no policy at all. He was not even frightened by the possibility that equilibrium might only be reached 'at a zero level of output' (TS, 1989, No.26, p.5). Another perhaps more surprising ally was the long-standing dissident and newly appointed Minister of Labour Jacek Kuroń. The latter, however, promised that there would not be too drastic a fall in living standards as protective measures, such as unemployment benefits, would be introduced for those losing their jobs. Nevertheless, he was convinced of the need to take the 'jump into the dark'.

Some others had reservations, continuing to see self-management as a possible option or favouring a 'Swedish' model of social democracy. Others doubted whether hopes for speedily controlling inflation would be realised. The likely social costs encouraged subsequent warnings against a possible 'jump onto concrete from a great height' and questions as to whether there should not be consideration of a more gradual strategy with a more active role for the state in the transition (Jeziorański, 1989). Balcerowicz, however, survived his parliamentary grilling reasonably comfortably and went on to formulate a more detailed government programme.

This speedy acceptance of what became known as the Balcerowicz programme poses two important questions. The first is how it could triumph within a movement based originally on a trade union. Balcerowicz himself had been a research economist rather than a political activist, but Kuroń had a lifetime's experience of left-wing opposition activity. He nevertheless explained some time later how he had been attracted to the new line.

The change had little to do with a profound study of its economic merits. The point was rather the political situation. The new government could have simply taken the policies from the Round Table, but the ultimate attraction was obvious, from the point of view of consolidating domestic support, of adopting the ideas current in the 'best' US universities. While listening to Sachs speaking Kuroń heard his Solidarity colleague Bugaj whisper 'what nonsense that chap talks' and replied 'I don't know much about what he is arguing for, but listening to it I know that it has political value'. Its principal attraction was that it could fill a policy vacuum for a government with no ready-made programme which was unsure of the international situation with the USSR still a super-power. Kuroń's instincts seemed to be confirmed when the group of economic experts around Beksiak reached what seemed to him to be similar enough conclusions while those around Balcerowicz effectively agreed in total (Kuroń, 1991, pp.17-20, and *ŻG,* 1991, No.23, p.4).

The second question is whether the programme corresponds to a serious critique of previous reform attempts. Kuroń (*ŻG,* 1989, No.38, p.7) tried to claim that it did, suggesting that Rakowski's mistake had been to adopt a 'gradual' approach 'conceding to pressures from society'. That contrasts strangely with the widespread criticism of the 'second stage' for trying to adjust prices too quickly and of Rakowski generally for ignoring the need to reach a consensus with society. The issue, in fact, is not really one of speed but of the political context. On some issues, such as wage indexation, Rakowski could not have been any firmer. What was politically impossible for a government representing a discredited, old system seemed to be politically essential for a government wanting to show that it was breaking dramatically from the past. It too, however, was ultimately to find itself hemmed in by 'pressures from society'.

In purely economic terms, however, the crucial question is whether price liberalisation and convertibility logically come on their own before other measures. Many sceptics argued that systemic change, including certainly demonopolisation and possibly even privatisation, should come first. Balcerowicz's deputy minister Marek Dąbrowski (*ŻG,* 1990, No.4, p.7) rejected this maintaining that 'examples demonstrate' the impossibility of demonopolising until the administrative system had been abandoned. This view could be derived from the bad experience of the 1980s but that cannot be taken as proof. A determined attempt by a popular government to break up monopolies could have been more successful than the vaguely directed reorganisation under the special powers of 1988. Moreover, bad experiences from the past could not prove the correctness of a new and completely untried strategy.

Shock Therapy Begins

The big day for the 'shock therapy' to start was set for 1 January 1990. The emphasis was entirely on bringing inflation under control as quickly as possible within the context of general market equilibrium.

That, of course, meant an initial burst of price rises, but after that there was to be approximate stability. The five key elements of the policy included, first, a roughly balanced budget: the deficit of 7.4 per cent of total public spending in 1989 was to be transformed into a 1.6 per cent surplus. The second element was to be the final freeing of nearly all prices. The third was to be a restrictive monetary policy finally achieving positive real interest rates, at least after a first wave of price rises had passed. The figure was set at monthly levels amounting to an annual average of 432 per cent in January but dropping steadily to 48 per cent by June.

The fourth element was to be a wage control policy with punitive taxes on enterprises for transgressing defined norms: these allowed wage rises only as a set proportion of the previous month's retail price index. The level was set at 30 per cent for January, falling to 20 per cent for the next three months. It was raised to 60 per cent for May and June, to 100 per cent in July, and then cut back to 60 per cent for the rest of the year. The fifth element in the programme was the establishment of internal convertibility at a unified exchange rate of 9,500 zł to the dollar. This, roughly the free market rate, amounted to a further devaluation from the official rate of 503 zł in December 1988 and 6,500 zł at the end of 1989. It was way below any rate based on conceivable estimates of purchasing power parity. It was a case of playing safe at a time before standby credits had been negotiated to weather possible deficits as imports were liberalised. It was also in line with the standard IMF package of setting a firm 'anchor', or rigid target against which other policies could be judged. There was also a 20 per cent import duty and various additional taxes could raise the cost of imports by 44 per cent in all.

Thus the alternative for a more gradual transition, or one that incorporated structural and institutional changes alongside price liberalisation from the start, was firmly rejected. A letter of intent to the IMF, the basis for a standby agreement reached on 5 February to cover the possible balance of payments deficit, gave the government's forecasts. The 'shock', it was believed, would eliminate inflation fairly rapidly after an initial 75 per cent rise in prices. National income would fall by only 5 per cent and recovery could begin as early as mid-1990.

There were early successes with unexpected budget and balance of
payments surpluses, but as Table 4.1 shows, things did not run
smoothly. There was a reduction in inflation after the first two months,
but the level remained consistently higher than forecast. There were
even signs of renewed acceleration towards the end of the year despite
hopes of a 1 per cent monthly rate from July onwards.

Table 4.1 Polish macroeconomic performance in 1990

	Prices	Wages	Consump-tion	Employ-ment	Ind. output 1	Ind. output 2
Jan	79.6	1.8	4.3	−1.0	−31.5	−30.5
Feb	23.8	15.0	15.7	−0.2	−2.1	−30.3
March	4.3	36.7	26.3	−1.0	0.9	−30.7
April	7.5	−5.8	7.7	−1.4	−1.5	−28.5
May	4.6	−3.0	0.8	−1.6	0.3	−28.0
June	3.4	2.3	10.7	−0.9	4.9	−27.3
July	3.6	10.8	3.2	−1.3	−12.2	−23.5
Aug	1.8	5.0	4.6	−1.3	7.6	−17.9
Sept	4.6	7.6	11.3	−1.0	8.0	−21.0
Oct	5.7	13.6	9.1	−0.9	0.4	−19.5
Nov	4.9	12.0	2.8	−1.0	0.0	−17.9
Dec	5.9	3.1	31.0	−2.6	3.2	−24.3
Whole year	560.9	398.0	439.6	−9.3	−24.2	−24.2

Figures show percentage changes on the previous period except for Industrial Output 2
which shows percentage changes over the same month in 1989. The whole year figures
show changes over the whole of 1989.

Source: *BS*, various issues.

The fall in industrial output was also much worse than expected
and, as confirmed by the figures comparing with the same months in
1989, most of the fall came in January. There were possible signs of
recovery later in the year. Employment fell substantially more slowly

than output which, as will be argued, is consistent with minimal restructuring and adaptation within enterprises.

The significance of the divergence from the figures in the letter of intent has to be put in context. The targets relating to inflation were conditions for the IMF and poor performance led to conflicts in the autumn. The figures relating to output and living standards were never intended as part of a rigid programme. The important point was the commitment to what was essentially the standard IMF 'stabilisation' package with a willingness to bear whatever costs might be required. Thus Balcerowicz admitted that the forecast drop in output was only a guess, based on the expectation that some enterprises would be forced to close. The timing of the recovery was never very precise with 'hopes' that it could come in late 1990, or in 1991. The social costs were not a major concern. Dąbrowski foresaw unemployment of anything between zero and 30 per cent. He suggested that the actual figure could be anywhere between the two (*ŻG*, 1990, No.2, p.8). It was the sort of detail that made no real difference to his conviction that no other policy could work and that the depression itself would herald a natural return to growth.

Nevertheless, the first months' results, with the unexpectedly deep depression and some successes in relation to inflation and the state budget, stimulated discussion over economic policy for the second half of the year. Broadly speaking there were three possibilities. One was to continue with the existing restrictive policy. Despite accusations from critics that the Balcerowicz programme was based on a dogmatic and unyielding faith in depression bringing recovery, this option was rejected at least for a time. A second was to switch to an anti-recession policy with a substantial expansion of demand. This was rejected on the grounds that macroeconomic control was still weak.

The third option was to aim for recovery from the supply side, by concentrating on 'systemic' changes, while keeping a firm grip on inflation. Although this was seen as the best approach, it was felt to be too slow on its own and the decision was therefore taken for a 'controlled relaxation of fiscal and monetary policies' (Gomułka, 1991b, p.6). The IMF was sceptical but the idea was incorporated into a second letter of intent allowing for a 10-15 per cent increase in real wages over the level of the first six months of the year, but there were no new policies for stimulating investment or exports and no details on how systemic changes were to be accelerated (Rosati, 1990).

The Economic Council, an expert advisory body containing a wide range of opinions and expected to make informed comment on policy issues, discussed this so-called 'second phase' in early 1991 and concluded that it had been a failure. They were, however, never able to produce an agreed analysis which could explain the continuation of inflation without a clear resumption of economic growth. The switch was criticised even more strongly by Dąbrowski who resigned as Deputy Minister of Finance in protest. There is considerable truth in his criticism that, while publicly claiming to be following the third option mentioned above, the government was actually drifting into an eclectic mixture of all three (Dąbrowski, 1991). Thus the anti-inflationary aspect was maintained with the continuation, albeit in a less severe form, of the wage control policy. As it operated through a tax on the total wage bill it effectively prevented expansion even in enterprises which faced buoyant markets: it thereby restricted structural adaptation and recovery. A further anti-inflationary element was a delay to the liberalisation of coal prices, and then implementation in a very partial way: this could hold back visible inflation but at the expense of the need for continuing subsidisation and of tensions within the mining industry which are discussed below in Chapter 5.

The anti-recession element was introduced in June 1990 with an expansion in the money supply, higher state spending, and a reduction in interest rates. The annual equivalent refinanced credit rate was reduced to 34 per cent from July to September, which suggests a negative real rate. The first half's budget surplus was used up, largely on preferential credits into the food industry and agriculture. Funds were made available for 'restructuring', but typically found their way into supporting bankrupt enterprises. This was cited as a partial explanation for the continuation of inflation. In Dąbrowski's view there was an alternative, based on more vigorous application of the market across all sectors, including health and other state services. That would help reduce public spending and, Dąbrowski continued to believe, would lead to rapid improvements in efficiency.

Weighing Up the Results

In the words of Grzegorz Kołodko (1991b, pp.15-16), one of Balcero-wicz's most consistent critics, 'the stabilisation policy of the first post-Communist government led to the deepest recession in post-war Poland, and at the same time to the deepest recession in the European Community with inflation stabilised at the highest level in Europe in 1990'. Before accepting a purely negative verdict, there has to be a discussion of the accuracy and significance of the statistics on which it is based and a recognition of the successes that were achieved.

Table 4.2 Percentages in Poland giving various reasons for failure to satisfy household needs in consumer goods

	Not enough money		Goods not avai-lable		Low quality of goods	
	Dec 1989	May 1990	Dec 1989	May 1990	Dec 1989	May 1990
Garments	44.6	60.9	21.8	2.8	6.5	10.5
Footwear	32.4	48.0	38.3	7.5	7.1	19.0
Radios and televisions	48.0	58.7	15.3	0.8	0.7	3.0
Cars	46.5	56.9	6.9	-	1.0	2.0
Food	27.1	39.3	13.3	2.6	2.8	2.8

The figures do not sum to 100 because further reasons were possible.

Source: Kramer, 1991a, p.9.

The main successes included establishing market equilibrium, maintaining a stable and unified exchange rate, achieving a balance of trade surplus and reversing the budget deficit. The last two of these were to prove to be temporary consequences of the macroeconomic situation and are discussed later. The first two were very significant changes with an immediate and generally positive impact on people's daily lives. Survey evidence showed 80 per cent pleased that queues had gone, 64 per cent happy that they no longer needed to hoard goods and 66 per cent welcoming the wider range available. Inevitably, 80 per cent also noted that they could not afford much of this new range (ŻG, 1992, No.27, p.8). The figures in Table 4.2 show the extent of the change with lack of money becoming an ever more important reason for not purchasing goods. Other survey evidence shows, if anything, a fall in the numbers regarding prices as unnecessarily high compared with 1989 (Karcz, 1991). The implication is that price rises could be accepted if shortages were eliminated.

It has been argued that the government's policies caused a catastrophic 'over-shooting' as equilibrium could have been achieved with far less pain (Kołodko, 1991a). As the depression of demand led to a substantial cut in output, it clearly did not need to be so severe just to eliminate shortages. It is nevertheless remarkable that opponents of the government have tended to be shy about criticising the first four months of 1990. People were prepared to accept sacrifices when something visibly positive was being achieved at the same time. Moreover, the dramatic and visible change could encourage the strong belief that a major break was being made with the Communist past and, irrespective of any careful weighing up of costs and benefits, that was a major factor encouraging either support for, or acquiescence to the Balcerowicz programme. One of the main psychological protections for continuing stiff restrictions was the argument that nothing should be done that could put the gains from those sacrifices into jeopardy.

Exchange rate stability, also claimed as a major success, was associated with a retreat from 'dollarisation' of the economy and a massive drop in the real free market exchange rate. As a result it was no longer worth taking an unskilled job abroad. Instead, Poland became the host to an unknown number of *gastarbeiter* from the Soviet Union and its successor republics working mostly on private building schemes with pay probably around half the level for Polish workers. Part of the 'disintegration' of the late 1980s seemed to have been reversed with Poland looking a little more like one of the advanced countries.

The issue of the credibility of statistics has been pressed by a variety of supporters of harsh measures, including Sachs. They have tried to argue that much of the decline in output has been illusory, reflecting the ending of useless and unwanted productive activities that never contributed to living standards. There are, moreover, problems with official statistics, the first being that they relate primarily to the state sector and there definitely was some balancing growth in the private sector. 516,000 new firms registered during 1990 while 154,000 went out of business leaving a total of 1.35 million employing nearly 2 million. 1991 saw a further growth to 1.366 million firms with a total employment of 2.48 million. Their contribution is included in the official figures only as a rather unreliable estimate.

Industrial output figures are not dramatically altered by including the private sector. The drop for 1990 moves from 25 per cent to 23 per cent, but internal trade's performance could be improved a lot. Indeed, the traditional Net Material Product measure of national income maximises the impression of decline, with an official figure of 17.5 per cent. GDP, stabilised by 'non-productive' activities, fell by only around 12 per cent. Indeed, the most dramatic indication of growth was an explosion of small trading in street stalls many of which need not have registered. There are no accurate estimates of how many people were involved, of the turnover or of the prices charged.

Casual observation points to prices around 20-25 per cent lower than in official outlets, a reversal from the pre-1990 position when unofficial were always higher than official prices. This points to an official figure on output maybe slightly below the true level and, more significantly, an exaggerated figure for inflation. A rough estimate, taking account also of price changes in former hard currency shops, pointed to a retail price index possibly a tenth below the official figure (Górski and Jaszczyński, 1991, p.60). Updating the weights used for calculating the index to those corresponding to the structure of consumption at the end of 1990 might take a similar amount again off the figure.

The most important area of controversy concerns living standards. The nominal drop in real wages for the whole of 1990 was 25.1 per cent, but this must be a deceptive measure as the former prevalence of shortage meant that many goods were either available only at inflated black market prices or not available at all. The drop in sales from state and cooperative shops for 1990 was 35 per cent while official statistical sources estimate the growth from the private sector to have been around 350 per cent. That points to a 16 per cent drop in sales overall, albeit with a wide range of uncertainty over the contribution of unofficial street trading.

Some check on changes in consumption is provided by household expenditure surveys. Although the Polish statistical office has not considered these accurate enough to replace its other methods of estimation, they should at least indicate the direction and approximate scale of movements. Comparisons of consumption in physical terms of various goods suggest a small drop only in consumption of food and various categories of modern consumer goods that were newly available from imports. Purchases of clothing, footwear and many other traditionally domestically manufactured consumer goods showed declines of around, and often over 30 per cent. With food accounting for around 50 per cent of consumer spending, this is compatible with a fall in real consumption of over 15 per cent, which is in line with the official estimate for the total drop in retail sales from all outlets. 1991 then showed some signs of a slight recovery, but nothing like enough to hold out early hopes of reaching the 1989 level again in the near future.

Berg and Sachs (1992) have estimated a drop in consumption of less than 5 per cent on the basis of the 60 per cent of household spending accounted for by the physical goods mentioned in expenditure surveys. They have then used this to suggest a drop in GDP also of less than 5 per cent, although this is substantially lower than their own estimates derived from a questionable reinterpretation of output data. The confidence they place in the household surveys is surprising, but their claim that official statistics have exaggerated the extent of decline cannot be ruled out.

Further questionnaire evidence also points to a growing feeling among households that they were buying less than a year before (Śmiłowski, 1991, and Kramer, 1991b). Some individuals were more satisfied with the new market conditions, but there was an almost total collapse in spending on cultural and recreational activities alongside polarisation in consumption of many manufactured goods: some felt satisfied with the situation and were buying more while somewhat more were buying less. These responses are compatible both with the view of the statistical office and with the Berg and Sachs estimates.

A final area of differing interpretations is the growth in unemployment. Figures first appeared in January 1990. The number increased steadily, reaching 6.1 per cent of those economically active by December 1990, rising to 11.4 per cent by the end of 1991 and then stabilising at least for a time at slightly under 13 per cent in mid-1992. Nevertheless, journalists' investigations in June 1990 suggested that up to 40 per cent of those registering had not been working before (ŻG, 1990, No.25, p.4). A remarkably generous benefit system — enabling even those actually earning from small trade to claim up to 90 per cent of previous earnings — could mean that the majority were 'voluntarily' unemployed.

However, a toughening of rules in December 1990 marked no break in the trend and a comparison between the growth in unemployment, the growth in private sector employment and the loss of jobs from the state sector does not suggest a major mismatch either in 1990 or in 1991. Those who had never worked were probably a small and ever decreasing proportion of the total. Moreover, surveys of the registered unemployed tended to indicate a picture of desperate poverty which diverged markedly from the popular perception of an easy life on state benefits (Graniewska, 1991).

The Macroeconomics of Depression

The disappointing results of 1990 can be explained around three aspects of economic behaviour. These are price setting, consumer spending and adaptation within enterprises, the last of which is covered in more detail in later chapters. All deviated substantially from the explicit or implicit assumptions on which the Balcerowicz programme was based. Price increases at the start of the year were close to the forecast level, but the causes were not universally appreciated. The principal impetus was from cost increases following the elimination of many state subsidies, the results of higher prices of energy and the sharp devaluation. Liberalisation was not an important factor as most prices had already been freed by December 1989. There were no controls at all on almost 60 per cent and only vague regulations covering another 20 per cent, while around 10 per cent continued to be controlled in various ways in the following year.

Evidence on consumer behaviour shows no significant role for temporary high demand as pent-up purchasing power was exhausted. This must cast further doubt on theories of chronic excess aggregate demand under central planning. Savings are difficult to follow as the trend in the late 1980s was to seek inflation proofing by holding dollars to an extent that cannot be estimated accurately. Nevertheless, the figures in Table 4.3, which compare incomes with expenditure, actually suggest that the first months of 1990 saw an *increase* in the savings rate from a figure of 16.9 per cent in 1989 which had already been high in comparison with earlier years. It seems that aggregate spending continued to be accounted for entirely from current incomes while inflation encouraged higher savings at least for a time.

Table 4.3 Consumer spending as a percentage of personal incomes in Poland in 1990 and 1991

	1990	1991		1990	1991
Jan	79.7	85.8	July	80.1	91.0
Feb	69.6	76.0	Aug	86.4	90.7
March	71.1	82.8	Sept	84.0	92.7
April	82.9	80.6	Oct	89.1	100.7
May	84.3	90.8	Nov	86.5	91.6
June	81.1	87.7	Dec	88.8	
First quarter	73.4	81.5	Third quarter	83.7	91.0
Second quarter	82.7	86.3	Fourth quarter	88.1	n.a.

Source: BS, various issues.

Possible reasons would be that savings, severely cut in real terms by the price rises, had fallen below the precautionary minimum, or that the sudden price increases put many people off buying all but the most absolute necessities. A further contributing factor could have been an accumulation of substantial stocks of consumer goods during panic buying in late 1989 stimulated by the expected price rises. The population seems to have adapted later in the year to a higher rate of spending as a proportion of incomes — averaging 82 per cent for 1990 as a whole and therefore still below the 1989 level — while all the time increasing the money value of savings. Figures for 1991 are consistent with survey evidence suggesting a growing percentage of the population with effectively no scope for saving (Kędzior, 1991).

The macroeconomic events of at least the early parts of 1990 cannot, then, be explained by the elimination of an inflationary overhang. In fact, the dependence of spending on incomes meant that the wage control system, by restricting wage rises below the rate of inflation, could have a rapid and massive impact on the real level of demand whenever prices had risen substantially.

This point warrants further explanation as there was controversy, fuelled by some of the most enthusiastic supporters of the free market, as to whether the wage control system was effective at all. Critics argued that monetary policy alone was the effective instrument and the wage increase figures in Table 4.1 do not appear to show an exact application of the indexation system. The January figure is deceptive as pay in December is boosted by bonuses from a share in profits. It looks as if the rules were applied pretty effectively in February, but various other months showed deviations one way or the other. This, however, was compatible with the rules which allowed an increase forgone in one period to be made up later. The high growth in wages in the later months of 1990 was therefore permissible in view of the low growth in April and May.

Moreover, although the policy of tight money and high interest rates may well have restrained wages in some enterprises, financial situations were so varied that it could not have had the blanket consequences of the wage control system. At best, monetary controls were effective only in the politically weaker enterprises while the bigger ones especially were able to circumvent such restrictions by running into debt. Wages were frequently regarded as the first priority, coming even before taxes or payment of interest on debts.

Moreover, even if the figures on wage increases were in some months below the level allowed, the wage control system could still

Table 4.4 Changes in industrial output, prices and profits in Poland in 1990 and 1991

	Non-food spending	Industrial prices	Net profi- tability	Industrial output
Jan 1990	−9.3	109.6	12.8	−31.5
Feb	32.3	9.6	15.4	−2.1
March	33.6	−0.2	15.9	0.9
April	−3.9	2.1	11.5	−1.5
May	3.3	0.6	12.9	0.3
June	10.6	1.5	13.1	4.9
July	4.2	3.3	10.1	−12.2
Aug	8.2	2.9	11.5	7.6
Sept	17.3	2.7	10.2	8.0
Oct	10.2	4.9	8.6	0.4
Nov	6.4	3.6	5.6	0
Dec	31.3	3.3	−0.4	3.2
Jan 1991	−21.1	9.8	2.2	−17.6
Feb	7.8	5.4	0.2	0.8
March	27.2	1.4	−0.3	0.1
April	−9.0	1.0	−1.7	−8.3
May	11.0	1.6	−1.1	−1.6
June	6.5	3.1	2.1	2.2
July	−5.7	2.1	−1.3	−12.1

All figures show percentage changes on the previous month apart from net profitability which shows net profits for all whole state enterprises as a proportion of sales. Non-food spending is calculated from figures for employees' households only.

Source: Biuletyn statystyczny, various issues.

have been the dominant restraining factor. By leading to lower spending from the start of the year onwards, it contributed to a worsening of financial situations such that many enterprises lacked the funds even to meet the permitted wage increases. It is therefore likely that, in the absence of the system used, wages would have risen more rapidly in some cases leading to a higher level of overall demand. The wide and arbitrary variations in wage increases could also have stimulated very general feelings of injustice leading to more social unrest.

Turning now to the behaviour of enterprises, figures for the decisive period of 1990 and early 1991, shown in Table 4.4, are partially consistent with a continuation of the past practice of automatic cost-plus pricing (cf Rosati, 1991). The price rises of January 1990 were associated with cost increases in that and the previous month, although they were more than adequate, leading to an increase in profitability. Most subsequent price rises, however, show little obvious relationship to immediately preceding cost changes. They were anyway clearly not enough to maintain profit levels.

Indeed, once the very specific month of January 1990 is excluded, the usual statistical methods show the relationship between cost increases and price rises to be extremely weak. By 1991 it is nonexistent. A reasonable hypothesis is that enterprises started in 1990 with mark-up pricing, although allowing generous mark-ups in view of the uncertainty as to how costs would move. Survey evidence confirms that a gradually increasing number of firms recognised that raising prices led, via lower sales, to a further drop in profits (Belka et al, 1992a). At the start of 1991 the enterprise sector was hit by price rises of 25 and 15 per cent for coal and electricity respectively. To maintain profit levels it needed to increase prices by 16 per cent, but could not even manage 10 per cent. February and July saw further cost increases but enterprises lacked the ability to pass them on in higher prices and profits disappeared altogether.

This initial effort at mark-up pricing alongside falling real spending led inevitably to a drop in output. This differs from the behaviour assumed in economic theory for a competitive market in which prices can be adjusted as rapidly as output. Lower demand should then lead to lower prices as well as reduced supply. It is also not identical to normal monopoly behaviour. Although there were some fanciful suggestions that some enterprises might be holding back output to push up prices (C.Józefiak, *ŻG*, 1990, No.37, p.4), it seems that behaviour was less subtle.

The point warrants closer examination in view of the importance for economic policy over the whole period of the argument that enterprises took advantage of demand increases to push up prices rather than restoring output levels. The theoretical basis was a claim that enterprises developed under central planning had become so 'deformed' in their behaviour that they would be motivated only towards short-term profit maximisation with no view to a longer time horizon (C.Józefiak, *ŻG*, 1990, No.45, p.6). This, however, actually assumes quite a sophisticated appreciation of how to exploit market power.

The figures in Table 4.4 can help to identify the reaction of manufacturing industry to changes in demand. Essentially, higher or lower consumer demand can be met with changes in stock levels, in prices or in output. Stocks are difficult to follow and published figures may be very unreliable in this period of rapid inflation. The general conclusion is that higher spending in an individual month does not induce an immediate corresponding, or even lagged increase in the price level. The usual statistical methods actually indicate no relationship at all. Neither is there any relationship if monthly are replaced by quarterly figures, which might be expected to allow for a slower reaction of prices to demand changes. There is, however, a significant relationship between manufacturing output and non-food spending. A simple regression shows a change in spending leading to slightly under half as large a change in industrial output. The relationship explains over 40 per cent of the variation in the latter over the 1989 to 1991 period.

This, then, is consistent with a very short-term adjustment from enterprises to demand changes that centres on output rather than prices. However, the monthly figures suggest, and the usual statistical methods confirm, that this relationship applies only during a fall in demand, while there is no sign of higher demand encouraging an immediate increase in output any more than an increase in prices. There clearly are more factors at play including a combination of normal seasonal variations, break-downs from shortages of inputs, which continued to affect some enterprises dependent on imports especially from the Soviet Union, and lags while stocks adjusted.

It seems possible to conclude that the dominant influence behind inflation was cost rises and that the main response to lower spending in early 1990 was to cut output. Gradually, however, enterprise behaviour underwent adaptation with the recognition in ever more units that automatic cost-plus pricing was itself leading to financial catastrophe via the drop in sales. The ability to raise prices was therefore more consciously linked to actual and expected demand. The relaxation of restraint in mid-1990 might therefore have stimulated some price rises, but only in so far as it could encourage the expectation that better times were coming. Sharper restraint, along the lines advocated by Dąbrowski, would probably have led to substantially lower inflation only by deepening the depression and hence by leading more enterprises to give up hopes of higher demand in the future.

From Shock to Disappointment

These general explanations for macroeconomic behaviour in 1990 can be extended into 1991, a year of continuing macroeconomic disappointment, and used to illuminate the apparent, but temporary successes over the state budget and the trade balance. 1991 saw inflation of 70 per cent alongside a 76 per cent increase in average wages. Industrial output fell by 12 per cent and real GDP was down by 9 per cent. This can be set against forecasts of 36 per cent inflation and at least 3 per cent growth in GDP contained in a letter of intent to the IMF dated 25 March 1991.

1991 also saw serious balance of payments problems stemming primarily from a worsening in the foreign trade position. Part of the reason was the chaotic situation in relations with the USSR. Problems were already clear in 1990, as many Soviet customers failed to pay their bills. The situation worsened dramatically in January 1991 when all payments were to be in hard currency. Soviet enterprises simply lacked the ability to pay. The Polish government responded by informing its enterprises that they would no longer be covered for exports from public funds. A few continued, with the aim of keeping a foothold in the potentially important Soviet market.

It can be added that the impact of all this on Polish industrial output remains unclear. Estimates in 1990 suggested that around 5 per cent went into exports to the USSR. Nearly half had no prospect of finding a market elsewhere. Sachs has seized on this as an explanation for the continuing drop in industrial output, although it cannot be the most important, let alone the only factor. Moreover, the drop in exports to the USSR has been almost exactly balanced by growth into other markets, albeit generally not by the same firms. The fall in output in 1991 was therefore, as in 1990, a result of depressed domestic demand induced primarily by the cycle of inflation and the wage control system.

Results for 1990 appeared satisfactory with convertible currency trade and balance of payments current account surpluses of $2,214 million and $668 million respectively. Exports were 13.7 per cent up on the 1989 level, with a fall of 7.0 per cent to the 'socialist' and a rise of 39.4 per cent to the 'non-socialist' countries. Imports were down by 17.9 per cent with a 35 per cent drop from 'socialist' and a 4.2 per cent rise from 'non-socialist' countries. These figures are based on reporting through customs and therefore take no account of private individuals who brought in goods for their own use or for street trading.

The growth in exports could appear encouraging, but the breakdown by sector reveals that the best results were achieved by raw materials or the least processed products which were able to increase the share of their output that could be exported. They alone faced no substantial quality barriers and could therefore take advantage of the devaluation at once. There was no major shift to becoming an exporter of more sophisticated products with the share of output exported actually declining in the more modern sectors.

The dramatic fall in imports was due primarily to the domestic depression and the exchange rate. The effect of the latter began to wear off throughout 1990 as the nominal exchange rate remained stable alongside a threefold increase in domestic prices: comparisons of prices between Poland and various advanced market economies in early 1991 actually showed many goods, ranging from food to sophisticated consumer durables, to be more expensive in the former (*Polityka*, 1991, No.8, p.18 and No.50, p.24). It was therefore no surprise when 1991 saw a 39 per cent increase in imports alongside a

1.4 per cent fall in exports. The 1990 success of convertible currency trade and balance of payments current account surpluses of $2,214 million and $668 million respectively were transformed into deficits.

A crucial factor for Poland's overall balance of payments was the scope for negotiating better terms with creditors. At the end of 1990 Poland owed over $30 bn to governments, represented through the Paris Club and $10.5 bn to commercial banks represented by the London Club. Negotiations with the Paris Club were conducted in the hope of achieving relief on up to 80 per cent of the total. Agreement was finally reached in March 1991 on a complex deal that was equivalent to a 50 per cent reduction, and there were hopes of persuading individual governments to be even more generous. Talks with the London Club reached no speedy conclusion, partly because private banks were unsure that it was their job to aid countries that were in trouble, partly because of the growing political uncertainty in Poland and partly because of doubts expressed by the IMF.

Indeed, the agreement with the Paris Club was itself only possible at a time when talks with the IMF were going well. Their outcome, in April 1991 was a package for a three-year period. Its provisions for 1991 included a reduction of inflation to 36 per cent for the whole year, a strict limit to the budget deficit and stabilisation of foreign currency reserves. The targets were already unrealistic at the time they were agreed.

Moreover, even the reduction in obligations to the Paris Club was not reflected in an improvement for the balance of payments because Poland had not been meeting its full nominal obligations since 1981. The balance of financial flows therefore saw a deterioration, with a doubling of debt service outflows contributing to an overall deficit of $449 million, even after the use of more foreign credits, including $322 million from the IMF.

Foreign economic relations had clearly become a danger area by 1991, but there was no major change in strategy. Instead, the government implemented a series of pragmatic adjustments in response to pressures from particular sectors of the economy. Thus May 1991 saw a 14 per cent devaluation of the złoty against the dollar. Superficially this appeared as the possible abandonment of one of the pillars of the Balcerowicz programme. In reality, however, in view of the level of inflation during that year, 1991 saw a substantial real revaluation of the currency while many exporters were demanding real devaluation. Moreover, the stabilisation of living standards during 1991, as indicated by the faster growth in wages than prices, was clearly dependent on the growth in imports. Restoring external balance would therefore threaten any government with further unpopularity.

This, however, is an almost trivial problem in comparison with the condition of the state budget where a surplus proved to be a very temporary blessing. Table 4.5 shows the changes, starting with the remarkable success of early 1990. The key to this was the cut in spending on subsidies while revenues benefited from the good financial position of state enterprises. The surplus was then partially dissipated in the second half of the year as falling enterprise profitability led to lower tax revenue after public spending had been increased slightly. The 1991 budget was to prove a different story. Its formulation in early 1991 was a tense and difficult process and required a compromise between the determination to continue with the Balcerowicz programme and the desire for an active encouragement of recovery. In the end, although it was still officially presented as deflationary, it was accepted that there would be a small deficit equivalent to 3 per cent of spending, or 1 per cent of GDP, if international debt repayments were included: had agreements been reached waiving those obligations in total, the deficit would have been halved.

There were some doubtful elements on the expenditure side, such as the hope that social security spending could be cut. There were also some question marks over the income side, including hopes for substantial revenue from privatisation. Ryszard Bugaj, who chaired the relevant parliamentary committee, described the budget as 'tragically stretched' (*GW*, 26 February 1991). The real weakness, however, was shown up by results for the first half of the year with a catastrophic collapse in revenues. The cause was the financial disaster in state enterprises and the failure to tax the private sector. The latter point, as discussed below, was partly the result of a policy decision aimed at encouraging privatisation. It was also partly a reflection of the lack of any experience of or apparatus for forcing the rapidly growing mass of private enterprises to pay taxes.

Table 4.5 Poland's state budget 1990-1992

	1990		1991		1992
	First half	Second half	First half	Second half	First half
Revenue	87.3	196.2	95.6	210.9	130.9
Expenditure	80.6	193.8	108.8	241.9	156.6
Balance	6.7	2.4	−13.2	−31.0	−25.7
Balance as % of expenditure	8.3	1.2	−12.1	−12.8	−16.4

All figures are in billion złoty unless otherwise stated.

Source: BS, various issues.

By the late summer of 1991 the government saw no alternative to introducing major corrections to the budget. Spending was to be cut by 21.5 per cent and a deficit equivalent to nearly 10 per cent of expenditure was accepted as inevitable. Hardest hit were the public services, such as health and education, where pay could no longer expect to keep pace with other sectors. Bielecki's government found it impossible to win parliamentary approval for these changes. The essential reason was not that there was any other way to resolve the problem of moving towards a balanced budget in the short term. The debate centred rather on the fundamental cause of the difficulties. Balcerowicz's Ministry of Finance pointed to an 'explosion' of expenditure, referring in particular to demands for state benefits in the light of rising unemployment. On the revenue side, the failure was attributed to the collapse of exports to the former CMEA countries hitting enterprise finances.

The implication was that the budget alone was at fault, or that it had been hit by unforeseen and unforeseeable circumstances. The government's whole economic strategy was therefore said to be free from criticism. Opponents of this view, obviously enough, saw the root of the problem in the recession and saw no prospect of achieving a balanced budget by continuing cuts. That, it was claimed could only lead to ever deeper depression alongside the destruction of much of the traditional activities of the state in a modern society. The only solution seemed to be to accept a substantial deficit for some time until a correction to the government's overall strategy could bring economic recovery. That view was not openly endorsed by any government in 1992. The talk was of accepting that a deficit of up to 5 per cent of GDP, the maximum allowed by the IMF, might not be dangerously destabilising. As the figures in Table 4.5 show, lack of control over the budget deficit in the second half of 1991 became still more pronounced in early 1992.

5. The Economy under Balcerowicz

The macroeconomic consequences of the Balcerowicz programme were ultimately the result of changes at the micro-level, in the individual units that make up the whole economic system. The initial assumption, as has been emphasised, was that shock therapy would lead to rapid adaptation and speedy recovery. When this failed to materialise, some put the blame on external factors. There was even the fatalistic belief, touched on in Chapter 4, that state enterprises were so irreparably deformed that they might never play any part in recovery. Results for the various sectors, however, do not confirm the view that the private sector could necessarily do better.

They were generally unable to raise outside finance and depended on the founders' savings, the reinvestment of profits and the goodwill of more adaptable state enterprises which did not demand immediate payment of bills (Garliński, 1992). Small private business, with a short time horizon, requiring minimal initial investment and offering a quick return, could prosper. The obvious example is street trade, but the small amount of research evidence available rather suggests that few traders have much prospect of developing larger businesses (Nowak, 1992). Beyond that, ownership made no real difference to performance. The important question was how the sector was affected by the fall in demand and how far it was able to adapt to changes in its environment.

Agriculture Demands Intervention

One of the worst-placed sectors was agriculture, dominated by private ownership. The outdated structure included 2.14 million private small-holdings, with an average size of 7.2 hectares, while another 1.7 million people owned allotments or farm animals but no agricultural

107

land. Most of the farms were under 5 hectares while only 6.9 per cent were over 15 hectares. The remaining 24 per cent of agricultural land was occupied by 5,500 large state or cooperative farms with 60 per cent over 1,000 hectares. They accounted for only 16 per cent of agricultural employment and 13 per cent of net output in 1989. The overall level of mechanisation was low with 1 million horses and 850,000 tractors: around 1.2 million farms had no means of traction at all. Tractors were generally concentrated into larger farms — 85 per cent of farms over 15 hectares had one — while horses were typical on farms in the 5-7 hectare range (Zarzecki, 1990).

It had long been taken for granted that a more efficient agricultural sector could emerge by concentration into larger units, the elimination of the smallest farms and a fall in the proportion of the labour force active in agriculture. The traditional Communist means to this end had been to encourage concentration into state farms, but that was largely discredited by the 1980s. By 1990 state farms, like other state enterprises, were generally burdened by debts that they could not hope to repay and the assumption was that their land would somehow eventually be made available for family farms (Leopold, 1991).

Any hopes for concentration into existing private farms in the 1980s had, however, also made little progress. Part of the reason was the depressed state of the economy generally which halted the flow of labour into other sectors. Agricultural output in the 1982-89 period actually increased by 16 per cent while the total number of farms, including individual owners of allotments or animals, grew by 2.7 per cent between 1980 and 1989. Private farms of over 15 hectares, the ones most likely to be able to introduce better techniques, did increase, but only from 145,000 in 1980 to 188,000 in 1987.

Contrary to what might have been hoped, the free market conditions of 1990 did not lead to speedier adaptation. Farmers were hit by the drop in domestic demand, particularly for meat, caused by lower real wages and freer imports. The fall in demand was smaller than for many manufactured goods, but farmers cannot adjust their output plans quickly. There is, of course, a logic to individual farmers even trying to *expand* output to bring in revenue when faced with falling product prices and higher input costs. This, plus good weather conditions, helped to keep the fall in real output in 1990 to 1.4 per cent, made up from a 3.2 per cent drop for animal products and approximate stability for crops.

Official figures suggest that 1990 saw a fourfold increase in output prices alongside eightfold and sevenfold increases for input and consumer goods prices respectively over the average 1989 level. Farmers' living standards inevitably suffered, but not by more than others'. From a position of equality with employees' families in 1985, farmers rose to be 12 per cent ahead in 1989 and were still 8 per cent ahead in 1990. That suggests, again using uncorrected official statistics, a fall in real spending of 21 per cent against a figure of 27 per cent in employees' households. A reversal took place after September 1990 and spending per head in farming households was 13 per cent below that in employees' households in 1991.

There have been some changes in the output profile, but no progress towards a major rationalisation of production (Leopold, 1990). The decline in employment prospects elsewhere in the economy is encouraging families to cling to any small plots of land that they still hold. Sixty per cent of farming households have other sources of income. As the depression bites elsewhere their efforts could be diverted back into agriculture. Indeed, in contrast to the situation in Czechoslovakia, unemployment in Poland is lower in rural than urban areas. Depression could therefore be hampering the transition to a more advanced and rational organisation of agriculture.

The response from agriculture has been to demand active government intervention. Surveys have consistently shown that farmers see their problems stemming not from the state domination of the rest of the economy, the structure of farm sizes or the profile of production. They blame price relationships and interest rates (Młynarczyk, 1991) and they typically place their hopes in government action to overcome the demand barrier (Bienkowski et al., 1990). Exports generally offer little scope for expansion in view of the low quality of many products of the Polish food industry. In fact, some food processing firms have been happy to boost their financial positions by importing quality goods, such as butter and yoghurts, and turning their backs on domestic agriculture.

The government's philosophy in 1989 was to accede to farmers' demands for marketisation of food. In 1990 public statements suggested that the new philosophy was essentially to avoid any specific agricultural policy. Although elements of a policy began to creep in, in response to farmers' protests, that remained the essential approach through 1991. When it was insisted that all other countries intervened substantially to help their agricultural sectors, the typical response was a dismissive one. US agriculture 'might be the most regulated [sector], but is it the healthiest?' asked Balcerowicz (1991, pp.6-7). He added 'inflexibly high prices are maintained for political reasons'.

This position was ultimately untenable when agriculture provided the livelihood for 10.5 million people. It was a political voice that could not be ignored, especially as the rest of the population could be sympathetic to the view that the sector providing its food should not be left 'to collapse'. There was, however, no prospect within the new market environment of providing a solution through high prices to consumers, along the lines of income support policies in Western Europe. Food already accounted for over 50 per cent of consumer spending, compared with around 20 per cent in the European Community. The newly formed Agricultural Intervention Agency, with 1,856 bn złoty (around 0.5 per cent of the total state budget) therefore restricted itself to the gradual raising of tariffs, especially on the most processed items such as butter, state support to stabilise but not to raise prices and subsidisation of credits to enable purchase of fertilisers. This last measure was justified by the long production cycle in agriculture such that operating credits simply could not be repaid for several months.

By the end of 1991 officials from the Ministry of Agriculture had taken to insisting that the depression in agriculture 'must' end in 1992 (Tański, 1991), but their policy options were very limited. There was still no enthusiasm for price support rather than just price stabilisation policies. The state budget was clearly in no condition to offer such help. Commitment to a more active agricultural policy has therefore come as the ability to implement it has declined.

This leaves agriculture with a very uncertain future. The spring of 1991 saw a threat of serious regression as farmers cut costs by reducing the use of industrial fertilisers from 160 kg per hectare to 75-80 kg per hectare, roughly the same level as in the second half of the 1960s. On this basis the grain harvest could fall by 40 per cent. Thanks probably to good weather conditions and the continuing benefits of past investment, output fell by only 0.7 per cent from the

1990 level. Less favourable weather in 1992, and deepening financial difficulties on both private and state farms, led to a drop of around 15 per cent in output with predictions of a similar fall to come in 1993. This obviously has serious implications for price stability and for the balance of payments.

Coal Might Like the Market

At the opposite extreme from agriculture, a sector which demanded state help because it could not adapt, were those sectors which felt continuing state controls, particularly on prices, to be the cause of their difficulties. These were the scene of the first major industrial conflicts after the collapse of Communist power. There were protests from railway workers and bus drivers in May and November 1990 respectively. Potentially the most serious case, however, was coal-mining which provided around 75 per cent of the country's energy needs. Hard coal output fell in 1989, after the Round Table agreed to improve working conditions, from 193 to 178 million tons. It fell again by 17 per cent in 1990 and by a further 5 per cent in 1991, largely because of the restrictions on demand. It was, of course, not initially one of the government's priorities to develop a coherent energy strategy. It was nevertheless concerned that price rises in energy could fuel inflation throughout the economy. It therefore continued to control prices in this sector and actually increased subsides to the sector as a whole during 1990 even though their level was being reduced very sharply elsewhere in the economy.

Two further factors contributed to miners' problems. The first was that bonuses related to profit made in 1989 were not paid during that year: they were then blocked in 1990 as the government insisted that they amounted to a wage increase within the terms of the new wage control system. The second factor was that a tax was paid on coal for export thereby reducing revenue to mines from potentially lucrative sales abroad. There was a logic to this strategy as the government might have feared, at the chosen exchange rate, a rush to export at the expense of crippling the domestic energy system. A partial freeing of coal prices in July 1990 was therefore also accompanied by restrictions on exports.

Mining had previously been firmly protected from any logic of the market and its finances were totally incomprehensible. There was a baffling heritage of past subsidisation, with seemingly illogical variations between individual mines, which made it very hard to predict how finances, and hence wages, would move if steps were taken towards a market economy (Jezioranski, 1990). Miners, however, were aware only that their relative pay was slipping. At one time nearly twice the average level for industry, relative pay in 1988 was 75.5 per cent ahead while by December 1990 the gap was only 51.7 per cent. It should be added that there were clear signs of a narrowing of wage dispersion generally and the miners were still safely around the top. Nevertheless, their relative pay was a figure they watched closely as their wages had typically been used in the 1980s as a basis for other sectors' claims.

Discontent came to a head towards the end of 1990. Delegations to the government in mid-November went back with nothing. The OPZZ unions appeared more militant at first, but Solidarity organisations were soon pushed into advocating strikes and took up the role of 'hawks'. One-day strikes broke out in 30 of the 71 mines, with indefinite hunger strikes by small groups of miners in some, on 20 November. The demands included payment of the past bonuses, an elimination of the burden of debts which were draining finances in interest payments, an end to the 20 per cent tax on coking coal for export and even 'the liquidation of the unjustified pay disparities between mines'. This last one was a double-edged issue as, even if many existing disparities were inexplicable, others would arise once wages were related to the highly variable productivities of individual mines. It is clear, however, that Solidarity organisations were taking a militant position against 'their' government by arguing in pro-market terms. The problem, they claimed, was 'a centralisation of management and of the economic and financial system unprecedented in history' (Dryll, 1990f).

Solidarity organisations warned that the government and parliament had either to 'choose the road of systematic, controlled growth in pay in mining, or there will be total chaos'. The threat was that managements would pay out wage increases and refuse to pay the punitive tax to the state budget. Negotiations, however, brought enough concessions from the government to head off such a potentially disastrous conflict. Balcerowicz refused to yield on issues relating to 1990 but made offers for 1991 which would allow for the freeing of all coal prices and the abolition of the tax on exports in June 1991 at the latest. At the same time there was to be a reduction in subsidies for the industry from the state budget.

In practice, price controls were maintained even in 1992 quite explicitly as an anti-inflation device. Subsidies continued in 1991, but their level was reduced from the equivalent of over 40 per cent of sales revenue in 1990 to only 11 per cent in 1991. Some of the gap was made good by price increases, while some was covered by growing levels of debt. Representatives of the industry continued to complain that coal-mining was being asked to pay for the government's anti-inflation policy while it could, they claimed, be highly profitable if freed from constraints. The workforce was, however, among the more docile in 1991. Despite the government's original tough stand, wages climbed back to a level 60 per cent above the average. The arena for industrial conflict shifted from those sectors that suffered from continuing central controls towards those that suffered from the pressures of the market.

Manufacturing Loses its Profits

Manufacturing industry was the key to the disappointments of the Balcerowicz programme. Practically all the evidence, right from the start of January 1990, suggests that it failed to stimulate a positive process of adaptation and restructuring. The emphasis on an anti-inflationary policy caused a deep depression, but in a form that hampered and distorted rather than promoting a reallocation of resources into the most promising enterprises or sectors. The chosen package was arbitrary in its impact and, if anything, favoured enterprises with out-dated equipment and no desire to expand output (Maj, 1990, 1991a, 1991b and 1991c).

The first impact was felt by enterprises in January 1990 when higher costs came from three sources. The most important were fuel, energy and raw materials affected both by changes in domestic regulations and by devaluation. There was also a sharp rise in interest rates. Although intended as a restrictive, anti-inflationary measure its most immediate impact was to raise costs: it therefore depressed real demand only indirectly by raising prices first. The impact of high interest rates varied enormously, ranging from a negligible proportion of costs to a figure greater than wage payments. The difference was partly arbitrary, depending on whether large investments had been financed by credit, and partly dependent on the sector: those industries with a long production cycle were more likely to need credits to finance current production.

The third element raising costs was an increase in the tax burden. The great bulk of state revenues in the past had come from taxes on enterprises and several elements remained unchanged in 1990 and 1991. Turnover tax was deducted before profits were calculated. Net profits were recorded as the difference between gross profits and various further taxes including an 'income', or rather a profits tax, which remained unchanged. There were, however, two major new elements including an adjustment to the so-called dividend, introduced in 1989 as a tax on the value of assets. The logic, obviously enough, was to encourage efficient use of the capital stock. This was promoted still more vigorously in 1990 when new rules eliminated any relationship between the level of dividend obligations and profitability. Moreover, new rules suggested that failure to maintain dividend payments could become a cause for enterprise liquidation.

Had assets been valued in a sensible way, and if enterprises had had the means to dispose of unwanted capital, then the dividend could have encouraged greater efficiency. In practice, under the conditions of deep depression and in the prevailing institutional climate, the latter of these conditions rarely applied. The former was also contravened by a revaluation of assets at the start of 1990 based purely on their age. In the absence of any means to arrive at a market valuation, this was the only feasible way to proceed. The result, however, was a system which penalised those with the newest equipment. Dividend obligations varied enormously from negligible levels to a substantial share of costs.

The second controversial tax change was the stiffening of penalties for exceeding the wage increase norm. The initials of its formal title, PPWW, were adapted into the familiar name of *popiwek*. This sounded in Polish as if it was associated with the effects after drinking too much beer. At the start of 1990 very few transgressed but the figure rose, probably passing a third of enterprises by the end of the year. It was an option available to those able to achieve a good financial position by price rises and bore no relationship to the ability to increase productivity (Maj, 1991a).

Enterprise profitability was no guide either to its past performance or to its future prospects. Even published results, which were based on the assumption that all bills would be paid, were not an accurate guide to the real financial position of an enterprise. They were seriously distorted by the ability of many enterprises to mask their problems by the simple device of running up debts to suppliers. So widespread was this that it was often very difficult to identify the primary cause of bad debts. Moreover, when identifiable they often turned out to be the largest enterprises closure of which would unleash a chain of further disasters throughout industry. For those enterprises that were profitable the only reward was often the privilege of becoming an unofficial creditor forced to subsidise the losses of others (J.Dąbrowski et al., 1991b, p.8).

The extent of even the paper financial difficulties reflected to a great extent the arbitrary ways in which the new tax and credit systems affected particular sectors. Profit rates in 1989 were roughly equal between sectors, but had diverged widely by 1991. Those with a short production cycle, an inelastic product demand and generally old equipment were likely to be well placed. A high share of labour costs was an advantage in view of the wage control system restricting their growth below the rate of inflation. A real success story was the food industry, showing a rise in profit rate from 17 per cent in mid-1989 to 26 per cent in mid-1991. It was uniquely well placed in view of the relatively small drop in consumer demand and of the industry's ability to exploit its position as a monopoly purchaser of the produce of domestic agriculture. It was farmers and not food processors that suffered during depression.

The worst placed were consumer electronics, which faced possible extinction from competition with higher quality imports, and the textile industry. The latter, accounting for 12 per cent of industrial employment, was concentrated into Łódź, the country's largest industrial city. Market concentration was low, with 393 state enterprises in 1989 employing on average 321, but lack of monopoly power seems to have been of little importance. Prices were soon held in check by imports while exports could not be increased permanently, owing to the low quality of products, the low level of technology and a cut in orders from the USSR. By the end of April 1990 Łódź was reporting a 30 to 50 per cent fall in sales, a 30 per cent reduction in output and a 50 per cent cut in real wages. Many factories had switched to a three-day week as very few enterprises could escape the collapse in demand and, increasingly through the year, profits.

Manufacturing Tries to Adapt

The hope had been that enterprises would adapt to the new conditions by becoming more efficient and enterprising. In the event, as suggested in Chapter 4, enterprises' first reaction was overwhelmingly defensive, based on a wait-and-see approach and on hopes that the depression would lift quickly. Defensive in this context means passing on higher costs in price increases whenever possible and responding to lower demand by cutting output. There are at least four good reasons for suggesting that this was their most logical first reaction.

The first is the extreme uncertainties of their situation. At the start of 1990, as so often happened during previous attempts at economic reforms, many were not even clear about the new regulations. They were also able to make only the vaguest estimates of future demand or of what price the market could bear. Even current sales were often not trusted, as households were believed to have stock-piled goods during the former years of sporadic availability. Moreover, there were often doubts about the availability of the required raw materials, particularly if they had to be imported from the Soviet Union. A typical management's view was 'What it will be like in a week, a month, in half a year — I don't know. I am afraid that demand will fall' (Brach, 1990, p.4). Some shared these fears and were proved right; others dismissed them and were often proved to be sadly mistaken. It made little difference. With such immense uncertainty enterprises could only respond to the immediate problems that confronted them. That meant raising prices and waiting to see what happened next.

The second reason for a 'defensive' reaction was the hope that things would soon improve. The psychological appeal is obvious, when no alternative presented itself. The justification from past experience is clear, as state enterprises were never left to go bankrupt in the past. It was also, ironically, a view encouraged by the government itself with its confident assertions that inflation would soon be fully under control and output growing again. Although possibly 30 per cent of enterprises could have been declared bankrupt by mid-1990, as they were behind with tax payments, they were pretty confident that they could survive: one survey showed only 8 per cent seeing bankruptcy as a possibility at all (Caban, 1990).

The third reason is that management lacked the abilities or expertise necessary for an approach based on rapid adaptation. They were not prepared with a background in market research or with a range of new products. Neither — and this is the fourth reason — did they have the financial resources necessary to take such steps. Even the partial reforms of the 1980s had not given enterprises the ability to build up independent financial reserves. They had to raise funds from scratch at existing rates of interest, with the main information available to banks being their catastrophic current financial position. Their first passive response was therefore the only one that could reasonably be expected.

Gradually, enterprises did try more ambitious forms of adaptation, but they were still essentially limited and based on the implicit hope that there was no need for a fundamental change in their behaviour. Thus, having recognised demand as a limiting factor, they tried a range of measures to promote sales or to cut selling costs. These included offering credit terms and other inducements to customers, by-passing existing wholesalers, setting up outlets run by the manufacturer and selling goods through street traders. Many enterprises tried to take advantage of the devaluation of January 1990 by expanding exports of existing products but interest in this declined throughout the year as domestic cost increases led to an effective revaluation. A more active approach was developed towards suppliers, with enterprises negotiating, often successfully, for price reductions. This was obviously likely to be most successful when there were competing suppliers, as in agriculture, but was completely pointless for imported materials.

Surveys covering the latter months of 1990 indicated that many enterprises believed that they were adapting to the new environment. Output increased again, possibly in response to expectations of a recovery in demand especially after the slight relaxation in the restrictive policy but also, it seems, as a reaction to success in eliminating the stocks built up in the first couple of months. The next few months, however, saw a reaccumulation of stocks and a further reduction in output. One survey of 49 manufacturing enterprises, and another of 166 in light industry alone, suggested even a period of growing optimism and a decline in fears of bankruptcy (Caban, 1991, and Pościk, 1991). Enterprises were claiming to be diversifying and taking steps to improve efficiency. Many were willing to accept that their organisational form was outdated and needed changing. One third were able to boast of contacts with a foreign partner and half were aiming to boost exports substantially.

Much of this, however, must be interpreted as wishful thinking or even mere rhetoric. The initial hopes of recovery from changing government policy were to some extent being replaced by a new and equally shallow belief than an easy panacea could be found abroad. In terms of real action there is not much sign of urgency. Despite hopes of higher efficiency hardly any were committed to significant further investment. The overwhelming majority, although claiming to want a better management structure, did not believe that the current one was negatively influencing performance. Neither were hopes for exports backed up with permanent international contacts. Links were irregular and sporadic and aimed broadly at selling the existing range of products. There were no cases, for example, of entering an agreement to produce under licence from a foreign firm. These activities still amounted to a 'short-run' adaptation to the market. They were a step forward, but were not based on any fundamental rethinking of strategy, of production programmes or of employment needs.

In fact, employment policy provides the clearest indication of the continuing hopes of better times to come. Firms were prepared to impose unpaid holidays or shorter working weeks, but were reluctant to make employees redundant. The behaviour of employees changed somewhat with a halving of absenteeism — the usual tokenistic act of compliance at times of rising unemployment — but productivity per man-hour declined. With employment falling by 9.2 per cent, the average hours worked per employee fell by 6.5 per cent in 1990.

The reluctance to take decisive steps to reduce employment is also reflected in the slow but steady rise in unemployment — neither corresponding to variations, nor as rapid as the drop, in output — and the similar fall in manufacturing employment. Jobs were going by natural wastage, often with individuals moving to better employment elsewhere, and were rarely part of a coherent strategy for employment reduction. Enterprises were frequently trying to keep their work collectives together, despite the massive drop in output. They even seem often to have continued recruiting manual workers while only wanting to lose 'indirectly' productive employees. Moreover, a survey covering 50 firms in the first half of 1990 showed that this was hardly ever associated with any reorganisation or rationalisation in the use of labour. The issues of employment and of production are in most enterprises treated 'separately and in isolation from each other' (Smuga, 1991, p.3).

In fact, despite some rhetoric about adapting, Polish enterprises continued to see the solution to their problems in the relaxation of the government's restrictive policy. The problem, to them, was the low volume of demand. The notion of 'over-shooting' in the restrictive policy could thus be given a further meaning. Not only did it mean a deeper depression than was necessary to achieve market equilibrium. It also meant a depression so obviously engineered and so arbitrary in its consequences as to encourage enterprises to stick to old modes of thought developed under central planning. Rather than seeing the solution in terms of changes in their own behaviour, they were naturally led to see it as stemming from a change in the rules applied from the centre.

The Failure of Adaptation

A survey of enterprises undertaken by the economic weekly *Życie Gospodarcze* in mid-1991 suggested that attempts at adaptation had come to a dead end. All kinds of enterprises could face bankruptcy with no obvious link to long-term prospects. Indeed, the first four to be put into a state of liquidation would not obviously have done worse than the average within another tax and economic policy framework. They were all from light industry, hit especially hard by the fall in domestic demand but within any plausible structural policy a sector that could be expected to grow. Some could even have hoped to reach viable agreements with Western firms which in time might have opened up new prospects for development. The trouble was that they could not expect to survive that long (Dryll, 1990g).

The most spectacular cases, however, were among the country's largest enterprises. Their size could itself be a protection as the government would think at least twice before moving to closure. The one that raised the questions of a new industrial policy most forcefully was the Ursus tractor factory in Warsaw. Employing 24,000 it was the capital city's biggest industrial enterprise. The history of its plans to expand output to 100,000 tractors a year, the resulting purchase of a licence from Massey–Ferguson and a subsequent massive investment programme, stands as one of the most famous blunders of the 1970s (Myant, 1982, pp.108-9).

These hopes had long since been abandoned, but the aim in 1990 was still to complete the investment and to reach an output of over 60,000 in 1993. This, it was claimed, was in line with any 'reasonable' estimate of the needs of domestic agriculture. It was, however, irrelevant to the immediate problems of 1990. Ursus was hit by high dividend payments, by high interest payments as its production cycle required substantial operating credits, and by falling demand. A collapse in sales, reflecting the crisis in agriculture, led to a 40 per cent drop in capacity utilisation in the first four months of 1990 (Dryll, 1990c). Over the year as a whole sales fell to 35,500 — tractor prices had increased over twice as fast as purchase prices from agriculture — and then plummeted to a monthly level of 300 in early 1991. The end of the road seemed near when, amid bitter internal conflicts, the electricity company threatened to cut off supplies in August. By then Ursus was in debt to possibly 1,000 suppliers and to the state budget and owed wages to its employees. Even its bank account had been frozen so that any payments had to be in cash. The events that followed are referred to later.

The *Życie Gospodarcze* survey generally appeared as a catalogue of externally generated difficulties which were often so massive and so sudden as to make the scale of a necessary restructuring almost unimaginable. Particularly enterprises used to selling military equipment or with traditional markets in the USSR could find the great majority of their demand wiped out. Many consumer goods manufacturers, particularly in electronics, stood no realistic chance against foreign competition. There were a few survivors, warding off the threat of bankruptcy. Among these were some managers who viewed the Balcerowicz programme very favourably, although often still wanting changes to enable 'good' firms to develop.

There were also a very few real success stories. Managements in such cases seemed unaware of why everybody else could not stop moaning and start to follow their example. They enjoyed, understandably, excellent labour relations and their only complaint against Balcerowicz was likely to relate to the wage control system. In the only cases publicised, however, these firms had started to develop contacts with the West years beforehand. This had been exceptional and in a sense even irrational behaviour as exporting to the West had generally been *less* profitable than exploiting the comfortable domestic or CMEA markets. Exports to capitalist countries had in one case been 'a hobby of the management, rather than the result of rational considerations' (Fronczak, 1990, p.6).

It seems clear that, taken as a whole, the government's policies did not lead to a process of restructuring and adaptation appropriate to the new market environment. It is, however, also pretty clear that simply conceding to pressures from enterprises would only restore the protected environment of the past. There are, then, three questions that need to be tackled once the failure of the first policy framework is acknowledged. The first is whether *some* reflation would be possible and beneficial. The second is whether some kind of more active industrial policy is not essential. Both of these questions were to become central to policy debates in 1991 and are addressed later. The third question is whether various changes within enterprises, possibly still in the context of the tough macroeconomic environment, could not make them more willing and able to adapt.

Caught in the Bermuda Triangle?

The main target of criticism here has usually been the weak position of management. Past support for self-management led to a structure within which an elected employees' council could effectively veto the directors' plans. A political atmosphere in which people appointed under the old system could be distrusted further weakened directors' standing. Once Solidarity organisations had been firmly reestablished in late 1989, elections were held to employees' councils. Many directors were then changed, although it should be added that they had usually fulfilled their term of office so that this all occurred within an orderly, constitutional framework.

There was, however, no basis for managerial legitimacy from outside — for example derived either from private owners or from a firmly stabilised state apparatus — and directors therefore had to rely on support from employees' representatives. That meant both the employees' councils and the trade unions. Of these the OPZZ unions probably represented around 30 per cent of the labour force with Solidarity enjoying a lower membership. Some employees belonged to both union groupings and slightly under half the labour force were in no union at all.

These unions were likely, it was assumed, to favour higher wages and full employment. They would certainly not welcome rationalisation involving redundancies. Competition between representative bodies, with none wanting to appear weak in front of management, could strengthen that tendency. The result was a management unable to take any decisive action. The three groupings created a 'Bermuda Triangle' into which responsibility and decision making could disappear without trace.

This assessment of management's position was supported by many respondents in the *Życie Gospodarcze* survey. Directors saw the system blocking progress in contacts with foreign firms. None would contemplate investing and taking a share in a firm if employees could control the subsequent use of their resources. Directors were therefore the most consistent supporters of major changes in ownership relations. Opposition from employees could thus be presented as the major barrier to the creation of firms that could survive in the open market environment. There was a change in 1991 towards an apparently more vigorous attack on over-employment with surveys showing the bulk of enterprises at least in light industry undertaking major structural changes. These involved the sale or closing down of parts of their operations. Nevertheless, redundancies were still motivated primarily by the need for immediate cost savings rather than forming part of a strategy for long-term growth. An 11 per cent fall in employment in 1991 was not far behind the drop in industrial output, but the 16 per cent fall over 1990 and 1991 together is still way below the 35 per cent reduction in output over the two years.

There is, moreover, indirect evidence that more ambitious rationalisation was blocked by opposition from employees as the total redundancies implemented by employing enterprises was half the level originally announced to employment offices (Belka, et al., 1992b). There are, however, two partial reservations to the argument that the 'Bermuda Triangle' was the major barrier. The first is that various other factors severely hampered the scope for rationalisation. In particular, there was a legal requirement to six months' redundancy pay. With enterprise finances already in a catastrophic state, this was often simply beyond their means. They therefore opted for the alternative of maintaining nominally higher employment levels while failing to pay their bills. This was safe enough as only the government, in the form of the Ministry of Industry, could instigate bankruptcy proceedings against them. That is actually the only power it had to intervene directly in an enterprise's affairs, but it would then be left to pay the redundancy money itself. It lacked the financial resources for this, and it also lacked the administrative staff to cope with the legal complexities of liquidating bankrupt state enterprises. By the end of 1991 only 11 such liquidations had been completed while estimates suggested that 1,400 enterprises should have been declared bankrupt (ŻG, 1991, No.51-2, supplement). It is therefore likely that changing management relations would on its own solve very little in these more extreme cases.

The second reservation relates to an evolution and considerable variation in industrial relations within enterprises. Studies covering the first half of 1990 rather suggested that employees were aware of the need for sacrifices (J.Dąbrowski et al., 1990 and 1991a, and Pościk, 1991). Trade unions were often passive on the wage issue, even when profits were high. OPZZ, despite some aggressive noises from its national leadership, was not particularly militant. Both union groups, although with Solidarity usually the more forceful, actually criticised directors for failing to produce strategies for adaptation. An energetic management seemed assured of backing, while those removed were usually accused of doing nothing to enable the enterprise to survive in the new conditions. Some were actually criticised for being too hesitant over wage and employment reductions.

It would, however, be wrong to generalise from this across all enterprises. The evidence seems to suggest that employees recognised the need for some unpleasant changes, but often could not accept the full extent of changes needed. Some enterprises were well placed in the market — such as many raw material producers able to export — or could keep going with minor adjustments only. In those cases industrial relations were likely to be good. The problems were greater if falling demand suggested the need for complete reorganisation and, as was often the case, labour reductions of 30 or 40 per cent, or even more. Management tended to shy away from decisive action in such cases, particularly as directors had often established their credibility upon claims that they could lead the workforce towards prosperity.

Indeed, whenever restructuring looked like being difficult and painful, there were almost certain to be different views on how it could be achieved. Any view that the management might be wrong could encourage employee militancy. Thus in Ursus bitter debates raged through 1990 and 1991 over the likely future demand for tractors. The director's view was that, once normal conditions returned to agriculture, sales could reach 50,000. Others, using international comparisons, saw 30,000 as the maximum. The employees' council reckoned on a figure of half that level and therefore advocated switching to producing cars. Others, predicting that agriculture would continue to be dominated by small farmers, favoured producing smaller tractors (Sonntag, 1991). It can be added that none of these plans offered speedy prosperity and all were based on guesses about future demand. The director's view, however, amounted to changing nothing and that could not increase his credibility in the eyes of the employees. Frustration was expressed in a string of protests that were expanded to cover all areas of employee discontent, including persistent demands for higher wages.

Managements seem to have been trapped in a situation where there were no 'good' options. Generally among firms facing a complete collapse in demand, redundancies were the management's last resort. They came after the failure to pay debts and taxes, weeks without wages and then lengthy 'enforced holidays'. They could come amid bitterness as employees no longer knew whom or what to protest against.

The first protests from the sectors hit by the market were usually aimed against the government's policies and need not have implied a worsening of industrial relations in the workplaces. An early arena was the Łódź textile industry. The unions, at first with the OPZZ and Solidarity operating completely independently, began pressing the government by the late spring of 1990. Warning of 'bankruptcy for the branch', they accused Syryjczyk and Balcerowicz of simply doing nothing. Protesting was somewhat awkward for Solidarity — 'it is not easy to be a pro-reform trade unionist', their local leadership admitted (Dryll, 1990a, p.5) — but their position was in harmony with what management wanted. For all of them the issue had to be a revival of demand for domestic industry.

Throughout 1991, however, the 'union for survival' between management and workforces of early 1990 collapsed amid the acrimony and disillusionment of the economic depression. Hardly a day passed without a strike or some form of protest. In all, there were 132 strikes during 1991 with 192,000 taking part. In terms of disruption their impact was probably less than in 1990, when there were 250 strikes. The important point, however, was the change in character of the protests. The main issues of dispute in 1991 were the restructuring of state enterprises, over which employees openly clashed with their managements, enterprises' poor financial positions, and pay restraint in the public sector. Interestingly, 60 per cent of strikes were organised by groups of employees without reference to a union centre. Thirty per cent were organised by Solidarity, 3 per cent by OPZZ unions and the remainder by joint action between the two groupings.

Throughout most of 1991 strikes appeared largely as isolated events and demands were often highly confused. Employees in enterprises facing financial catastrophe had no idea whom they should protest against. They often resorted to general declarations against, for example, 'the current policy of putting the burden of the costs of reform mainly on the weakest social groups' or against 'all those who pilfered state property under the veil of privatisation' (Dryll, 1991c, p.1).

By the end of the year protests were taking a more desperate form, often involving a hunger strike by groups of employees, and typically demanding government help to prevent redundancies and closures. There were also clear steps towards coordination with, for example, the reestablishment of a Regional Strike Committee in Łódź, where wage payments were very erratic in many enterprises. The aim was to force the government to give aid to the city's industries.

This, then, was the legacy in manufacturing of the Balcerowicz programme. Enterprises had proved unable to adapt to the new environment in such a way as to initiate renewed growth. The barriers included their lack of financial resources, their lack of experience within a market system and their expectation, encouraged by the government, that things would soon be getting better. Gradually, labour relations emerged as a further barrier. By late 1991 they seemed to be worsening both when management did nothing — leaving enterprises to head towards bankruptcy — and when they tried to impose major reorganisations. The next chapter discusses the consequences of these growing problems in, and protests from, industry and other sectors for the development of economic policy.

6. The Search for Alternatives

The depth of Poland's economic and social problems encouraged a continuous search for alternative policies which could satisfy the initial hopes of a reasonably rapid return to rising living standards. Ideas revolved around the three broad issues of reflation, privatisation and policies for reviving firms while still under state ownership. Ultimately, no easy way out could be proposed from any side, especially after the Balcerowicz programme had plunged the economy into the depths of depression. Indeed, the search for alternatives often took a form that accelerated fragmentation, thereby contributing to the growing paralysis of political life.

Wałęsa's Alternative Programme

The Solidarity leadership became vocal in its criticisms during meetings with the government as early as March 1990. Its first targets were the rising unemployment, the new joint stock companies allegedly giving wealth to the *nomenklatura* and the presence of high officials of the old regime in many top jobs. The Solidarity congress, ending on 25 April, was dominated by the personality of its chairman, Lech Wałęsa, the leading figure in the Gdańsk strike of 1980 which led to the original creation of the union. Delegates showed the familiar contradictory relationships towards him, combining adoration, tolerance for his particular brand of demagogy, and violent criticisms of his alleged use of dictatorial methods. The final conclusion was that Solidarity should refrain from becoming a political party, but that it should continue an involvement in politics centred upon three principles. These were a commitment to creating a democratic political system, an aim to work towards an efficient economic system and a determination 'to minimise the social costs'.

This last point was becoming increasingly significant and dominated discussion with Balcerowicz who câme to the congress to answer questions. He was pressed to give some indication of when an improvement could be expected and of what was planned in relation to rising unemployment. He was warned of a possible 'social explosion' and was condemned for his 'shock programme'. His response was the very familiar one that there was no alternative and he challenged anyone to provide one.

A sort of alternative did emerge in the personality of Wałęsa. There were calls for him to become President and he could not resist promising to do something. As he accepted, his former supporters were beginning to say 'thanks to our struggle Wałęsa has the Nobel Prize, but what do we have?' (Dryll, 1990b, p.3). The same criticisms, and hopes in his personality, were expressed at a meeting on 8 July of MPs and Solidarity representatives in the Lenin shipyard. Zbigniew Lis of the shipyard's Solidarity organisation summed up the feelings saying that 'Wałęsa is our hope ... because he is saying again that things are bad but that they can be better' (Dryll, 1990d, p.3).

Wałęsa may to some extent have been swept back into political life on this tide of rising disappointment, but conscious manipulation may also have been important. Behind him stood an organised grouping within Solidarity which had shared his doubts about forming a government in 1989. They had started attacking the Mazowiecki administration from the end of that year, accusing it of a bias to the left. On 12 May 1990 they formed the Centre Alliance, intended to be a centre-right Christian Democratic movement committed to 'accelerating' changes.

Wałęsa's stand helped to confirm and accelerate a political disintegration of Solidarity around at least the three identifiable positions of his supporters, Mazowiecki's supporters and an embryonic left wing. His election programme gave a low prominence to economic issues, but referred to the need for 'radical changes' in the practice of reform by 'accelerating privatisation'. He had no clear strategy for achieving this, but was unhappy about allowing foreign ownership and made references to giving every Pole the financial means to buy shares. A possible help to this acceleration, facilitating rapid changes to the legal framework, was a call first made by Wałęsa in December 1989 for special powers allowing rule by decree. That would have meant waiving normal parliamentary procedures and was firmly opposed by the government throughout 1990 and even in 1991 after Wałęsa's election.

Much of Wałęsa's support came from his original working-class constituency, but the philosophy behind his political platform had a right-wing and Polish nationalist flavour. There were actually several identifiable positions among Wałęsa's economic advisers. The most remarkable, and surprising, was provided by Stefan Kurowski, his close confidant and a supporter of the market economy over several decades. Carrying forward the views of economists in the Centre Alliance, he set the primary aim as 'opposing the recession with all our strength' (ŻG, 1990, No.45, p.4).

The method was to be 'classical, Keynesian', involving a loosening of the financial screws, a devaluation to a more 'realistic' exchange rate and public spending on infrastructure and social services. He supported privatisation, but ridiculed its elevation to the status of a 'magic spell'. He even accused the government of 'market dogmatism', in the sense that it had imposed restrictive policies and then seemed to believe that the market would emerge on its own. His view seemed to be that it would require a helping hand from an expansionary macroeconomic policy. A final point to his proposals was a call to refuse to repay foreign debt, which he trusted the forthcoming President would have the international standing to proclaim to the world: he claimed that the Balcerowicz programme had been implemented on the implicit understanding with the IMF that a major debt relief would be arranged.

The main and most obvious criticism of Kurowski's programme was that raising demand would lead to no significant increase in output and only price rises (Józefiak, ŻG, 1990, No.45, p.8). This ties in with the debate over the causes of inflation in 1990. Kurowski assumed, implicitly as much as explicitly, that it derived from the practice of cost-plus pricing under conditions of rising costs while changes in the level of demand were met primarily by adjusting the level of output. The evidence from Chapter 4 would tend to support the suggestion that prices might have kept roughly in line with cost increases even within a less restrictive policy framework. Unfortunately, experience during 1990 and 1991 cannot be used to state definitely what would have happened under these hypothetical circumstances. With demand expanding enterprises could have learnt to behave as classical monopolies in a market system and responded with higher prices. There would also have been strong pressure for higher imports. It has to be accepted that the simple Keynesian solution might have required a considerable step back towards centralised price and foreign trade controls.

The more typical backers of Wałęsa, at least among more sophisticated economic opinion, were the Liberal Democratic Congress. This was a small group — 3,000 members in 1990 — that emerged in Gdańsk in 1983 and only extended its activities beyond that city in 1989. They described themselves, with considerable justification, as 'pragmatic' liberals, firmly believing in a free enterprise system but not turning a blind eye to all the obstacles on the way. They advocated, as an ultimate aim, 'democratic capitalism', or even 'capitalism without excesses', and wanted to represent the interests of a 'middle class', once one had been formed. On 15 November they produced a programme 'dedicated' to Wałęsa which had some common ground with Kurowski, but also an implicit recognition of the terms needed to satisfy the IMF. That was to leave scope for continuing with the Balcerowicz programme.

The government was criticised for inactivity over unemployment, and for doing nothing to improve the infrastructure while there was said to be a need for 'a much more resolute industrial policy'. The main attack, however, was on 'the lack of a coherent programme for the stimulation of the private sector'. The preparation of institutional reform had been 'delayed' and without this, it was claimed, there was no way out of the recession. The way forward was to start with 'small' privatisation, rather than concentrating on grandiose schemes for rapid and total privatisation of all big enterprises. In all, the approach was presented as 'a correction to and bringing to life of the Balcerowicz programme and not its rejection'.

Balcerowicz Keeps Control

As Prime Minister, Liberal Democratic Congress member Bielecki continued for a time to echo much of the rhetoric of the Wałęsa campaign. His choice as Prime Minister was, however, the result of his own willingness to keep Balcerowicz as Finance Minister. The latter's power was actually increased as he became the sole Deputy Prime Minister and therefore effectively the overall supremo in economic policy. There seemed little option at the time if there was to be progress in reducing the burden of debt repayments as nobody could match Balcerowicz's standing with the IMF.

At first it seemed that there could still be a shift in policy emphasis. Balcerowicz's adviser Stanisław Gomułka argued for 'increasing economic activity' provided it was achieved by means 'which do not lead to the return of hyperinflation or to a catastrophic collapse of the trade balance' (ŻG, 1991, No.1, p.10). That sounded close enough to the views of others such as the newly appointed Chairman of the State Planning Office Jerzy Eysymontt who suggested that 'stabilisation' should now be followed by 'recovery'. Kurowski, of course, was particularly firm on the dangers of continuing with an unchanged strategy: 'God forbid', he exclaimed, 'that is a policy for the murder of the economy' (ŻG, 1991, No.4, p.8).

The Economic Council meeting of 9 February set the scene for a shift. A profound schizophrenia was visible in individual members who could try to argue for measures to bring about revival but then backed off fearing renewed instability. The key point this time, however, was a growing scepticism about the 'Keynesian' method of bringing about a recovery. This had seemed a possibility worth considering in mid-1990. The judgement now, albeit not a unanimous one, was that the relaxation of controls on pay and on the money supply had caused the higher inflation of late 1990 (Kowalska, 1991).

Gomułka shifted his emphasis and put the point very forcefully. Monetary policy might have been 'excessively restrictive' in early 1990. The latter half of the year, however, saw an expansion of credit and a 25 per cent growth in real wages. His claim is accurate and the same figures were used by the IMF. This, however, was not evidence of demand running ahead of supply when set in the context of the collapse in real wages in the preceding months. Nevertheless, Gomułka (1991a, p.6, and 1991b, p.6) suggested that the government had lurched into an 'electioneering economic policy' culminating in a situation in early 1991 when 'the whole reform programme was under threat'. He still hoped for rapid growth in investment in the near future, after a process of 'creative destruction' had demolished obsolete capacity and restructured the economy. His optimism was not based on an analysis of changes within enterprises themselves, where there were no signs of the creative side of the process beginning, but he still assumed that there could be speedy economic expansion. He foresaw the attainment of the current Western European level by the year 2010.

This kind of continuing support for the restrictive policies, and the widespread assumption that the IMF took the same view, helped Balcerowicz settle any uncertainty on economic policy in early 1991. The first test of who really controlled economic policy related to the wage control system. The most free-market-oriented economists had always opposed this, believing that control of the money supply was enough to defeat inflation and they formed the core of a new committee of presidential advisers. In a statement in 18 February they condemned the *popiwek* for being, 'like all means of controlling wages, an ineffective instrument'.

The new government went some way towards this position by abolishing the *popiwek* outside the state sector. The justification was partly a deliberate favouring of the private sector, and encouragement to privatisation, and partly a theoretical argument that firms with a private owner would not give wage increases beyond their means. The most immediate economic consequences were to worsen the position of the state budget while encouraging protests from employees in the state sector against what they saw as unfair discrimination. Whatever Wałęsa's advisers might have thought, employees generally saw it as the main obstacle to higher pay. Moreover, the system seemed to have accentuated the perceived arbitrariness of wage determination with some enterprises mysteriously able to offer huge increases and pay the financial penalties (Chmiel, 1991).

The *popiwek* became the 'hero' of protest actions and strikes in early February 1991. The OPZZ unions organised an 'anti-*popiwek*' demonstration, targeting the presidential palace on 15 February. A week before that Bielecki and Balcerowicz had met delegations from both unions. Balcerowicz indicated a willingness to relax the wage indexation from 60 per cent to 90 per cent, acknowledged that 'in general' he was for abolishing the system, but insisted that it would be a total disaster to do so at once (Dryll, 1991a). He argued forcefully to Solidarity representatives that wages would rise in the most profitable enterprises leading to protests and strikes in others, a drop in profitability generally and ultimately the collapse of the state budget.

Solidarity organisations seem to have been convinced if not by all the arguments then at least by the government's outward determination. Bielecki addressed the Solidarity congress on 24 February 1991 speaking very much Balcerowicz's language about the need to combat inflation and keep international trust if there was to be any relief on debts. This, it should be added, was consistent with Liberal Democratic Congress pre-election statements. Moreover, it seemed clear that the government would defend the *popiwek* 'to the last minister' (Dryll, 1991b, p.1). Promises that other means to control inflation would be found as soon as possible helped further sweeten the pill. There were a few calls to 'reprivatise' Balcerowicz, but the government's credibility survived.

After this Balcerowicz could retighten the screw. The refinanced credit rate of interest rose again to an annual figure of 72 per cent in early 1991, which was above the rate of inflation for that year. Ideas of any substantial changes in industrial or agricultural policies were forgotten for the time being. Far from a shift to a more active government, policy seemed to be heading in the direction advocated by Dąbrowski, and backed by various of Wałęsa's advisers who had not followed Kurowski's Keynesian road (e.g. Winiecki, 1991). The criticisms of the attempt at reflation in the latter half of 1990 had effectively won official acceptance. The interventionist option, however, was to be brought back to the centre of attention as continuation of tight wage controls deepened the depression and as privatisation policies drifted into a dead end.

The Rise of Privatisation

The idea of privatisation had had a relatively short history in Poland. Economists were beginning to mention it in the mid-1980s and it began to find a firm place in public discussions around the end of 1988. Right from the start it was recognised that personal savings were woefully inadequate for the task of buying the bulk of the state's assets. Estimates varied, suggesting that they might suffice for between

3 and 11 per cent. Solutions had been suggested involving support from government credits, but all discussions seemed to end with the recognition that privatisation would have to be a slow process.

The most ambitious plan, aiming to overcome the familiar objection of inadequate personal savings, was for almost total privatisation based on vouchers. Every adult citizen could be given vouchers of equal value and these could then be exchanged for shares in enterprises of their choice. The authors of this 1988 proposal were the neo-liberals Janusz Lewandowski and Jan Szomburg from Gdańsk.

The disadvantages of the scheme were to be referred to repeatedly in both Poland and Czechoslovakia. It would deprive the state budget of a possible source of revenue and leave highly dispersed, and hence 'inactive', owners with no obvious commitment to 'their' firms. It could also hamper sales to desirable foreign investors. The likely subsequent sale of substantial numbers of shares would flood the market, making it very difficult to raise capital by new share issues. It would also be likely to fuel excess consumer demand strengthening inflationary pressures. Blocking this latter danger by preventing share trading for a set period would rule out the emergence of a functioning capital market without which the benefits of private ownership would be very small.

The Round Table bequeathed the ambiguous generalisation of 'a pluralist ownership structure'. Privatisation was to be under parliamentary control — unlike what was frequently described as the 'pathological' form of 'quasi-privatisation' of the Rakowski period — and dependent on 'the consent of the employees' council following a referendum of all employees'. The implication of this was more likely to be a slowing down than an acceleration of the process. The Solidarity election programme contained no clear commitment to privatisation which opinion polls at the time suggested could be a highly unpopular measure. The Mazowiecki government accepted a general commitment to systemic change, but it was some months before there was agreement upon clear proposals, and even that was to prove unstable.

The implicit assumption behind the debate was that the only important issue was the form of ownership. Little was said about how the commercialisation of state enterprises should be achieved, in other words about the criteria that should be set for management prior to privatisation. There was also little discussion of the possible role of foreign capital. This was a persistently touchy issue with some seeing an influx of foreign capital as the key to economic growth while others warned against 'selling out' the country to foreigners. During the debates over privatisation, however, the dispute was effectively polarised between neo-liberals, favouring ownership by individual Polish shareholders, and advocates of a self-management option, still hankering for some kind of group ownership.

This latter position had some grassroots support as new elections to employees' councils generally confirmed the dominance of former Solidarity activists. Following the Round Table various attempts were made to revive a nationwide self-management movement. Its position amounted to a rejection of joint stock companies, which were seen as a means of eliminating the employees' voice and giving all power to management, but it found itself in conflict with 'a hard, dogmatic group of advocates of privatisation' (Dryll, 1989b, p.2). They were, however, aware of the danger of being labelled as the last defenders of state ownership when no other form could be thought up compatible with their existing powers.

The initiative was clearly with the neo-liberals from the start and supporters of self-management could only hope to moderate some of the proposals. Thirteen draft laws were worked out in the newly created Office for Ownership Transformation between September 1989 and March 1990. They concentrated on what was later known as 'big' privatisation, meaning the transfer of the bulk of large-scale industry into private hands. The issues of privatising smaller units first or encouraging the emergence of new private enterprise were largely ignored. At first, there was firm opposition to 'handing out' shares but the same logic as before gradually reasserted itself. If privatisation was to be rapid, then shares would have to be distributed somehow at below any plausible assessment of their true value. The drafts therefore gradually incorporated more possible methods.

The debates in parliament produced some concessions to the self-management lobby. The government's proposal for a single controlling body, the Agency for Transformation, was attacked as being too bureaucratic, allowing insufficient control by parliament. In the final version parliament was given the right to discuss an annual privatisation programme, but not to vote on each enterprise concerned.

There was also acceptance of an advisory council attached to the Ministry for Privatisation, seen as somehow representing the 'social' element. Its powers would be very limited and its membership appointed by the Prime Minister.

The final law also allowed for a slightly enhanced role for employees in privatisation decisions. Employees' councils were given the power to apply for transformation into a state-owned joint stock company, the necessary first step before full privatisation. This did not rule out such proposals from the Ministry, which employees' representatives would have to accept. They could, however, veto an alternative road to privatisation based on the Ministry liquidating an enterprise's assets and disposing of them as it wished: that could be the best method, especially for smaller enterprises where major restructuring was deemed essential.

There was also a slight relaxation of the stipulation that practically all shares were to be sold for their full value: there was a clearer recognition of the possibility of at least some privatisation by voucher. There were concessions to the self-management lobby with 20 per cent of shares to be made available to employees on preferential terms. More significantly, although employees' representatives were to lose the powers over the director enjoyed in existing company law, they were to take one-third of the seats on enterprise supervisory boards. These were to run state-owned joint stock companies prior to their full privatisation. Once over 50 per cent of shares had been sold, employees would lose all powers unrelated to share ownership.

The debate ended with the passing of two laws on 17 July 1990. Their legal significance was largely to make possible a variety of forms of privatisation while clearly ruling out some options (Gruszecki, 1990). Thus the extent of employee shareholding was clearly limited and the full self-management option effectively rejected. The growth of *nomenklatura* companies was hampered by a legal stipulation preventing directors from also being shareholders in a new company. Perhaps most important of all, however, was a continuing implicit acceptance that employees' goodwill was required. The formal structures of self-management were to disappear, but nobody doubted that privatisation against the will of the workforce would be politically highly dangerous if not a practical impossibility in larger enterprises.

The assumption was that, once the legal framework was in place, privatisation would proceed extremely rapidly. This seemed even more likely after the appointment of the Bielecki government. In practice, however, achievements were very limited. The process began with the sale of shares to the general public in a carefully selected group of viable companies after a massive advertising campaign. The first five flotations were of firms enjoying excellent contacts with the world market and therefore, it was hoped, able to do well even through the domestic depression. Support for privatisation among employees was extremely high, running at 90 per cent in two of them in referendums. The outcome of the share sales in January 1991 was to leave ownership highly dispersed among probably some 30,000 individual shareholders each. The dominant voice was likely to go either to employees, with a 20 per cent share giving probable control amid such dispersion, or in one case to a management consortium allied to a foreign partner.

The Dilemmas of Privatisation

The first attempt at privatisation by orthodox means served to confirm just how slow a process it would be to sell off most of industry. The offer was over-subscribed for only one of the five while for others the deadline for share sales had to be extended. The problems with relying on orthodox means of privatisation were further emphasised by opinion poll results. It was pretty clear that even those people with savings could find better uses for them than share purchases. Preference often went, for example, to developing one's own business and, from the point of view of developing a market economy, that would seem a very laudable objective. Others, of course, preferred to keep their small amount of wealth in a more liquid and intelligible form.

There were also differences within enterprises over the degree of enthusiasm for privatisation and over what it was expected to achieve. Surveys confirmed a 'verbal' acceptance throughout society, as there had been for economic reform in general beforehand. There was, however, really solid support only from directors and Solidarity activists (Jarosz, 1991, and Karpińska-Mizielińska, 1991). The former saw it as an escape from the 'Bermuda Triangle' and as the key to new investment from the sale of shares to a Western partner. Enthusiasm among managers was therefore greatest in those enterprises seeking an escape from bankruptcy. A joint stock company allowing foreign ownership was their usual preferred option.

The Solidarity activists' position was based largely on their militant anti-Communism: they were the only group in one substantial survey who could generally see nothing positive in the socialist past. The workforce they represented was more circumspect, particularly in enterprises facing difficulties, often remembering past job security and fearing the consequences of private ownership.

Privatisation was most attractive to employees when it offered a means of escape from the wage control system. Indeed the idea was pressed by groups of employees from 1989 onwards even when hopes of higher wages seemed absurdly unrealistic. An early example was a bizarre manifestation in the Piast mine in Silesia. Frustrated that they could not win a satisfactory pay increase, a third of the employees declared themselves shareholders. The idea came from the Solidarity organisation with the rather simple notion that it should be possible to negotiate a better deal with the new owners (Dryll, 1989a). A later example was a strike in Ursus in February 1991 demanding 'accelerating the privatisation of the factory' so as to get rid of the director, regarded by Solidarity as inadequate, and so as to escape from the pay restraint system.

Privatisation policy, then, faced three major dilemmas. The first was the problem of how to transfer ownership to private individuals when the method of direct sale of shares had more or less exhausted its potential as soon as it had started. The second was the problem of gaining a consensus of those most directly affected when there clearly were widely divergent, and even conflicting, hopes and expectations. The third, which was closely related to the second, was the link of privatisation to rationalisation and reorganisation within enterprises. Examples from foreign experience, such as the privatisation of some major industries in the UK in the 1980s, suggested that the latter process often came first, particularly in those enterprises facing the greatest difficulties.

The trouble with that, as leading Polish officials frequently admitted, was that they simply lacked the resources to intervene in this way. There was also the distrust, well known from neo-liberal theory, of leaving such responsibility to state officials who it was assumed would yield to pressures to protect the inefficient, as under central planning. Leaving all reorganisation until after privatisation, however, was hardly a safe option either. Newly privatised firms would be at least as incapable as state bodies. Moreover, if the first acts after privatisation were to be sweeping closures and redundancies then that would hardly help to encourage support in the cornerstone of the government's policy. Krzysztof Lis, the official in charge of privatisation throughout 1990, summed up the dilemma at a major seminar in Warsaw in February 1991. He was convinced that property relations had to be transformed before the market could start to function. Unfortunately, although 'all can prove that it is essential', it also seemed that 'all can see and prove it to be impossible'. He was beginning to resign himself to the view that privatisation had become 'a magic word' surrounded by 'excessive expectations'.

The nearest to a solution to this dilemma was provided by Lewandowski and Szomburg (1990) of the Liberal Democratic Congress, the original authors of the scheme for privatisation by voucher. Their 'Decalogue for Privatisation', published just before the Presidential election in 1990, tried to formulate a list of proposals that would establish active owners, maintain public support and be linked to a programme for economic recovery. This link was to be satisfied by emphasising the privatisation of smaller firms. These too had a better chance of finding 'active' owners. The need for support was to be satisfied by the widest possible distribution of ownership through a voucher system. That, however, as was recognised, would create highly dispersed ownership and was therefore not considered suitable for the bulk of large and middle-sized enterprises. The suggestion was that perhaps only 500 should be disposed of by the voucher method, while other schemes might be tried for the remaining 7,500.

Commercialisation under state ownership was not rejected in total. The problem, however, was said to be the impossibility of directors winning legitimacy within the workplace under existing state ownership. This argument followed from research on relations within enterprises referred to in Chapter 5. A change therefore had to be made to guarantee enterprises' independence from purely internal pressures. Only then could they be expected to take a longer-term view and begin serious enterprise restructuring. The suggested solution was to give directors' shares, as an incentive to guide their behaviour. For the biggest enterprises even this was judged inadequate. The suggestion for them was that the state might 'refrain' from directly controlling management. Instead, the role of active owners could be taken by a variety of institutional investors and even state-owned holding companies.

Taken singly, each of these points was a sensible reaction to real problems. Competing state holding companies had actually been proposed in the late 1980s, but were rejected by privatisation purists on the grounds that only 'active', individual, private owners could bring about a real change in enterprise behaviour. It is, however, unclear whether the different objectives were mutually reconcilable. Public support could be greater for a system giving equal shares to all, but it seemed that other considerations were leading to a continual limitation in the scope of privatisation by voucher. A few shares in some unknown firms were hardly likely to make much difference to people threatened with wage cuts or redundancy. The real problem, however, was the possible link to restructuring within enterprises.

To some extent this was clarified by Szomburg (1990) in an article that seemed less flexible than the Decalogue. Full private ownership, he maintained, was an absolute precondition for recovery. However, as it was clearly going to take a long time, he concluded that 'it will be necessary to wait many years ... so as to create the necessary conditions' for recovery. To this he added the suggestion that 'big' restructuring would involve immense social costs for which 'we are not prepared'. He therefore suggested 'postponing' this 'probably to the second half of the decade'. By then new small enterprises might be able to absorb some of the unemployment. In the meantime, 'big' privatisation could continue, predominantly by the voucher method, but without much effect until a 'process of concentration of ownership' had established the possibility of active control over management. All of this was admirably logical. If nothing could be achieved without privatisation and privatisation was going to be either impossible or ineffective for years to come, the conclusion had to be that recovery for the state-owned core of the economy was simply not foreseeable. It was an excellent theoretical justification for the government's lack of decisive action.

1991 saw a further complicating factor with the emergence of the idea of returning nationalised property to its former owners, or their heirs. Pressure built up from mid-1990 with claimants appearing throughout the country. An estimated 70,000 had registered by the end of 1991 asking for the return of property valued at around 200 billion złoty, equivalent to 0.3 per cent of the country's total fixed assets.

The idea did not arise as a logical element of economic reforms. It was rather part of the political aim of 'de-Communising' society. It could threaten to complicate and delay economic changes by creating scope for possibly endless legal haggles as property was traced back over two generations. Some had been transformed, some had been rebuilt after the war, some was never rebuilt and some had been allowed to fall into decay at a later date. The public reaction to returning this to long-forgotten and often aristocratic owners was highly variable, depending on the kind of property concerned. The legal implications were also unclear as the idea, according to some of its supporters, was based on the view that everything done since 1944 had been illegal. That carried the dangerous implication that even Polish statehood could be up for question.

Wałęsa, however, rather liked the idea and his interventions made it harder for the government to resolve the issue quickly. It seemed to him a very simple way to solve the problem of finding owners. Moreover, the government was committed to the view that private property should be the foundation of society and the economy and its credibility would not be enhanced if it ignored the claims of those who felt their past rights had been transgressed.

On 2 April 1991 the government discussed what Lewandowski, appointed Minister for Privatisation in the Bielecki government, described as 'a difficult compromise'. Its basis was the view that 'the injustices of history have to be put right, but it cannot be reversed' (Baczyński, 1991, p.1). Moreover, in view of the government's minimal financial resources it could hardly put right all past wrongs: such a commitment, it was suggested, might bring demands for compensation from almost the whole population. In reality, of course, the burden of compensating former owners would fall on those who had not owned anything and they had not obviously gained out of the previous 40 years either. Returning physical assets might seem to save money, but raised all sorts of further problems when their nature and use had often changed so much. Lewandowski had therefore preferred, in contrast to Wałęsa, various forms of financial compensation, ideally with shares in newly privatised firms.

Not all in the government shared his desire to limit the return of property to a minimum, and no final decision could be taken. Delays continued and a different government produced a draft law in June 1992 putting the emphasis back on the return of physical assets. The weight of opinion in parliament seemed more likely to support a development of Lewandowski's original view. Indecision over what rules would be decided obviously contributed to general uncertainty in enterprises and held up privatisation in any cases where claims were a serious possibility.

A New Way Forward

Lewandowski tried to break out of the deadlock with the 'programme for general privatisation' presented at the end of June 1991. Contrary to earlier promises, the main emphasis still seemed to be on 'big' privatisation. His plan was to select 400 state enterprises, judged to be in a 'good condition', representing 25 per cent of the total value of production and 12 per cent of total industrial employment. These were then to be converted during August into joint stock companies with the aim of privatisation in December. Sixty per cent of the shares would go to the public, 10 per cent to employees and 30 per cent would remain in the State Treasury. The real novelty was that the 60 per cent for the public was to be put into the hands of between five and twenty National Property Boards. These were to be supervisory bodies made up of 'publicly trusted' individuals with specialist knowledge. They would then take steps to improve the condition of the enterprises. In the spring of 1993, with more information available on firms' internal situations, the first free trading in shares would begin. Until then, the public's only means of involvement would be passive registration with the National Property Boards.

Lewandowski (1991) justified the scheme with the assertion that 'there is no alternative for large-scale industry'. He could still see no possible improvement without the creation of 'active' owners.

'Commercialisation' under state ownership was therefore useless and irrelevant. Privatisation by voucher was also rejected as creating 'passive owners' only who would contribute nothing to 'a mechanism conducive to restructuring'. The need, he now recognised, was to bring in new expertise on management, marketing, financial policy and the like. The new holding companies, he believed, would achieve this by importing 'foreign' experts mostly, it seemed, from Japan and the USA.

Criticisms came from all sides, including other ministers, and the programme was never adopted as the collective policy of the government. The Economic Council invited foreign advisers to a meeting on 5 October 1991 and ended with the conclusion that, but for the political implications of the whole privatisation programme visibly collapsing, it could argue for 'abandoning the experiment' (*ŻG*, 1991, No.41, p.6). The most incisive attack came from an advisory body on privatisation, the Council for Property Transformation, chaired by Marek Dąbrowski (Dąbrowski and Błaszczyk, 1991).

The central target, reflecting fears that former methods were reentering by the back door, was the nature and motivation of the holding bodies. They would not be under anybody's direct control and could therefore take arbitrary decisions in response to lobbies and political pressure groups. Lewandowski's reply was to affirm that he hoped this would not happen, but he could indicate no mechanism that would impose a motivation distinct from that of the civil servant, allegedly trying to represent the 'public interest', but so often denigrated by neo-liberals.

Critics also warned of a possible immense concentration of economic power. Lewandowski responded that he hoped for the creation of a large number of holding companies, with shares randomly allocated between them. He also confirmed that the holding companies would not be organised so as to control complete sectors. That could provide some reassurance against fears of excessive monopolisation, but it would also mean that restructuring was to be limited to the individual enterprise level while ruling out rationalisation across sectors. The future of the boards was also unclear, as they might become entrenched and immovable power bases. Lewandowski replied that they might dissolve themselves after ten years, but he had no clear view of how they would develop.

The essential problem was the conflict between neo-liberal ideology and the realities of the Polish économy. Dąbrowski and his colleagues, wanting a scheme that would be widely comprehensible, politically appealing and leading to identifiable private owners, could not see why Lewandowski had abandoned the original voucher method. Lewandowski, boasting with some justification of being a 'pragmatic' liberal, had recognised the limitations of speedy privatisation alone. He recognised the voucher method, the only way to bring quick results, as at best irrelevant to recovery in large enterprises and at worst positively harmful. He was scathingly critical of Czechoslovakia's 'big' privatisation programme, discussed in Chapter 11.

Nevertheless, he could still see absolutely no point in trying to bring improvements under state ownership. Moreover, it would have been difficult to renege completely on Wałęsa's commitment to give shares to every Pole. The resulting programme was a bizarre hybrid born of neo-liberal ideology and some tentative pragmatism. It still left many open questions and failed to attract much interest from the general public. Lewandowski later admitted to having plenty of doubts and defended the programme on the uninspiring grounds that no perfect method exists (*ŻG*, 1992, No.15, p.7).

The Balance Sheet of Privatisation

Under the Bielecki government the private sector made substantial advances. By the end of 1991 private enterprises accounted for 24 per cent of industrial output, 83 per cent of retail trade and was well established in services, catering and construction. There were, however, continual complaints about the dishonest means by which new firms were being established — using the assets of existing state enterprises to enrich a few individuals — and about blatant tax evasion from the new private sector. Indeed, its contribution to national income may have been underestimated as figures provided by firms themselves probably understated their output.

The biggest disappointment, however, was in the slow progress towards the privatisation of state-owned industrial enterprises. Official figures for the end of 1991 showed 15 per cent on the way to privatisation, but few of these had got beyond the preliminary stage of conversion into a state-owned joint stock company. Moreover, the uncertainties over how, when and whether enterprises would be privatised were reinforcing the tendency to concentrate on a very short time horizon and thereby hampering chances of economic recovery. The disappointments over privatisation can be considered in relation to the four broad methods of liquidation, flotation of shares, Lewandowski's programme of general privatisation and partial or complete sale to foreign owners.

The greatest success seemed to have been achieved by privatisation through liquidation, a method considered appropriate for small enterprises and initiated in 791 cases by November 1991 (Grzegorzewski, *ŻG*, 1991, No.49, p.4). There were delays due to difficulties in valuing larger firms and in some cases employees had used their powers to veto a sale especially when sections were to be closed down or transferred to other owners. There had in all been only 12 sales of complete enterprises to the public. Evidently there were not many individuals with the necessary financial backing. Moreover, those with funds could also have been in a position to set up in business by means of the kind of deals that had led to the *nomenklatura* companies of the past. That was still an easier route to becoming a capitalist.

There were, however, encouraging results in 300 enterprises that had been liquidated and then leased out. In these cases there was typically little conflict: the new partners often came forward with investment of their own and the firms seemed to be doing well in keeping to their financial obligations. Dąbrowski's committee expressed strong doubts as these firms had often been leased to employees and therefore had no dominant owner. Practice again seemed to conflict with ideology.

Share flotations proceeded slowly. By April 1991 ten private enterprises had been created by this means and a stock exchange was opened in Warsaw. An assessment of performance of the opening year of the first five is, unfortunately, not very encouraging. Like all firms, they had to cope with rising costs and falling demand and were generally unable to pay dividends to shareholders. The most popular at the time of privatisation had been the Exbud construction firm and its share prices held up well throughout 1991. However, it suffered from the collapse of markets in the Soviet Union, Czechoslovakia and elsewhere. It was, somewhat mysteriously, still able to record a small profit for 1991 as a whole. It had also halved its labour force, despite an assurance from the management before privatisation that no job losses were expected. Wages, however, had risen from well below to over 50 per cent above the average (Wróbel, 1991).

The best that could be said was that in this, the most attractive of the enterprises offered to the Polish public, it was too early to write off the exercise as a failure. There was still an experienced labour force and management team which now had full independence from the state. With an upturn in demand, it might be able to develop a long-term strategy for growth. Nevertheless, any hopes of selling off a substantial proportion of industry to domestic purchasers were clearly unrealistic under the prevailing conditions of deeply depressed demand.

Lewandowski's original intention of quickly handing 400 firms to holding companies made little progress in the latter part of 1991. No law had been passed even by mid-1992. At the start of 1992 the only achievement was the conversion of 15 of the chosen enterprises into state-owned joint stock companies. The rationale behind the choices made was, however, somewhat mysterious as can be illustrated. There was strong evidence that fears of mass protests were leading the government to select some potentially bankrupt large enterprises, including one of the largest textile firms in the Łódź area. Privatisation, by allowing exemption from some taxes, was thus becoming a means to yield to pressure for keeping firms afloat without restructuring (Grzegorzewski, 1992).

The unstable interregnum after the demise of the Bielecki government created more uncertainty for 'general' privatisation. Tomasz Gruszecki, Lewandowski's replacement, was openly critical of past policies and referred to the need to slow down privatisation and sort out ideas before it could be accelerated. Wałęsa, however, made another of his interventions into economic policy in April 1992 with the announcement of a new proposal for giving every adult Pole a credit of $10,000 with which to buy shares. The effect of such a scheme could have been similar to that of the voucher privatisation tried in Czechoslovakia, but he left the details vague and the idea was not developed in the government. Indeed, July 1992 saw the return of Lewandowski to his former ministerial post and a revised version of his programme was finally approved by the government on 18 August.

Foreign capital was also slow in coming. The legal framework had evolved over three stages. Foreign enterprises of small production, owned by foreigners with Polish ancestry, had been permitted in the 1970s and employed 83,000 by the end of 1990, declining to 45,000 at the end of 1991. The first joint venture law of 1986 allowed firms with a minority foreign share. A modification in 1988 allowed majority foreign ownership and total joint venture employment reached 129,000 in December 1991. These enterprises were mostly small, with very few employing more than 1,000. They spread across a number of sectors, but were best represented in services, consultancy and trade. There was a small presence in manufacturing, but mostly in low technology areas such as the garment industry.

By the end of 1990, the total foreign capital invested had reached $179 million in 2,799 firms (Sadowska-Cieślak and Olszewski, 1991). By the end of 1991 there were 4,796 firms with a foreign share in ownership, but the total volume of foreign investment, at only $670 million, was below the level achieved in Czechoslovakia, a country with less than half the population (Kleer, 1992). It was also way behind the $1,050 million achieved by the even smaller Hungarian economy. Moreover, employment in all firms with a foreign share in ownership was still only 1.5 per cent of the total for the Polish economy and financial results were only marginally better than for state-owned enterprises. It was not an impressive picture if the aim was a rapid transformation of the economy.

These poor results did not reflect lack of effort from the Polish side. Surveys confirmed that an enormous number of contacts had been made especially from those sectors facing the greatest financial difficulties or with a history of international contacts. The prospective foreign partners, however, were often interested only in gaining information with which to strengthen their competitive position. When genuinely planning to invest, they naturally wanted only the profitable parts of existing firms and even then there were suspicions that they might be aiming just to control, and then close down, a competitor. Some had hopes of using Poland as a base for a later penetration of the Soviet market, but that led only to small-scale investment with which to secure a foothold for the future (Belka et al., 1992c).

These attitudes from foreign firms only served to strengthen suspicions on the Polish side. Foreign consulting firms acquired a particularly bad reputation as they seemed always to be proposing swingeing cuts in employment, sometimes to the extent of 80 per cent of an existing labour force. To some extent, these problems were present also in Czechoslovakia, as shown in Chapter 11, but Poland seems to have done significantly worse both in attracting foreign capital and in ensuring that it would come on terms that were acceptable to domestic employees. This was somewhat surprising as Poland appeared to have the advantages of a larger domestic market and lower costs. The former point, of course, was likely to be particularly relevant to a firm with a long time horizon which could see beyond the current recession. The latter point was possibly becoming less relevant as all costs were rising with the ending of subsidies on energy and of cheap raw material imports from the USSR.

A number of factors may have contributed to this disappointing performance. The legal framework was a possibility but, although there were divergences over some significant details such as the rights to repatriate profits, by 1991 this differed little between Poland, Czechoslovakia and even Hungary. A second possibility is the institutional framework and there is evidence that foreign firms saw Poland falling down in terms of the efficiency of its administration and its ability to cope with foreign contacts (Kleer, 1992). The 'Bermuda Triangle' was also a discouragement, although that problem should disappear with privatisation. The third possibility is the lower level of Polish technology and managerial expertise meaning that there are fewer enterprises offering prospects to a foreign partner. The fourth possibility is the general perception of political instability and uncertainty, and this was judged to be an increasingly important factor by 1991.

In so far as these factors led to less interest from potential foreign investors, they forced the Polish authorities to accept worse terms than were necessary in Czechoslovakia. They were even less able to insist on maintaining employment levels and had less ability to get a good price for the assets. This in turn encouraged more domestic doubts, making Poland appear again to be a less attractive location.

Could an Industrial Policy Work?

The failure to achieve economic recovery on the basis of speedy privatisation encouraged the search for an alternative within the framework of a continuing predominance of state ownership. The key notion here was 'industrial policy', a term that was often used in juxtaposition to the *laissez-faire* approach but which was rarely given a precise definition. Indeed, it was supported from two distinct angles. In many enterprises it was seen as a lifeline for survival and amounted to little more than a cry for financial assistance. From some professional economists it was seen as a process of selecting for help only those sectors or even individual enterprises that were judged to have good prospects for the future.

The great fear, of course, was that government officials administering such a policy would yield to pressures from below and give ample support to the 'no-hopers'. A possibly even more serious problem, particularly as the state budget headed towards collapse, was the inability of the government to give any meaningful help to any enterprise. Thus various agencies were established, but their funding was trivial when set against the financial problems faced by state enterprises.

The issue was forced to the centre of attention by events in Ursus in the summer of 1991. Financial catastrophe there led to the resignation of the Minister of Industry and his replacement by Henryka Bochniarz who seemed committed during her short time in office to a genuine switch towards a more active industrial policy. The first step was an enquiry into whether Ursus should be kept open at all. The conclusion, reached at the end of September, was that it should be given a chance to work out a business programme that could convince the banks that it had prospects. The proposal, however, did no more than retrace the familiar old ground reaffirming that there were long-term prospects of a recovery in demand for tractors and for some alternative products. There was, in short, a commitment neither to the sort of radical surgery that could eliminate Ursus's short-term losses, nor to the massive financial help that could enable restructuring while retaining the bulk of the labour force. It was another exercise in delay and indecision.

In general political terms the most natural supporters of an industrial policy for state-owned enterprises were the Solidarity of Labour group, a left-wing body that took shape around Ryszard Bugaj. They were suspicious of the Balcerowicz programme from the start, but never advocated its reversal. They claimed to be trying to give a voice to the 'waged worker' through the original Solidarity philosophy of 'justice, solidarity and self-management', but it was not easy to develop a serious economic programme from this starting point.

Thus Solidarity of Labour referred to an objective of a 'social market economy' which was to be achieved by 'an understanding between a workers' movement and a new entrepreneurial movement' (Poprzeczko, 1991). The trouble is that this could not realistically be achieved without at least some workers suffering. One alternative view, accepted for example by Kuroń, was to put off any thoughts of becoming a social democrat until after Western-style capitalism had been achieved. That he took to mean accepting and supporting the Balcerowicz programme.

Those in Solidarity of Labour wanted to find another way partly because some of the costs seemed to them unnecessary and partly because the non-interventionist approach was not bringing recovery. It is, however, pretty clear that simply strengthening the workers' voice could bring harm as well as benefits. It could hamper restructuring in enterprises and encourage state subsidies and support both when justified in terms of a long-term strategy and when such action would only serve to protect inefficiency. An actively interventionist approach is not universally a pro-worker approach.

Steps towards resolving this dilemma were slow in coming. At the May meeting of the Economic Council the Vice Chairman and Solidarity of Labour supporter Jan Mujżel (1991) presented an idea for a selective industrial policy that could give scope for enterprise restructuring without allowing a full return to the paternalism of the past. The key was to be a special last chance status, lasting six months but open for extension during which, following a referendum of the employees, an enterprise would be exempt from bank credit charges and dividend payments. It would be run by a special commission, dominated by employees' representatives. Failure to use this time to work out a restructuring programme, or failure to pay other bills, would lead to definitive bankruptcy. The idea was received with interest, but scope for such a policy was already limited by the efforts to balance the budget. The government could only come up with a scheme in December 1991 whereby enterprises could enter a competition to formulate the most convincing restructuring programme: state funding was explicitly excluded.

The Solidarity of Labour group also tried to put forward a general alternative to Lewandowski's privatisation scheme. Given the starting assumption that state enterprises would dominate for some time to come, it seemed obvious to Bugaj (1991) that economic recovery depended on recovery within them. In contrast to the neo-liberals, he believed this to be a possibility. There therefore had to be, alongside policies for the privatisation of small and medium-sized enterprises, measures to stabilise conditions in the state sector. That had to include an end to various forms of discrimination against state enterprises, and a clear statement on whether they were to be privatised over the coming two to three years. Management should be stabilised with firm contracts, possibly for two to four years, based on an agreed programme for the enterprise's activity.

This, then, was a scheme that might start to overcome the problems of the Bermuda Triangle and enable firms to develop a long time horizon while still under state ownership. Privatisation could then proceed, especially in smaller firms, by sales of shares, by handing over to employee control, by leasing deals and by a range of other available means. This could proceed more rapidly in the context of a controlled reflation which would also increase the domestic savings potential. The important point, however, was that there was no need to assume that the economy would only start to live once it was predominantly in private hands.

Realistically, in view of the state budget and balance of payments problems, this strategy depended either on very substantial external aid or on the acceptance of a budget deficit and possibly of some form of stronger restrictions on imports. Changes in microeconomic policy were therefore dependent on substantial corrections to the basics of the Balcerowicz programme. Even at the end of 1992, no political force had won major backing for so radical a break with the recent past. An account of how far policies had developed is taken up in Chapter 12 when possible alternatives can be discussed against the background of experience in both Poland and Czechoslovakia.

PART III

Economic Transformation in Czechoslovakia

Czech

7. The Paralysis of Reform

Stagnation with Stability

Czechoslovakia's position at the end of the 1980s differed from Poland's in terms both of the economic situation and of the political background. The structure of the economy, with effectively no private sector and a closer dependence on trade with the Soviet Union, suggested a longer road to a market economy. Against this, the economic situation seemed to be less disastrous. Annual growth rates were considerably below a 3.5 per cent target set in the five-year plan for the period 1986-90, but official statistics still showed positive figures. Net material product increased at a rate of over 2.5 per cent per annum for the period 1986-88, then falling to 1 per cent to 1989. The main reason for that final drop was a fall in exports, particularly armaments, to the Soviet Union and other CMEA countries. If allowance is made for hidden inflation this suggests overall approximately zero growth, as in the first half of the decade. The leadership, however, did not need to admit this and continued to boast that there had been no 'period of stagnation' in Czechoslovakia.

The gross debt figure of $7.9 billion at the end of 1989 was also satisfactory when set against hard currency exports of $5.7 billion and a slight surplus of credits over debits, although some loans to developing countries would never be repaid. The situation on the consumer goods market was also incomparably better than in Poland. Surveys conducted by the Ministry of Internal Trade showed general satisfaction with supplies of food but persistent complaints about shortages of many manufactured goods. Supplies could be erratic and unpredictable and the problems were worsening towards the end of the 1980s. This was a warning to the authorities who regarded the limited range of consumer shortages as the key factor in maintaining political stability.

The roots of the 'disequilibrium' were a subject of considerable controversy with several professional economists trying to find evidence of forced saving or forced substitution. It was possible to find individuals who could not spend all that they would like, but the savings rate was generally fairly low at around 4 per cent of disposable incomes in the 1980s. There is no evidence of a significant volume of pent-up purchasing power. It is likely that aggregate consumer supply and demand were broadly in balance with specific shortages notionally cancelled out by surpluses of other goods. The culprit was 'the low adaptability of economic units' and the absence of 'flexible mechanisms' (Klacek et al., 1989, p.15).

From a policy point of view the distinction between forced and voluntary saving need not be decisive. Personal savings were almost equal in value to annual retail trade turnover in 1988. Should the stability of the consumer goods market be seriously threatened, there was the ready potential for a devastating wave of panic buying transforming the localised imbalances into undeniable global imbalance.

There were the first signs of possible panic when the savings rate dropped from 4.4 per cent in 1987 to 3.6 per cent by 1989. The authorities blamed the problem on 'one day' tourists, primarily from Poland, and reacted quickly to plug any danger points as they arose. Steps taken included an emergency ban on the export of a range of consumer goods, including some food products and even building materials, in November 1988. Tough customs checks on individuals brought strong protests from the Polish government and more polite complaints even from the Soviet Union. Despite that, the trend was to keep putting the blame on foreigners. In some areas temporary rationing systems were even introduced for some goods.

The general picture, however, was of stability. The consumer price index showed 0.3 per cent inflation in 1988 and 1.4 per cent in 1989, and most basic goods were available. It was quite possible for the leadership to encourage the feeling that Czechoslovakia was something of a crisis-free zone while other neighbouring countries which had set out allegedly on the road to reform were degenerating into chaos. In the absence of reliable opinion polls, or of any accurate means for assessing public feelings, it was far from certain that there would be massive support for a major change in policy. The authorities' clear objective was to buy social peace without too much concern for any longer-term economic consequences and the available evidence suggested that they might have been succeeding.

A Final Attempt at Reform

Despite these apparent economic advantages, Czechoslovakia suffered in relation to Poland from a more rigidly authoritarian political structure within which effectively no questioning of official policies was allowed. The official position until 1987 had been to defend the stultifying ideological construct of 'existing socialism', a term used to imply that the only socialism that would be allowed was the one that existed: no consideration of other 'models' could be tolerated (Sochor, 1984). Even the term 'reform' was effectively taboo. The ageing leadership might have continued in that frame of mind had it not been for the arrival of Gorbachov on the Soviet scene. In a sudden switch, barely concealed hostility to the changes in the USSR was replaced in 1987 by barely credible exhortations of total support. Economic reform, or 'restructuring' to use the term borrowed from the Soviet Union then became, as in Poland and Hungary, the official creed of the leadership (Myant, 1989a).

Unfortunately, this was not accompanied by a sincere desire to introduce a radically different system. The Czechoslovak leadership was happy to mouth support for reform, but was not prepared to admit either that the economy faced serious difficulties or that past policies, themselves the responsibility of the existing leadership, might have been mistaken. They were not even prepared to allow free and open discussion among professional economists who were deeply distrusted as a potential source of political trouble. The formulation of reform proposals was entrusted to officials within the existing economic hierarchy who came with no coherent critique of the past system, and generally made no effort to create one.

Nevertheless, some changes were introduced that could have found a home in a more radical reform. Some ideas were lifted directly from the newly radical Soviet Union, but the experiences of Hungary or Poland were still regarded as unacceptable examples. In the words of one critic, it was 'a reform without theory and without unambiguous blueprint' (Klaus, 1989, p.25), but that still left scope for it to develop in many different directions.

Pride of place goes to the Law on the State Enterprise passed in 1987. The general objective was to clarify the independent status of the enterprise, thereby overcoming one of the basic barriers to past reform attempts. The formulation of its first draft was secretly entrusted to a group including Zdislav Šulc, an economist relegated to manual work after 1970. The final version was watered down by various government officials and was anyway rendered partially ineffective by the absence of other elements to a reformed system. Indeed, an accompanying Law on State Planning introduced in June 1989, and giving scope for the centre to intervene in enterprise affairs as in the past, was felt necessary as an explicit reassurance that the role of state planning was not to be weakened in the face of 'apparently progressive adventurist opinions about the free operation of the market'.

The fate of the Law on the State Enterprise was a typical example of how the entrenched bureaucracy could ensure that apparently radical measures ended up altering nothing. The key changes were to be elections of self-management bodies and directors within enterprises and the breaking up of multi-enterprise associations. The latter were effectively an intermediate link in the hierarchical chain which had no relevance if enterprises were to be given full responsibility for their own affairs. Nevertheless, their demise saw fierce struggles with some able to continue in existence by the trick of renaming themselves enterprises. Some others were split up into their constituent units, but the overall effect was to reduce the number of industrial enterprises from 884 in 1987 to 588 in 1989 while the average number of employees increased from 2,090 to 3,155. A debate in parliament, following investigations by MPs, concluded with the euphemistic formulation that the controlling ministries 'did not make full use of the possibility to eliminate the high degree of undesirable monopolisation' (*RP*, 11 October 1989). The whole operation used up a great deal of managerial time and energy without contributing in any way to raising the economy's flexibility or level of competitiveness.

The election of employees' councils could again have been part of an attempt to strengthen enterprise autonomy. In reality, their impact was extremely limited. A survey after more than a year of their activity, covering 53 state enterprises, showed that the 'effective nonexistence of any directives' had led to enormous individual variations in how they were constituted (Czíra and Munková, 1989). On average 60 per cent of representatives were party members, with the party organisation effectively controlling nominations. They generally lacked funds, received no help from outside the enterprise and had inadequate information with which to judge their enterprise's long-term plans. They usually met once every three months and seem to have spent their time wondering what they were meant to be doing. It would be difficult to agree with one representative who suggested that 'somebody might be surprised that we have so far taken no important decisions in relation to the enterprise's activity' (L.Friml, *RP*, 25 October 1988).

The creation of these councils was linked to the election by the workforce by secret ballot of enterprise directors. The only justification given in public was a desire to be seen to be democratising economic life as the ailing dictatorship liked to claim was happening in other spheres. Party organisations, however, controlled nominations and often put forward only one candidate. They could then be told from a higher level to find another, as contested elections had become the practice in the USSR, but often seemed able to dig up a clone of their first choice. When there was a genuine contest it only aroused complaints that the 'wrong' candidate had won. There were calls from within the economic hierarchy to end the 'time and money-wasting' elections (*RP*, 11 October 1989), but they were continued right up to November 1989. It is possible that the turnover of enterprise directors, sometimes bringing forward a younger generation, could have been a useful step. On its own, however, without a whole range of other measures to change enterprise behaviour, it could achieve very little.

The impact of other changes was also very limited. An administered wholesale price reform was implemented on 1 January 1989 in much the same way as price revisions in former years. Enough enterprises were able to manipulate the prices they could charge to ensure an increase in average profitability. There was some relaxation of the foreign trade monopoly and more scope allowed for private enterprise. The latter, however, was still restricted by a refusal to allow the employment of others following a veto from the party leadership to allowing 'exploitation'.

Two other changes were potentially important. One was a law allowing the establishment of joint ventures with foreign firms. A first version in 1985 yielded absolutely no results, but a few firms were established after amendments in 1987. By allowing such a development the authorities were yielding to the view that only by allowing foreign ownership could they gain modern technology. They then restricted their chances of achieving this by more severe restrictions and regulations than in laws that had been introduced in Hungary and Poland. The authorities had accepted the need for a new approach in general terms but, frightened of further loss of control over economic processes, retained strong powers over the establishment, appointment of leading personnel and foreign trade and payments activities of the new joint ventures (Štěpánek, 1989). Only after 1 January 1989 was the foreign partner allowed majority ownership.

Hopes that this would lead to an inflow of modern technology proved unrealistic. Fewer than 30 joint ventures were formed before November 1989 and most were involved in hotel modernisation. In manufacturing joint ventures were either a means to find sales outlets for credible Czechoslovak products or a means for Western firms to sell off outdated technology to a gullible partner. There was no interest in Czechoslovakia as a base for high technology production for export into advanced countries and therefore little chance that joint ventures would contribute much to a modernisation of the economy as a whole.

The other significant development was a splitting of the 'monobank' system set for January 1990. The State Bank was to retain its functions as a central bank but was no longer to be involved in the granting of credits to enterprises. This task was to pass to two Commercial Banks, one based in Prague and one in Bratislava, and to an Investment Bank which was to start by specialising in long-term loans. Ultimately these banks were to be allowed to operate over the whole country in all legitimate spheres and new independent banks were to be allowed to emerge. There were already in late 1989 clear signs that several would be founded, led by an Agricultural Bank promoted by large cooperatives. The prospect, then, was of competition leading to the imposition of financial criteria on investment decisions. Banks would no longer be subordinated to planning authorities with the limited role of checking that plan targets and limits were adhered to.

This measure stands out as being the most consistently market-oriented of all changes. To some extent it was possible because of backing from within one of the main pillars of the existing economic apparatus, namely the banking sector itself. A variety of bank officials had seized the chance to fight for an enhanced role as soon as talk of reform became officially permissible. Other parts of the economic apparatus were less interested in significant changes and ensured that nothing went beyond 'corrections to the previously existing central planning' (Komárek et al., 1990, p.79).

Towards a Reform Programme

Outside the economic apparatus itself a slight political relaxation facilitated the reemergence of some professional economists who had been victimised after the Soviet invasion of 1968 had led to the end of earlier reform attempts. Others too began looking more energetically for means to reform the system. It soon became clear that, despite a widespread acceptance of the need for major changes, there were substantial differences in approach and no satisfactory or ready-made alternative to the fumblings of the authorities.

Three broad approaches could be distinguished. In one view the principal need was to change the system of management, meaning the incentive structures confronting enterprises. That did not prove an attractive starting point for an overall reform strategy and came to be seen, on its own, as a dead end. It corresponds to the 'pragmatic decentralisation' discussed in Chapter 2.

A second view placed the immediate emphasis on restoring or achieving macroeconomic equilibrium. Nobody was opposed to this. Government spokesmen and their critics warned repeatedly of the need not to disrupt the delicate balance on the consumer goods market, but that was not generally set within the context of a full reform strategy. Others consistently accepted that even while implementing a reform strategy the centre should retain some powers of direct intervention, for example in ensuring supplies of goods in short supply, so as to maintain confidence on consumer goods markets.

The key figure in formulating an alternative approach which placed equilibrium at the very centre was Václav Klaus, an economist who had been removed from the Economics Institute of the Academy of Sciences in 1970 but continued to work in the State Bank. He pressed the view that reform had to start with equilibrium and, more controversially, that it was 'possible by means of macroeconomic instruments to bring supply and demand into harmony on all the most important markets' (Klaus and Tříska, 1988, p.825). Questions of efficiency, growth, structure or innovativeness were therefore all secondary.

He backed this up with the suggestion that at least 'a part of the economy' was coordinated through the market. He implied that it could be a substantial part when he suggested that 'only a few minor corrections' were needed to the institutional framework for the standard monetarist methods to be effective (Klaus and Tříska, 1988, p.825). Thus, to him, the greater independence for enterprises and reform in banking meant that 'we are already in a transitional process' (*Chicago Tribune,* 20 August 1989). Given a restrictive monetary and fiscal policy and a more active approach from the banking sector, he seemed to believe that a great deal could be changed in enterprise behaviour even under state ownership.

A number of questions were left open, such as the possible need for price liberalisation. On this Klaus gave only the hint that 'suppressed' would have to be converted into 'open' inflation before the price mechanism could ensure full equilibrium (Klaus and Tříska, 1988, p.825). His last substantial article before elevation to ministerial status was only slightly clearer. It referred to 'the creation of a non-inflationary climate' and means to ensure that price rises from the elimination of subsidies were interpreted 'as an essential, rational partial step in a deep economic reform after which further steps will follow, this time less unfavourable to the consumer' (Klaus and Rudlovčák, 1989, pp.77-8).

The third view among economists put the main emphasis on structural change. The key figure in this was Valtr Komárek, an economist who had fallen from favour after 1968 but regained some friends at the top as changes in the Soviet Union brought pressure for the beginnings of reform. By 1987 he was heading his own Institute of Forecasting and was able to bring together a variety of formerly banned researchers. He even persuaded the authorities to allow him to employ Klaus and the latter, after some hesitation, abandoned his job in the State Bank in November 1987. The breadth of views and a multi-disciplinary approach implied by the choice of personnel leave little doubt that Komárek recognised the complex and multi-faceted nature of the transition that lay ahead. At the same time, his own skills were rather as a populariser and as a political operator. There were gaps in his own personal theoretical position which suggested an almost exclusive emphasis on structural change.

His starting point was a forecast for the Czechoslovak economy and society to the year 2000. It was commissioned by the party leadership, but Komárek used the opportunity to make detailed comparisons with the most advanced countries of the world. He could thereby demonstrate that Czechoslovakia had fallen behind the best in terms of national income per head. His estimate, based on calculations by the institute's deputy director Vladimír Dlouhý, was of a level 15-25 per cent behind Great Britain, Austria or Belgium (Komárek et al., 1990, p.44). It was still well above the level of the more backward Western European countries. These estimates are over-optimistic, but a figure nearer to the truth might have been even less acceptable politically. The value of Komárek's position was that it could reassure the leadership that the past had not been too disastrous and that a change in economic policy now could bring a rapid rise in prosperity.

The key to this was to be a reorientation away from the traditional basic industries. Komárek argued, for example, for a halving of steel production. Reallocating resources to newer sectors, in line with the structures of advanced Western European economies, would be the motor for growth. Continuing with the existing growth strategy would prove ultimately unsustainable in view of the ecological damage caused, the impending exhaustion of the country's coal deposits and intensifying competition from newly industrialised countries in markets for the least sophisticated products.

Some parts of Komárek's argument were, at least verbally, taken seriously. The only visible result, however, was a decision in July 1988, confirmed in October 1989, to run down the highly uneconomic uranium mining, although that was largely dictated by a complete halt in Soviet purchases. Beyond that individual sectors fought back with their usual heroism. Although he obviously enjoyed some degree of official protection, Komárek and his institute soon found themselves subjected to a hail of criticism.

The minister in charge of energy publicly warned that, even though there was a temporary energy surplus in mid-1989, sinking a new mine could take up to 20 years (A.Krumnikl, *HN*, 1989, No.35). With this pessimistic view on the efficiency of the investment sector, he suggested that it would be safer to keep on expanding capacity. The chairman of the miners' union took a slightly different line warning that the workforce was becoming nervous to the extent of a 'lack of understanding for the basic principles of restructuring' (V.Poledník, *RP*, 20 June 1989). Similar fears came from the steel industry, alongside reminders that a reduction in its capacity would lead to a drop in exports with no new sectors ready to take its place (M.Hocko, *RP*, 17 June 1989).

At the more general level State Planning Commission officials verbally associated themselves with the need for a dramatic change in economic performance but effectively dissociated themselves from Komárek's means to achieve it. The strongest attacks were for his institute's clear estimate of a loss of up to 700,000 jobs in industry, 24 per cent of the 1989 total, in the period up to the year 2000 (Komárek et al., 1990, p.291) with no more than a general hope that new jobs could be created in services. Even a loss of 150,000 jobs was regarded by state planning officials as so difficult and potentially painful as to warrant consideration only as an open question (Kánský, Glaser and Ungermann, 1989, p.9).

Fully aware of the increasingly dangerous political climate that they faced, the leadership never publicly accepted Komárek's position in full, preferring to promise 'a climate of economic certainties and guarantees' (L.Adamec, *RP*, 12 December 1988). Stability of everything seemed to be the essence of the strategy. Komárek, of course, warned that although this could appear to be 'less full of conflict and less politically risky', it actually contained immense risks in the medium term and was 'unattainable in the long term' (Komárek et al., 1990, p.31). By the middle of November 1989 the government was still unable to decide on how to treat Komárek's forecasts and may even have been on the brink of abolishing his institute.

Attempts at a Synthesis

Although Komárek was at the centre of controversy over economic policy before November 1989, his arguments were not particularly sophisticated. Others in the reform camp criticised him both at the time and subsequently. One claim was that he was intending to do everything by central planning while successful new growth was possible only on the basis of market-determined prices and greater scope for a new private sector. Without this, investment could not be directed into the right enterprises.

This criticism is half justified. In response Komárek could prove a whole range of products, especially many raw materials and the least processed goods, to be unprofitable on any reasonable estimate of prices. He could also demonstrate the hopelessness of continuing with many kinds of manufactured goods that could never become internationally competitive. His kind of approach did seem adequate for showing up the sectors that should decline. It was far less clear how it could be a basis for encouraging growth. For this Komárek noted a few sectors and product ranges and pointed to the importance of tourism and services generally without explaining how their growth could be achieved.

A further problem with Komárek's approach was the attempt to interpret all problems within the structure paradigm. Thus he was as concerned as anyone about equilibrium, without which he recognised that no price mechanism could work. Disequilibrium, however, he interpreted as a consequence of economic structure. Thus the overgrown energy sector demanded high levels of investment which in turn were the root of further disequilibrium. The validity of this argument has already been questioned in Chapter 1. There was a strong bias towards investment in basic industries, but that need not cause general disequilibrium when other investment was strictly curtailed and wages controlled. Komárek was confusing two distinct types of imbalance. He used his questionable interpretation to argue for a fairly long transition process in which 'the centre must help significantly' and which was 'objectively linked to the process of restructuring' (Komárek et al., 1990, pp.217 and 245)

This, then, was the great ambiguity of Komárek's strategy. He was opposed to 'unrestricted and uninformative market romanticism' and saw real dangers of Polish-style instability if the centre abandoned its powers too quickly. At the same time he recognised the need for 'a real full-blooded market'. The trouble was that his means to get there, involving central intervention and structural change, required the prior existence of a market both in terms of a price system and in terms of a capital market to allow successful firms to raise funds for investment.

Komárek occupied centre stage in the reform debates before November 1989, but various economists tried to fill the gaps in his approach. This gap in his thinking was recognised by sympathisers with reform both outside and within his institute. Some, accepting that the current price system could give no guidance for selective renewal, suggested seeking alternative criteria as 'we cannot wait passively for what the new economic mechanism brings' (Kupka and Špak, 1987, p.63). Others saw no alternative to seeing 'free prices of both goods and factors of production' as the 'core' to creating a system distinct from central planning (Kouba, 1989). Others, by the continuing detailed study of individual sectors, were led to conclude that foreign ownership could be the key to growth. Thus, it was suggested for the key engineering sector, the only way forward might be the sale of 30 per cent to Western firms involving the likely loss of traditional trade marks such as Škoda or Tesla (Kolanda, 1989, and Dittert and Kolanda, 1989). The question of whether this could be achieved without first freeing domestic prices remained to be answered.

Nobody, then, had been able to formulate a comprehensive and convincing reform strategy prior to November 1989. Possibly the closest was Otakar Turek (1989), one of the leading figures in the reforms of the 1960s who had been banned from publishing in the 1970s. In 1987 he was brought into the Institute of Forecasting. On the basis of an assessment of the reform strategies of past decades, he began to construct an embryonic programme covering a wide range of institutional and policy changes. Thus the initial steps towards a new banking system and enterprise independence would be strengthened with the beginnings of a genuine capital market in which existing enterprises could raise additional finance without prior central approval.

Prices would gradually be freed alongside the break-up and control of monopolies and the Ministry of Finance would become the supreme government body for economic policy. The State Planning Commission could continue with a role in restructuring, but operating within a budget allocated from the Ministry of Finance. Sectoral ministries would be abolished but their apparatus would need to be kept intact for a time until enterprises had had a chance to adapt to the market environment. Alongside these changes there would have to be the gradual creation of a social security network: without this enterprises could not abandon their responsibility for current employees' welfare and impose redundancies when the market so dictated. Full privatisation of large enterprises was not envisaged — Turek was not convinced of its necessity and was fully aware of the political sensitivity of the issue — but there were suggestions for handing over small businesses to private individuals, either by leasing or on low interest loans.

Turek was working out a strategy for transition to a market that was intended to be as complete a basis as possible. It accepted the need for various forms of state intervention both in the specific transition period and in the longer term. It accepted the interdependence between these fields of policy and gave no promises of an immediate total transformation.

Some of this thinking found its way into a collective report from the Institute of Forecasting completed in December 1989 (Komárek at al., 1990). Unfortunately, the document as a whole was a confused and eclectic amalgam of theoretical positions. It bore Klaus's imprint in its emphasis on the primacy of equilibrium. It contained some of Komárek's thinking, but also attacks on Keynesian economics and expressions of faith in the applicability of theories of monetarism, property rights and public choice. The work confirmed its own claim that, with Communist power already collapsing, 'no complete economic programme as a whole has been unambiguously formulated'.

8. The Triumph of Monetarism

A Hesitant Start

The formulation of economic policy was transformed after the mass demonstrations and 'velvet revolution' of 1989 had effectively demolished the old political system. The playwright and long-standing dissident Václav Havel became president in December and his newly formed Civic Forum, a broad coalition of all opposition groupings spanning the political spectrum from far right to far left, led the rapid transformation of the power structure. The new 'government of national understanding' contained nine Communist Party members out of 20, but the number was quickly reduced as ministers left their old party. After the general election of June 1990, the Communist Party was completely eliminated from power.

Meanwhile, with the full backing of Civic Forum, control of key economic ministries went to former employees of Komárek's Institute of Forecasting. Komárek himself, resigning his party membership, became a Deputy Prime Minister with overall authority for formulating the reform. Klaus, never a party member, became the Minister of Finance and Dlouhý, resigning a party membership which had implied no support for the old system, headed the State Planning Commission. There was no reason for these new ministers to want to build on the basis of the minimal reform steps instituted by the former regime. Moreover, they soon felt themselves pushed towards more decisive action.

The immediate stimulus was a sharp fall in industrial output. Over 1990 as a whole it dropped by 3.7 per cent, but the first three months at first seemed to point to even worse results. The cause was partly the fall in exports to the CMEA countries. It was also widely attributed to disruption following the dismissal of directors who had been too closely identified with the old system.

Sometimes they were replaced by clearly well qualified but politically less objectionable alternatives. The Czech government appealed for an orderly process, using the existing Law on the State Enterprise and leading as quickly as possible to a restabilisation of management structures. Nevertheless, the immediate economic effect was a breakdown of the interpersonal relationships between officials in the economic hierarchy which had been so helpful to what smooth running was possible under the old system. Thus, as frequently reiterated by Vladimír Dlouhý, the collapse of the old power structure based upon the Communist Party brought with it a collapse in economic relationships. 'The standard central planning is not functioning', he reported, adding that it had fallen apart quite independently of the government's intentions (*RP*, 16 May 1990).

Dlouhý's reaction was twofold. On the one hand it confirmed him as a supporter of rapid economic reform. He hoped, somewhat naively, that some basic reform steps could have been taken by the autumn. A new system could begin to emerge and function. On the other hand, and far less naively, he advocating intervention to 'keep the core of the economy functioning with the aid of a plan'. Thus emerged the idea of a 'minimal plan' which was approved by the government on 26 April 1990. It contained no attempts at balancing, covered priorities only, and accepted the constraints imposed by the state budget. It was 'minimal' in that it concentrated on securing only the most essential inputs. The hope was that it could be developed into a stabilisation programme for the whole 1990-92 period. In practice it was soon forgotten, as was Dlouhý's hope for a 'much more detailed state industrial policy'. Instead, increasing emphasis was placed on solving problems by rapid systemic change.

This was associated with political defeat for Komárek who was widely judged to have been a failure as Deputy Prime Minister. Despite massive popularity at the start, he quickly lost the confidence of his fellow ministers. Following an intervention from President Havel, he was replaced in April 1990 by Václav Valeš, a veteran of the 1968 reform movement who had been active in opposition activity over the following years. Komárek was handicapped by an inability to organise his work, but a further factor was the inappropriateness of his reform strategy at a time when people were expecting visibly radical changes.

Thus, true to his earlier ideas, he took a firm stand against 'rashness'. He foresaw a 'specifically Czechoslovak' variant which would 'respect our own political and social reality and conditions'. There would therefore be no immediate jump to 'the theoretically faultless and elegant construction of a market economy', as that would mean 'sacrificing the trust of the people'. Instead, he advocated 'a seemingly slower approach' which would avoid 'galloping inflation and hundreds of thousands of unemployed' (Komárek, 1990, p.1). He was clearly warning against the 'shock treatment' under way in Poland.

In the meantime Komárek's strategy centred on creating what he saw as the organisational and institutional preconditions for a market system. That was said to mean breaking up monopolies, establishing enterprise independence, encouraging new private firms and welcoming foreign capital. There was some progress with new laws allowing scope for private enterprise without any limit on the number of employees. The law on the state enterprise was also revised allowing for three types of firms, including one based on self-management. The main option, however, was for a state-owned joint stock company based on the West German law. That implied a clear reduction in the powers of the assembly of the employees and Komárek described this as a switch back towards a 'managerial' conception. Without that, it was argued, employees could resist demonopolisation, and there would be little chance of encouraging foreign investment. The embryonic new trade union organisations tried to protest, but the logic of the government's steps was undeniable. Self-management was not deeply rooted enough to threaten to lead to the emergence of a 'Bermuda Triangle'.

There was, however, no dramatic progress that the public could notice and appreciate. There was no sudden influx of foreign capital, new private enterprises grew very slowly and continued to complain of restrictions while giant state enterprises still dominated the economy. Komárek's visible impact was in holding back suggestions for more radical changes.

At first he had the government with him. Prime Minister Marian Čalfa, addressing parliament in late February, warned against 'pleasant radical slogans' and confirmed that the government had rejected 'any over-hasty ideas of a price shock'. Already, however, Čalfa's address differed significantly from Komárek's position. It started with an extremely sober and negative account of the economic situation including an estimate of national income per head at only 40 per cent of the West German level, as calculated by the new chairman of the Federal Statistical Office Ivan Šujan (1990).

Although there is nothing in this that refutes Komárek's approach, this more pessimistic assessment of the economic situation encouraged the view that something pretty dramatic really had to be done and that there was very little positive to be preserved from the past. As Valeš later expressed it, there could no longer be any question of repeating 1968: at that time 'there was a gap between ourselves and a prosperous society. Now we can see a chasm' (*RP*, 29 May 1990). Moreover, there seemed little point in denying that there would be substantial social costs associated with the transition. To hesitate on that count might lead to a dissipation of goodwill and trust, making firm reform steps more difficult in the future. As Dlouhý put it 'the population is politically ready to bear the possible social consequences' (*Le Monde*, 7 April 1990). Opinion polls might show signs of possible opposition, but they also frequently showed a clear majority supporting a start 'at once'. Thus, as in Poland, one of the paradoxes was that a gradual approach, aiming to be politically acceptable, was actually out of tune with a political atmosphere and the popular desire to feel that, at last, real change was under way.

Klaus Takes the Initiative

The initiative quickly slipped into the hands of Václav Klaus with his straightforward conviction that 'economic science' had 'long ago demonstrated the superiority of the market' (1990, p.4). This he understood in neo-liberal terms as a self-regulating system based on the price mechanism within which any government intervention was purely a source of undesirable distortions. The aim, once the political transformation of November 1989 had eliminated any need to believe in possible reforms to the old system, was to be a market economy 'without adjectives'. He thereby rejected the rather vague notion of a 'social market economy'. The term had been used as the basis for the highly successful post-war West German economy and was revived in

Czechoslovakia, although it remained to be clarified how the 'social' and 'market' elements were to be combined. Klaus was soon suggesting that any such programme would amount to just another attempt at 'squaring the circle' (*LN*, 21 March 1991).

It seemed that Klaus's first conception was for a transition process starting with the establishment of equilibrium on all markets. This might be followed by demonopolisation and steps to define ownership. After that prices could be freed. The details varied a little from week to week and demonopolisation was gradually given a lower priority: competition was to be ensured by a freeing of imports. Despite this flexibility, two points remained dominant. The first was the need for a restrictive fiscal and monetary policy just as he had propounded before November 1989. The second was the determination to prevent inflation. This, rather than the belief that restoring equilibrium alone would lead to greater efficiency, became the main justification for deflationary policies. It could be the prelude and precondition for further changes including the possible privatisation of state enterprises.

Klaus left himself a lot of hostages to fortune, proclaiming that 'we consider inflation to be an economic evil and we are not aiming for any sort of managed inflation'. It was 'a cancer' and 'a socio-economic evil, which must be prevented at any cost' (*RP*, 11 April 1990). At the end of July 1990 he still maintained that 'even in the transition period' it should not 'go above a single figure value' (*HN*, 31 July 1990) and similar forecasts for 1991 were used within his Federal Ministry of Finance throughout the early autumn.

True to his monetarist beliefs, Klaus's first important economic policy change in 1990 was an attempt at 'a radical and painful reduction in the state budget' (*LD*, 5 February 1990). The first version, as approved by parliament on 30 November 1989, had visualised a deficit of Kčs 5.1 billion, around 1 per cent of net material product, with the budget accounting for 70 per cent of national income. In previous years it had been broadly in balance until 1989 saw a substantial worsening associated with an increase in the negative turnover tax on basic foods and fuels from 7.5 per cent to 12 per cent of total spending as the government battled to hold back open inflation.

Klaus would willingly have made dramatic reductions across the board, but was only able to get agreement for enough cuts to produce a Kčs 5.4 billion surplus in a budget approved by parliament on 27

March. The axe fell on defence and security, down 12.4 per cent, which almost any Minister of Finance might have cut, but a previous and highly popular commitment to higher health spending was maintained. Generally, investment subsidies were continued. Klaus confessed that he foresaw frowns from the IMF and claimed to wake up at night worrying over how small the cuts in spending were to be (Káňa, 1990). Indeed, it is difficult to see how the kind of cuts proposed could contribute much to the tightening of conditions facing enterprises, 'forcing them to search for means to raise efficiency'. If anything, although they had been vocal in their complaints about impending disaster, a 'compromise' seemed to have left the traditional nationalised industries with the least to worry about.

In practice, the deflationary effect of the budget was small partly because it proved impossible to impose all the intended cuts on subsidies. Its impact was also diminished by the failure to control other elements of demand. The budget was never as important in deter-mining aggregate demand as Klaus believed. Credit expanded more rapidly than planned and was supplemented by the uncontrolled growth of inter-enterprise debt, discussed in Chapter 10. Moreover, wages rose more rapidly than productivity and, particularly towards the end of the year amid fears of impending inflation, the savings rate fell to the unprecedentedly low level of 0.3 per cent.

The revision of the budget was followed by a few months of debate and dithering leading up to the June elections. The central issue was whether to press ahead with the elimination of food price subsidies. The case for urgency was reinforced after the easing of border restrictions enabled Austrian and German tourists to buy food at the expense of the Czechoslovak state contributing to significant shortages in some frontier areas. Klaus therefore made it clear several times that he wanted rapid changes, even before the elections. He won backing from Dlouhý who became convinced that, despite its unpopularity, 'there is no other way' (*SS,* 15 March 1990).

By the time of his removal, Komárek's opposition to this was leaving him isolated even from fellow economists who were not attracted by Klaus' free market radicalism. Thus Turek (1990) was highly critical of the apparently endless delays and advocated a rapid move to end some of the restrictive trade agreements and to liberalise all prices not under monopoly control (assuming monopolies could be defined). This, he suggested, would give real scope for new private firms.

This did not necessarily mean raising food prices first. There were arguments that, by international standards, food was actually relatively expensive. The high level of subsidies reflected the extreme ineffic- iency of many farms (Komárek et al., 1990, p.83, and Hejnák and Křovák, 1991). The really cheap services were housing, domestic heating and public transport. Nevertheless, pressure within the federal government for making a start was very strong and centred on food. The decision was taken on 24 May to eliminate almost all food price subsidies as of 9 July 1990. Price increases for food as a whole would amount to 24.6 per cent, adding 10 per cent to the overall inflation level. Within this beef prices would be the hardest hit, despite a small continuing subsidy to soften the blow, rising by 112 per cent. Consumers were to be compensated from 1 July with a flat rate monthly grant of Kčs 140 per head. Klaus had been opposed to this, preferring to give no compensation so as to boost his budget surplus. He managed to persuade his government colleagues to make the gesture of not claiming the grant for themselves.

The food price increases had three immediate effects. The first was to create very temporary instability on the consumer goods market. Spending for the month of July was 1.4 per cent above the level of personal incomes. Large amounts of meat bought at the old prices disappeared into domestic freezers. The second consequence was a drop in food, and especially meat consumption. In the first half of 1990 it was running comfortably above the 1989 level and the drop for the whole year was only 0.3 per cent. The figure for the last six months, however, was nearly 10 per cent down on the same period in 1989. The third consequence was the start to a serious crisis in agriculture which is discussed in Chapter 10.

The Debate over Economic Reform

The federal government approved in outline its reform strategy in early May and even produced a detailed time-table containing a legislative programme over the next two years which was to create the full legal, institutional and economic framework for a market system. There were still some open questions, with doubts from a group of experts under the Czech government over privatisation by voucher, an idea that had been seized on by Klaus in the late spring. They preferred a more gradual process with commercialisation and possibly forms of renting out enterprises to work collectives. Privatisation would be by sales starting inevitably with the smallest.

They were also more cautious over the pace and ordering of price and import liberalisations and over the speed with which convertibility could be achieved. These issues were anyway inevitably undecided as they depended to some extent on the ability to negotiate standby credits to cover for the possibility of liberalisation leading to a large trade deficit (Valeš, *RP,* 5 May 1990). Klaus was therefore disappointed in his aim of getting a programme approved *before* the election: success in this, in view of the likely election result, could have been taken as effectively ending the main debate. He succeeded, however, in ensuring that only one draft was presented, although it did contain some concessions to the views of the Czech government's experts.

The new federal government, firmly dominated by Civic Forum and its Slovak partner Public Against Violence, was sworn in on 27 June with the main task of implementing rapid economic reform. The programme, as prepared by the former government, became the basis for parliamentary discussions in early July. The aim was a market economy 'with all its positive and negative aspects' and this was to be achieved 'at the earliest possible date'. The implication was that this meant rejecting a transitional phase with substantial central intervention or regulation.

Speed was now justified by reference to three arguments. It would, it was claimed, lower the total costs to society. The same argument was put by Milton Friedman on a flying visit to the country (*SS,* 13 September 1990): it can most easily be justified within the view that a completely free market would work so well as to make all forms of intervention an undesirable obstruction. The second argument was that speed would prevent the bureaucracy from consolidating old structures. The third argument was that a slower process might be seen from the outside as a sign of indecision, making foreign assistance less likely.

There was no attempt from any quarter to present a systematic and coherent alternative. The most critical, not surprisingly, was the

Communist Party which no longer had any significant political weight, but warned of unemployment and inflation, complained about the absence of detailed figures and rejected the view that state ownership should be replaced by private ownership alone. There were, however, enough wider doubts to justify putting off a decision until 'expert' opinions had been sought from the five main research and teaching establishments in economics. Responses were received from the Economics Institute of the Czechoslovak Academy of Sciences, from the Institutes of Forecasting of the Czechoslovak and Slovak Academies of Sciences, from the High School of Economics in Prague and from the Czechoslovak Economic Forum. They varied from an effectively total rejection to generally strong support alongside some specific doubts.

The most critical was the High School of Economics in Prague which attacked the basic philosophy for centring on 'limited systemic changes which are expected automatically to generate positive material changes' (Kalinová et al., 1990, p.8). In its view, strategy should be based on past experience, especially of Japan and Scandinavia. That meant a far more vigorously interventionist approach with less attention to the price mechanism. There was an alternative programme in embryo, the feasibility of which is discussed later.

A somewhat less critical view was presented by Komárek's Czechoslovak Institute of Forecasting. Rather than a 'coherent' alternative, it issued 'warnings' on some points. At a general level it warned against trying to implement reform 'against the substantial opposition of a large part of the population'. That meant recognising 'the limits of society's tolerance' and incorporating a serious estimation of social effects into the proposals. There was also a less insistent criticism of the 'cabinet' decision-making process leading up to the formulation of the government's programme.

Criticisms along these lines had been made before and Valeš had recognised the dangers in decisions coming from only 'a relatively narrow group of economists at the centre' (*HN*, 16 July 1990). Klaus was on record as seeing no benefit in broad public discussion (*RP*, 27 April 1990). The Institute of Forecasting was clearly arguing for openness, discussion and wide participation of interest groups leading towards consensus. Broadly similar reservations were received from the Institute of Forecasting of the Slovak Academy of Sciences and from the Czechoslovak Economic Forum, a broad discussion group that had emerged in early 1990. The least critical was the Economics Institute of the Czechoslovak Academy of Sciences which raised some very specific reservations, such as the possible imbalance between expected unemployment and the proposed spending on unemployment benefits.

The final debate in parliament was handled as an issue of confidence in the government. If the programme were to be rejected then, Valeš warned, 'the government would have to resign' (*HN*, 4 September 1990). Criticisms and reservations were therefore treated as outright opposition. Klaus was particularly scathing about the Economics Institute's contribution which amounted to a detailed commentary. 'We cannot take its efforts very seriously', he remarked, as 'it does not take them very seriously either.' It had indeed failed to agree on a united platform, but its comments could still be seen as very helpful contributions to the ongoing development of a programme. Klaus was not interested in that sort of discussion, hoping instead for an effective blank cheque from the unconditional acceptance of the document.

The document itself contained seven sections. The first four represented the essence of the Klaus strategy. The remaining three, and a number of annexes, were of no interest to him (Kuehnl and Obrman, 1990, p.11), but their exclusion would have made it impossible for the government to unite around a single document.

The first section was concerned with the absolute priority of blocking inflation. This was to be done by a further tightening of fiscal and monetary restraint in 1991. There was hardly any disagreement with this from professional economists, although there is plenty of scope for regarding other issues as being at least as important. It could even be argued that inflation, in the sense of a rise in the price level, was not really regarded by Klaus and his colleagues as the main problem as their strategy quite obviously would lead to price rises.

Nevertheless, critics' reservations centred on the need for additional measures to maintain equilibrium. This included linking savings to inflation, raising the interest rate on deposits and intervening to raise the supply of some deficit goods. The consistent objective was to prevent a wave of panic buying. The High School of Economics, as on other issues, was more critical than the rest, advocating systematic 'supply side' intervention alongside macroeconomic demand restrictions.

The second section covered denationalisation and privatisation which were said to be essential or 'the destiny' of the reform would be jeopardised. A full plan was to be approved by October 1990. Small businesses could be auctioned or returned to former owners. Some middle-sized, locally-owned enterprises could be given to employee shareholders. There was a significant concession to the Czech experts in a commitment to 'commercialise' large enterprises by the end of 1990. Reorganisation to break up monopolies was also to proceed throughout the period and shares would be distributed in several ways, including the option of distribution 'below cost'. This, then, was a careful compromise.

Klaus had, since the late spring, clearly advocated distributing shares by the voucher method. The justifications were the familiar ones that 'national property belongs to all the people' (*RP*, 27 April 1990), that creating identifiable private ownership was the only way to improve enterprise behaviour and that savings were inadequate to buy a significant proportion of shares in state enterprises. He no longer maintained his earlier hope that restricting demand could on its own lead to changes in enterprise behaviour.

None of the five expert bodies was convinced by the voucher method, referring to the kind of problems mentioned in Chapter 6. The most coherent disagreement came from the Institute of Forecasting which was keen to encourage foreign investment, but foresaw substantial state ownership continuing for some time. The immediate need was therefore for 'commercialisation' of state enterprises, encouragement to participation from foreign capital and creation of employee share-ownership schemes. Complete sale to domestic owners would come much later after the careful creation of an institutional framework. This was presented as a realistic approach avoiding the new and innovative jump into 'people's capitalism'.

The third section covered prices with a commitment to continue with the abolition of negative turnover taxes. The date of 1 January 1991 was set for price liberalisation and the establishment of internal convertibility, discussed below. There was a warning of 'a slight increase in the price level', depending on the exchange rate. This was to be held in check by the well-known restrictive monetary and fiscal policies. It was also recognised that there would have to be a stern wages policy and some degree of administrative regulation of some particularly sensitive prices. The High School of Economics was more cautious, advocating price liberalisation 'only where signs of competition can be seen'. It was opposed to freeing imports, which it argued would lead to the destruction of domestic productive capacity (Kalinová et al., 1990, p.33). Others, however, saw little to object to with some enthusiastic support for the view that nothing much would be gained from any delay. The price system seemed so bad and so far out of line with international relativities that its reform was a precondition for sensible economic policies generally (Kotulan, 1990, p.17). The only open questions related to how vigorously residual powers to control prices would be used.

The fourth issue was 'internal convertibility'. This meant allowing enterprises to buy foreign currency while all would be forced to sell all their foreign currency earnings. It would replace the complex system from the past in which an official exchange rate of Kčs 17 to $1 left most exports unprofitable. The government therefore subsidised exporters while allocating hard currency to importers on an administrative basis. Reforms in 1989 led to more scope to keep hard currency earnings, but did not fundamentally change the system. In August 1989 a hard currency auction was introduced in which small amounts were snapped up at extraordinarily high rates. The peak was Kčs 134 to $1 when only Kčs 15.6 million were traded in November 1989. By May 1990 the rate was stabilising at Kčs 40 to $1 with Kčs 61.2 million traded and then fell as low as Kčs 33 to $1 in August. It seemed a reasonable guess that the equilibrium rate for full internal convertibility would be somewhat below this.

The justifications for full internal convertibility included the argument that the full abolition of the dual system with its accompanying administrative controls was the only way to ensure equality between all enterprises and sectors. There would anyway have to be a substantial devaluation as a result of higher raw material prices from the Soviet Union as all trade was to be converted to a hard currency basis as of January 1991. It was also claimed that the step was required by the IMF and that it would make it easier to attract foreign capital. It was therefore 'an absolutely essential step' for 'effective participation in the world economy' (Dyba and Charap, 1990, p.1).

Nobody doubted any of this as part of a longer-term perspective but, along with privatisation by voucher, immediate internal convertibility was generally not favoured in the expert commentaries.

Criticisms centred on four areas, the first being the inflationary impact. The programme contained a clear recognition of this and suggested two options. Defending an exchange rate of Kčs 20 to $1 would lead to an enormous growth in debt. Other estimates suggested that around 50 per cent of exports would still be unprofitable and require subsidies (Vít, 1990). A rate of Kčs 24-30 to $1 would lead, it was claimed, to a faster transition but at the expense of a sharp drop in real wages: it would therefore require 'a certain consensus' with trade unions and other representative bodies. Actual figures on inflation were not made public, but could be estimated on the assumption that all enterprises simply passed on higher costs. Valeš had long before given the figures of 3 per cent inflation at Kčs 17 to $1 and 50 per cent at Kčs 35 to $1. The obvious danger was that significant inflation would induce a wave of compensating wage demands culminating in a collapse into hyper-inflationary chaos.

The second criticism was that devaluation would not immediately stimulate manufacturing exports. Low competitiveness there related primarily to low quality and the low level of adaptation to demand. Growth was therefore likely to be substantial only after some internal restructuring and that would only be hampered if high inflation was encouraging an ever more restrictive policy. Nevertheless — and this was the third point — devaluation could help exports of raw materials and semi-finished products with a low import content. There was therefore the possibility of some shortages in vital inputs — Dlouhý even later announced that steps would be taken to control coal exports — and in some basic foods and consumer goods. Sharp devaluation could therefore be accused of creating specific disequilibria requiring new forms of central intervention to counter its effects.

The fourth objection was that this would have profound implications for structural policy. There would be highly uneven financial effects on enterprises. Some exporters would experience a huge boost to profits, measured in domestic currency, while sectors dependent on imports, such as the textile and garment industries, would face financial catastrophe. This reorientation towards raw-material exports and away from light industry would, of course, be justified if the new, devalued exchange rate could be considered permanent. In the background in all critical views was the belief that it could not.

Once manufacturing had a chance to adapt, it was assumed, the value of the Czechoslovak Crown (the Kčs) relative to convertible currencies would rise as new export markets were found. The immediate establishment of internal convertibility would therefore simply have given signals which from the long-term point of view were deceptive. Some critics even suggested that the government would be forced to intervene with subsidies — probably on a greater scale than ever before — to firms that had suddenly been pushed into financial catastrophe despite good long-term prospects (Pick, 1990). It would also, by setting a rate way below estimates of purchasing power parity of around Kčs 10 to $1 — even half that on some careful estimates (Kolář, 1992) — have allowed the continued loss of part of the country's output to foreigners who could buy basic commodities far more cheaply than at home.

The Czechoslovak Economic Forum proposed as an alternative a two- to three-year period with two rates, one of Kčs 17 to $1 and one set by the free market (V.Šlajer, *HN,* 13 September 1990). Exporters would keep a share of their hard currency earnings and the free market element could gradually be expanded. The Czechoslovak Institute of Forecasting produced a more comprehensive proposal on foreign economic relations starting with a suggestion for a small, but still significant, devaluation with the auctions continuing as before. Only some imports would be freed while high tariffs were to continue on others. There would have to be some unspecified measures for export promotion which would allow for a convergence of exchange rates.

Both this and the government's strategy, at least if its critics were correct, needed substantial state intervention for some time to come. It could therefore be claimed, as Komárek had tried to do when accused of wanting to delay reform, that this was not to be 'a slower, but rather a completely different adaptation of the economy' (*SS,* 7 June 1990).

This question of convertibility was probably the most openly controversial at the time. The remaining three elements contained potentially crucial issues, but attracted far less discussion. A final piece on agriculture was hardly criticised at all. A section on the social aspects of the transition was acknowledged by Čalfa to be rather brief.

It contained generalisations about the desirability of active measures and of 'forestalling the loss of work places' rather than 'passive care for the unemployed'. It was strangely out of line with laws in preparation which aimed to create a legal and institutional framework for social and employment policy. It passed largely without comment.

A remaining section covered structural policy and here there were more serious criticisms. Some of Komárek's former ideas seemed to have survived, albeit in watered down form while the need, in most critics' views, was for a substantially different orientation. The dilemma had already become clear beforehand when Dlouhý admitted that the basics of a structural policy being worked out in the State Planning Commission were 'not too impressive' (*RP*, 16 May 1990). It amounted to cutting armaments production and the mining of uranium and some other ores. The government's document reiterated a willingness to recognise responsibility for energy and waffled about the need to cut the economy's energy and material intensity. It also hinted at a more ambitious conception of structural policy 'supporting' other changes leading to the transition to a market.

From the Economics Institute came doubts about the 'intended scale of operation of structural policy' (Klvačová, 1990a, p.40). Within a planned economy the structure could be set by policy. In a market economy it was far from clear what a structural policy was to achieve. It would seem that it must involve a centre contradicting market signals and the danger was that that could degenerate again into one sector gaining advantages over another. At the minimum, then, it should be made clear what criteria and what instruments were to be used. More generally, it was not clear that less selective policies would not be more appropriate, for example supporting in general new enterprises or new technologies (Klvačová, 1990b).

The contribution from the High School of Economics took this further, wondering at the inclusion of the section on structure while there was no mention of policies for export promotion or technological advance. The most important issue, however, was raised most forcefully by the Institute of Forecasting. It called for active inter-vention in the market sector with 'temporary protection for viable enterprises, to give them reasonable time for adaptation'. This was not to be a continuation of the 'paternalistic role' of supporting those with no long-term chances under full market conditions. It was based on the belief that immediate market signals could not be a reliable guide to long-term viability. The guess was that the total volume of enterprise subsidies would actually have to be increased, although the basis for that expectation was never clarified. Such subsidies were to run for a limited period of possibly three to five years.

Was There an Alternative?

The extent and breadth of criticisms of the government's programme must raise the question of whether any real alternative was available. The point can be pursued in three stages, depending on the institution providing the criticisms on which it could be based. The strongest condemnations, from the High School of Economics, are not convincing at the theoretical level. It claimed to be trying only 'to clarify the role of government in the management of the economy' (Kalinová et al., 1990, p.13). It was probably justified in denigrating assumptions that the market alone would bring about recovery, particularly in the context of sharply deflationary policies. It was certainly justified in insisting, as its main author Milan Matějka had argued several times before (e.g. 1990), that there is no single kind of market economy. The problem, however, was that no effort was made to produce even an implicit conception of what market economies do have in common. Above all, there was never any discussion of whether or not the price mechanism has a central role.

Without clarity at this level it becomes very difficult to know whether the Matějka strategy was for active intervention within a market system or, effectively, for a continuation of an improved version of the old kind of intervention. If the real distinction is the use of price signals derived from a functioning market, then the reluctance to free prices would seem to point in the latter direction.

The need for a rapid freeing of prices was fully recognised by the Czechoslovak Economic Forum. The theoretical basis for their position had been worked out to a great extent by Zdislav Šulc. While working as a storeman he had produced studies of the economic system generally, of the post-war liberalisation in West Germany and of the strategy for reform in Czechoslovakia (1990a). His conclusions from German experience included two practical messages and one theoretical one with further practical implications. At the practical level he concluded that the rapid liberalisation of prices in 1948 alongside a currency reform followed by various anti-inflationary measures had laid the foundations for later successes. Even the Social Democrats who had been opposed to such a speedy abandonment of the war economy soon recognised that they had been wrong. This analysis pointed very clearly to the need to establish equilibrium on all markets as quickly as possible and that meant that Šulc was keen on price liberalisation. The German example, however, also suggested to him the need to be more cautious over freeing imports and establishing convertibility, which had been achieved fully only in 1958.

Šulc's theoretical conclusion concerned to the relationship between the price mechanism and private ownership. Studies of the administered economy in Nazi Germany suggested that firms had behaved in a very similar way to enterprises under central planning. They too had tried to maximise inputs while concealing their full potential in the interests of gaining easy plan targets. Šulc concluded (1990a, p.19) from this that the important distinction between economic systems did not depend on ownership. The classification into 'capitalism' and 'socialism' was less important than the distinction between a 'regulated market' mechanism and a 'centrally allocating' mechanism. He therefore concluded that widespread privatisation need not be a precondition for a market system to operate. The need was rather for 'commercialisation' with a clear delimitation of enterprises' financial independence.

Strictly speaking his evidence did not prove this at all. It suggested that state ownership was not essential for a centrally-planned system but private ownership could still be a precondition for the market. Šulc, in fact, was not necessarily opposed to privatisation and clearly welcomed both the emergence and encouragement of new private firms and the inflow of foreign capital. Nevertheless, he argued that privatisation in a single step was neither possible nor essential. He backed this with all the familiar objections to the voucher method, while also referring to the possibility of developing the idea of 'destatisation' (Šulc, 1990b).

He took pains to distance his conception from changes that had been implemented under the Law on the State Enterprise and the post-November 1989 purge of managements. A new means for selecting a director, he maintained, solved nothing fundamental. The need was rather for clear financial rules to break enterprises from their habits of maximising costs and wage payments. There therefore had to be a system of payment for capital assets, prices derived from the market and incentives for management tied to profits. These, he believed, were the necessary and sufficient conditions. Thus in early 1990 he joined with the other critics of Komárek's hesitancy and pressed for faster progress towards price changes.

His full strategy was for a modification of the 'shock therapy' of sudden liberalisation into 'a big package'. This differed from the government's programme in two respects. The first was the linking of price liberalisation to demonopolisation and a new tax system. In practice, as has been argued, the first of these was no longer considered in government circles to be a matter of urgency. The second was not to be ready until January 1993 which would mean a further adjustment to relative prices and profitabilities.

The second modification was the suggestion that the impact of price changes should be calculated carefully to see which enterprises would face particular difficulties. Variations between individual cases would be enormous, due for example to differing asset valuations, and to be unprepared would risk being bumped into correcting and adjusting unstable rules. That would devalue the reform, which had to be based on stable conditions, and discourage the inflow of foreign capital. The need was therefore for a clearly formulated system of temporary subsidisation. It would mean 'a substantial enhancement of the position and regulative role of the centre' (Šulc, 1990c, pp.8-9).

To build this towards a full alternative programme, various points from the Institute of Forecasting can be added. The key issues here are the exchange rate and the need for an industrial policy. On the former point, the arguments for a slower transition to full internal convertibility are clearly dependent on the dangers in the sudden shock method. As in Poland, the method of holding inflation in check involved a very sharp reduction in domestic demand and hence in output. Under such circumstances even potentially promising export sectors were to face severe difficulties. Moreover, an argument often used that trade with the USSR was to be based on convertible currency also proved unfortunate when exports suffered a catastrophic collapse anyway in the first month of 1991. A partial revival of trade with some former CMEA countries was largely dependent on a return to the old barter system. There was therefore clearly a strong case for a more cautious approach over the exchange rate.

Industrial policy, as in Poland, meant a selective approach between enterprises giving support where necessary to ward off bankruptcy. The case derives from the view that current market signals do not give an accurate guide to an enterprise's long-term prospects. The open questions relate to how much time should be allowed for adaptation and to the possible conditions that could be attached to the relaxation of financial stringency. The danger is always there of the same kind of manipulation as practised under central planning. Moreover, if substantial subsidies were still to be offered, then that might, depending on their scale, seriously threaten a restrictive budgetary policy.

There were a number of unresolved issues before a full alternative could be worked out. Nevertheless, the criticisms of the government's programme were pointing towards a clear message. The 'big shock' on its own would not create a system that could work and bring economic revival. It would need to be supplemented with a substantial range of new forms of intervention. That could still be a great step forward. A market system with a functioning price mechanism subjected to an array of explicit restrictions is better than no meaningful price mechanism at all.

9. The Big Shock

Following adoption of the government's reform strategy in September 1990, the date of 1 January 1991 was set for price liberalisation and internal convertibility. The small delay was intended to allow time for preparation in enterprises and government bodies, but the months of 1990 saw the first clear signs of the collapse of central control over short-run macroeconomic processes, encouraging calls for an even quicker pace of price liberalisation.

Enterprises began accumulating stocks of imported inputs, in anticipation of devaluation. They thereby exhausted the State Bank's hard currency reserves forcing a hasty devaluation to Kčs 24 to $1 in October. The stability on consumer goods markets was disrupted by minor chaos surrounding the food price rises in July and exacerbated by a simultaneous 35 per cent cut in oil deliveries from the USSR. Queues, some several kilometres long, formed at petrol stations and the government, appearing somewhat incompetent, was forced to raise the price of petrol and then to impose a temporary rationing system in October when the queues returned. This did not prevent panic buying of all goods believed to be derived in any way from oil.

The expectation of imminent price increases then led to the strongest bout of general panic buying at least since the currency reform and end of post-war rationing in 1953. Klaus continued to speak confidently of sufficient instruments to prevent an 'inflationary spiral', but the government was already publishing estimates of up to 50 per cent inflation, depending on the price of oil (*HN*, 16 October 1990, and E.Oswald, *HN,* 19 October 1990). As Table 9.2 shows, the savings rate fell to −5.6 per cent for the last quarter of 1990, averaging 0.5 per cent over the whole year.

The federal government held back from publishing a document with its forecast of what to expect in 1991, fearing 'that the possible variants for development of the Czechoslovak economy could even provoke panic' (*HN*, 10 December 1990). Such coyness proved untenable when parts were leaked to the press. The document, however, could only outline possible scenarios, described as 'catastrophe' and 'breakdown'.

The biggest unknown was the level of oil imports from the USSR which had peaked at 19 million tons in 1980. Negotiations during the autumn ended with a deal 'guaranteeing' 7.5 million tons and the possibility of negotiating for more from individual republics. In exchange for this and other raw materials Czechoslovakia would sell a range of industrial goods but it was far from clear how reliable guarantees could be or exactly how payment, to be conducted in convertible currency, would be made.

The catastrophic version, with oil deliveries running at below 11 million tons, would mean the administrative distribution of what was available and the closing down of energy-intensive production. The breakdown version, with 11-13 million tons of oil and likely cuts in other raw materials, would mean a likely decline in steel and chemicals contributing to an overall 10 per cent drop in national income. The reform, however, could still go ahead. There would be 35 to 45 per cent inflation over the first two or three months of the year.

If employees could accept wage increases of only 10 to 15 per cent, meaning a drop in real wages of up to 15 per cent, the price level could then return to only 30 per cent above the December 1990 figure. Bankruptcies would quickly ensue with unemployment rising to up to 12 per cent. Following a period of adaptation, growth might be resumed after 1992 and the 1989 level of national income could be restored around mid-decade. This, then, was more detailed and more realistic than the forecasts made in Poland at the start of 'shock therapy'. It was, however, ultimately to prove too optimistic especially about the prospects for speedy adaptation in enterprises. The crucial point, however, was that the main threat seemed to come from continuing dependence on the USSR. The need was therefore to press ahead with the reform as quickly as possible so as to help with a complete reorientation towards Western Europe.

Shock Therapy Begins

Table 9.1 shows the general consequences of price liberalisation and the introduction of internal convertibility at the rate of Kčs28 to $1 which was finally chosen. The overall picture is very similar to that for Poland in 1990, with figures suggesting an essentially similar process at work. Substantial price rises at the start of the year alongside wage restraint — the drop for January exaggerates the effect as December figures are boosted by end year bonuses — led to lower real spending and hence lower real output. Again as in Poland, unemployment rose rapidly, and the fall in industrial output was nearer to matching the fall in output.

The obvious difference from Poland is that inflation was not quite as severe and was more obviously stabilised by the end of the year. The timing of the fall in industrial output was also slightly different, coming a little later in the year: an explanation is suggested later in this chapter. The obvious difference from the federal government's prediction was that the latter foresaw a fall in output as a result of difficulties in trade with the Soviet Union and missed the link to domestic demand. This was to become an issue of major controversy in interpreting what really happened in 1991.

Price increases had been expected from five sources. The first was the direct increase in imported input prices. Added to this were the switch to accounting in hard currency in imports from the Soviet Union and the end to state subsidisation of some input prices. The effects of all of these factors were relatively easy to calculate, and account for roughly two-thirds of the increase in the price level in 1991. A final two sources of price increases were regarded as more problematic. These were the possibility that enterprises would exploit their monopoly power by raising prices above the increase in costs, and the effects of a unification of turnover tax rates. Previously there had been a total of 1,400 possible rates ranging from −291 per cent to +83 per cent, reflecting the requirements for balancing supply and demand on individual markets or the bizarre and ultimately arbitrary desire of officials to penalise or favour the consumption of particular commodities. As of 1 January 1991 there were to be four possible rates of zero per cent, 12 per cent, 22 per cent and 32 per cent. The change was intended to be fiscally neutral, but the suspicion was that it could raise the price level by up to 5 per cent.

Table 9.1 Czechoslovakia's macroeconomic performance in 1991

	Retail prices	Personal incomes	Consumer spending	Ind. output	Industrial employment	Unemployment
Jan	25.8	−23.2	−13.5	−4.3	−7.1	1.5
Feb	7.0	−5.4	−14.9	−6.1	2.5	1.9
March	4.7	2.6	9.3	−21.1	−2.2	2.3
April	2.0	10.1	−4.2	−15.3	−5.1	2.8
May	1.9	0.9	0.3	−22.4	1.5	3.2
June	1.8	−0.8	6.8	−22.6	−0.9	3.8
July	−0.1	5.0	−1.9	−21.5	−3.8	4.6
Aug	0.0	1.7	5.3	−31.1	−1.6	5.1
Sept	0.3	−2.9	−2.1	−29.0	2.8	5.6
Oct	−0.1	5.3	7.1	−27.8	−7.0	6.0
Nov	1.6	8.1	3.2	−32.0	1.5	6.3
Dec	1.2	41.9	1.4	−34.4	2.7	6.6
Whole year	53.6	14.5	5.1	−21.2	−16.0	6.6

All columns show percentage changes on the previous month apart from industrial output, which is the change for all industrial enterprises over the same month of the preceding year, and unemployment, which shows those registered as a percentage of the available labour force.

Source: SP, various issues.

There were three key instruments for controlling inflation. The most important, wage control, is discussed later. As in Poland, it is difficult to separate out the impact of the second, the restrictive monetary policy. This was based primarily on direct credit limits, an instrument which its supporters acknowledged to be in clear conflict with market principles (Vít, 1992). It probably did contribute to holding back wages and hence aggregate demand. Higher interest rates, however, also contributed to higher costs while the restriction on credit was to some extent circumvented by the growth in inter-enterprise bad debts. The third instrument, inspired by fears of uncontrolled instability leading into hyper-inflation, was the continued setting of upper limits for around 15 per cent of prices. The effect was to stabilise various food prices in particular at a level that the government guessed would represent a long-term competitive equilibrium. By December 1991 controls were retained on only 5 per cent of goods and services, although there had been periodic partial reintroductions of some limits and occasional warnings that any could be reimposed should market instability recur.

The government's expectation was that price movements would follow three stages. A rapid rise would lead into the build up of stocks followed then by price reductions. By the end of January Emanuel Šíp, the director of the Price Department in the federal Ministry of Finance, could claim that all these phases had been experienced for some products and even boasted of 'a Czechoslovak miracle' in achieving an inflation rate which, although higher than 'some forecasts', was lower than in some other Eastern European countries (*LN*, 30 January 1991). By the end of the year, he hoped, competition would have forced the death of 'productive dinosaurs' that could not adapt to the new environment (E.Šíp, *Práce*, 18 April 1991). Others also confidently predicted that the 'naive market behaviour' of industrial enterprises in raising prices 'only opens the door to the emergence and arrival of new competitors' (K.Dyba, *LN*, 18 April 1991).

As Šíp later admitted (1992), the last phase in his process occurred only for perishable foods. For other goods, as in Poland, adaptation could take the form of stock building and reductions in output enabling supply and demand to balance at a higher price. Moreover, although prices did stabilise, this was the result of a demand barrier and was not associated with the appearance of direct competitors as these optimists had hoped for.

In general, the danger of new competition was not very great. The exchange rate, supported by a 20 per cent import surcharge, reduced only gradually to 10 per cent, protected much of domestic production, while new competitors could not emerge from scratch so quickly. Anti-monopoly agencies did start to operate at the federal, Czech and

Slovak levels in March 1991, but they were woefully inexperienced and lacked the powers to undertake a systematic or coherent reorganisation of the structure of production. The aim was rather said to be to teach monopolies to behave 'decently' (I.Flassik, *RP,* 3 May 1991), while the legal means for achieving this were even weaker than in advanced economies of Western Europe (Bočinská, Straka and Šíp, 1992).

There were differences in price movements between sectors of the economy, but these related primarily to the timing of the rises and subsequent stabilisation. The most rapid increases came first in food. There was clear evidence in early price changes of some automatic cost-plus pricing, with output adjusting to the resulting lower level of demand. This, however, was a short-lived practice and cannot be the full explanation in any period as there were enormous and seemingly arbitrary regional variations. There were also some local fluctuations and still wider variations for individual food products, suggesting attempts by retailers to find the highest price the market could bear.

Their first guesses were often too high. The overall peak in relation to December was an index of 135 on 15 February. Meat prices were already falling from mid-January having met the demand barrier almost at once. The biggest and most permanent increases were for the most basic goods with potatoes peaking at 162 on 15 March. The mild revival of inflation at the end of 1991, shown in Table 9.1, was due again to food prices. It was partly a consequence of higher costs throughout the year that were passed on after the harvest and partly of the beginnings of new forms of state intervention in agricultural goods markets.

For non-food consumer goods there was a steadier increase lasting over several months, with prices reaching a stable level in the late spring. A more detailed breakdown shows considerable variations between sectors. For some, especially light consumer goods, the peak price charged by the direct producers came in February or even late January. Only a few sectors, especially energy with prices subject to central control, and engineering, showed substantial growth beyond the early spring. Prices charged to consumers followed a similar trend, suggesting a roughly constant mark up in the distribution system. Generally, however, retailers imposed price rises even before they could have experienced the higher costs. They may have been influenced by expectations on both the cost and the demand side in view of the consumer boom of the previous months.

Overall, pricing behaviour is even harder to explain in terms of higher costs than in the Polish case where enterprises had had some freedom to get used to the cost-plus principle over previous years. January 1991 actually saw a fall in enterprises' spending on inputs as they used the stocks built up at the lower prices of late 1990. Even accounting profit, a category that relates only to actual production undertaken in a period, doubled from 9 per cent of the value of output in December 1990 to 18 per cent in January 1991. Higher costs did soon feed into enterprise accounts, but monthly figures show no link between the timing of cost and price rises.

It seems likely that many enterprises, generally aware of a massive increase in costs, simply raised prices as far as they thought they could. As one management put it, when challenged that its price rises were way above the level of cost increases, 'these prices are not definitive ... we will see how the customers react' (P.Husák, *LN*, 14 February 1991). Either there were no possible competitors, or potential rivals were behaving in the same way. The result was somewhat higher inflation than the authorities — implicitly assuming simple cost-plus pricing — had predicted. When hit by the demand barrier, manufacturing enterprises cut output rather than prices. In one case the Slovak Ministry of Internal Trade itself intervened, claiming the right as the owner of the enterprises, to impose cuts of around 30 per cent in white goods prices in June 1991. There were accusations of returning to the arbitrary interventions of the past, but a helping hand to inexperienced monopolies may be the only way to achieve the third phase of Šíp's adaptation process.

Cutting Consumer Demand

The key to stemming price rises was, as in Poland, the restriction of consumer demand through cuts in real wages. This was achieved partly through a wage control system and partly through financial constraints on enterprises. The effectiveness of both depended on an explicit agreement with newly formed trade unions on the need for substantial cuts in living standards.

The old, Communist-dominated structures were replaced in March 1990 by the Czech and Slovak Confederation of Trade Unions (ČSKOS) as a loose coordinating body with no powers to dictate policy to affiliated unions. Thirty four out of the country's 60 unions affiliated quickly. Figures from a survey of 940 adults in 1991 showed that around 51 per cent were ČSKOS members while 5 per cent were in other unions, although later surveys suggest lower membership overall. Some of the members were pensioners or housewives and membership generally rose with the level of an individual's qualification, reaching 63 per cent for those with higher education (D.Rejlková, *Sondy*, 1991, No.38).

With no particular party affiliation, the unions' leadership stressed support for speedy reform. There was certainly no desire to defend the alleged gains of socialism. 'Those were not gains,' responded the first ČSKOS Chairman Igor Pleskot, 'they were inventions to bamboozle the people' (*RP*, 23 July 1990). His belief, however, was that the difficult period ahead would generate problems best settled within a tripartite 'council of mutual agreement' which would sign 'general agreements'. These would include acceptance of the right of trade union activity and of the right to strike. These were guaranteed in laws passed, not without some sharp disagreements over details, in December 1990. The government was also prepared to help solve problems of regional and sectoral unemployment. In return, the unions would accept cuts in real wages.

The federal government was at least as enthusiastic about this general strategy and a willingness to compromise on all sides made it possible to sign the 'General Agreement' on 28 January 1991. It embodied a complex indexation system whereby real wages were to fall by no more than 12 per cent over the year. Monthly figures leave little doubt that the wage control system was applied: significant rises came in the months of March and June, set as the dates for partial compensation for price rises.

Increases, however, were less than promised as real wages fell by 25 per cent in the first quarter and, despite some recovery in the last months, by 24 per cent for the year as a whole. The immediate reason was that few enterprises — possibly only 10–20 per cent — had the resources with which to adhere to the indexation agreement. Unions could have tried to insist on full compliance with the letter of the

'General Agreement', but accepted the situation with remarkably good grace. They also, albeit far more reluctantly, made concessions over further aspects of the agreement which had initially been formulated to embody the principle that the weakest members of society should not be asked to endure further sacrifices.

The most controversial concerned the minimum wage which had been set at 60 per cent of the January 1991 average industrial wage with almost 100 per cent indexation from that level. The direct cost of implementing this would not have been enormous. Nevertheless, price rises in early 1991, alongside the near-stagnation of other wages, would have brought over 20 per cent of employees under the scope of the minimum wage by April, compared with 13 per cent in February. There was an obvious danger that attempts to maintain traditional differentials would spark off cost-push inflation. Disagreements rumbled on until July when the federal government unilaterally abolished the indexation agreement on minimum wages. The ČSKOS made strong verbal protests, but its representatives were soon back talking reasonably amicably with the government.

This compliant attitude extended into workplaces. Union representatives could even accept complete closure, justifying inaction on the grounds that protesting would help nobody. Textile workers' representatives saw no alternative to major rationalisation and job losses and contented themselves with requesting provisions for early retirement. They explicitly distanced themselves from the forceful methods used by farmers (see Chapter 10 below), giving a reassurance that the predominantly female labour force would not be blockading central Prague with sewing machines (*Sondy*, 1991, No.46). Even steel workers in Kladno, after losing a third of the workforce, wanted nothing more than to be allowed to participate in helping former employees to find satisfactory new jobs.

The obvious question is why, despite the massive cut in living standards, it proved relatively easy to maintain social peace. Four factors could be mentioned to distinguish Czechoslovakia from, for example, the Polish case. The first relates to the less painful course of the economic changes themselves. Redundant workers in big cities were generally able to find alternative employment. Thus the potentially explosive issue of unemployment could be partially de-fused.

The second factor relates to the unions themselves: around 80 per cent of their officials were said to be completely new to the job. Moreover, unlike their counterparts in Poland's Solidarity, they had not established credibility and trust from years of underground activity. Taking a militant stand against government policies was not always unpopular, but those who did so risked being labelled as supporters of a return to the past.

Instead of active protests, unions have preferred 'the road of unceasing dialogue' (*Sondy*, 1992, No.25-6, p.8). In their determination to distance themselves as far as is possible from the Communist past, they have enthusiastically denounced any thoughts of a 'third way'. Many of the top union leaders are known to be sympathetic to the Social Democrats, but union representatives stood under all major political banners in the 1992 election. One survey of activists in the textile industry in 1992 showed only 9 per cent identifying themselves as standing politically on the left: 22 per cent saw themselves as right-wingers, 49 per cent stood in the middle and the remainder had no interest in politics. Although 77 per cent were 'dissatisfied' with political developments, fully 33 per cent supported the Civic Democratic Party, much more than its support in opinion polls at the time (*Sondy*, 1992, No.14). Leading officials have ruled out political cooperation only with Communists and the very extreme right.

A third factor, obviously related to the second, is the atmosphere among the wider union membership. As in society generally, there is a strong desire for radical change and that means general identification with the government's aims. Indeed, pressure from below was sometimes in support of the government rather than the ČSKOS position. Thus there were complaints from health workers and from the Prague underground that the obligation to pay the minimum wage was draining resources that could have been used to raise the earnings of more skilled employees (B.Svatoš and J.Schlanger, *Práce*, 23 September 1991).

The fourth factor was the government's strategy. Despite accusations of delay and inaction, the government did develop job-creation and protection policies, albeit with limited financial support, and did give some protection to the weakest in society. Moreover, the willingness to talk encouraged the view on the union side that dialogue was the best means to get results. Even Klaus, despite his hostility to the 'social market economy', soon overcame an early scepticism and joined with others in singing the praises of the General Agreement as a means to ensure a 'constructive' approach from unions.

It was, however, only one part of the explanation for the sharp reduction in spending. The Czechoslovak consumer goods market was also influenced by a major change in consumer behaviour as shown in Table 9.2. The first quarter of 1991 saw a continuation of the negative savings rate of late 1990, with spending 4.7 per cent below income levels, but later months then saw a sharp increase to the record savings level of 8.0 per cent for the year as a whole. These figures may be distorted by direct spending abroad, possibly accounting for 5 per cent of consumption by Czechoslovak citizens, and by foreigners' expenditure inside Czechoslovakia. High saving is, however, confirmed by a 4.5 per cent growth in savings deposits, compared with a 3.6 per cent drop in 1990.

Table 9.2 The personal savings rate in Czechoslovakia in 1990 and 1991

	Savings rate 1		Savings rate 2	
	1990	1991	1990	1991
First quarter	3.4	−3.7	1.6	−2.0
Second quarter	2.8	7.3	−0.8	−0.3
Third quarter	1.2	6.9	−3.2	1.6
Fourth quarter	−5.6	15.4	−11.4	2.4
Whole year	0.5	6.5	−3.5	0.4

Savings rate 1 shows the average monthly percentage of personal incomes not accounted for by personal expenditure. Savings rate 2 shows the average of the monthly changes in savings deposits as a percentage of personal incomes for that month.

Source: SP, various issues.

Behind this lay a change in the structure of consumption. Late 1990 had seen a typical bout of panic buying with substantial increases in purchases of manufactured goods such as textiles and footwear. Spending on food declined in real terms. In 1991, however, the sharpest falls in spending hit any consumer goods for which purchase could be delayed. Consumption from savings in the first three months was therefore associated with a clear shift in the structure of consumption towards food and other very basic goods. Then, after March, there was a return to high saving. A new pattern of consumer behaviour had already established itself with much of the population simply not spending if possible on anything that was not essential.

An implication of this is that high spending in early 1991 cannot seriously be interpreted as a sudden and welcome exhaustion of pent-up purchasing power as price liberalisation eliminated shortages. In this Czechoslovakia was following the Polish example. Some spending did go on newly available imported goods, but the general picture is of savings, built up as a protection against possible bad times, finally being used to fulfil that objective.

The overall effect of this on producers was to soften slightly the blow that would otherwise have been felt at the start of 1991 and then to accentuate it later in the spring. Many manufacturing for the domestic market probably entered the year with reassuringly low levels of stocks of finished products alongside useful stocks of inputs. This helps explain why the main cut in industrial output came later in the year than had been the case in Poland, as confirmed by a comparison between Tables 4.1 and 9.1.

Did Reform Cause Recession?

Three arguments have been produced to reduce the significance of the exceptionally sharp fall in output and living standards. The first is to suggest that output is not the crucial indicator. Thus the IMF concluded, on the basis of the first quarter's results, that 'the government has passed with a first class mark'. Bijan Aghevli, the head of its mission, pointed to successes in balancing the budget and restricting domestic credit and suggested that any difficulties could be overcome only by speeding up reform (*HN*, 3 May 1991). In effect, the IMF argument was that the restrictive policy was biting and that that in itself was the key to later recovery.

The second argument centred on the familiar claim that the drop in output was made up of goods that 'nobody would really miss' (J.Jonáš, *LN*, 10 June 1991). Its source was, again, the IMF. It was a flippant argument, familiar in Poland, that bore no serious relationship to the truth. Few inside Czechoslovakia, even among the most adamant supporters of the government's strategy, bothered to repeat it.

Table 9.3 Percentages in Czechoslovakia observing improvement or worsening in level of supply in shops over preceding year

	Better	Worse	Same	Don't know
Spring 1978	19.1	27.9	47.9	4.5
Spring 1988	14.7	31.3	49.5	4.2
Spring 1989	6.8	42.3	46.8	4.0
Spring 1990	7.3	29.2	60.7	2.8
Autumn 1990	4.4	72.5	20.3	2.8
Spring 1991	54.7	13.4	25.9	6.0
Autumn 1991	59.4	10.5	24.9	5.3

Source: Czech Ministry of Internal Trade.

Surveys conducted by the Czech Ministry of Internal Trade, covering slightly over 1,000 respondents, clearly confirm the perception of a fall in living standards. The 1980s, despite the official figures suggesting a small improvement, saw slightly more feeling their standards falling rather than rising while the majority perceived no significant change. The real break came in the autumn of 1990 with only a very small minority observing an improvement. In the autumn of 1991, 54 per cent felt themselves worse off than a year earlier, 9 per cent claimed to have seen an improvement and 30 per cent reported no change. Figures in Table 9.3 on the level of shortage are broadly in line with the Polish experience, although the transformation was less dramatic. More detailed figures suggest that there was no significant change for most basic consumer goods. The real improvements were associated almost exclusively with imports. A new range of goods was becoming available for those with money and, of course, all were now free to travel to Germany or Austria to buy high-quality consumer goods.

The small minority observing a worsening or no change could see the new range of imported goods counterbalanced by the disruption of existing supplies associated with privatisation, as is discussed in Chapter 11 below. Moreover, there were cases of declining demand leading, for example, to the closure of outlets and service stations for cars. More generally, industry and the distribution system still lacked either the technology or the managerial expertise to respond quickly to changes in demand. As the problem had been one of poor adaptability rather than gross excess demand, simply cutting demand need make little difference. Nevertheless, the awareness that new goods were becoming available meant that even those who were buying only the most basic necessities could keep faith with the government's policies and hope for the new system to bring its benefits in the future. There seemed to be nothing else to hope for.

The final argument to explain away the decline in output was that it was largely due to declining exports to the Soviet Union and other former CMEA countries. Klaus was particularly eager to suggest that this was more or less an adequate explanation. There is no doubt that it was a substantial problem. Fears of a possible failure of oil deliveries were to prove trivial in comparison as lower domestic demand meant that the country actually had a surplus for export after importing 11.3 bn tons over the year, less than 60 per cent of the peak level of the early 1980s. Exports of other goods to the Soviet Union, however, were hit hard by the conversion to trading in convertible currency. The problem was that Soviet enterprises had no hard currency with which to buy goods and negotiations at higher levels made only slow progress. The expectation for some time was that these were just teething troubles, but no firm solution has yet been found.

Various careful attempts have been made to estimate the significance of this factor (Klacek et al., 1991), but the margin of error is substantial. A reasonable guess is that the drop in exports to the former CMEA accounted for around a third of the 15.9 per cent fall in GDP, or 20.2 per cent fall in NMP, in 1991. This can be deduced partly from the weight of these exports within the economy's output and partly from the likely impact of cuts in domestic demand. On the first point, exports to CMEA countries in 1990 represented 13 per cent of GDP and are estimated to have fallen in real terms by between a third and a half in 1991. The direct affect on GDP would be a cut of between 4 and 6.5 per cent (Vintrová, 1992).

On the second point, the fall in recorded real personal consumption in 1991 was nearly 32 per cent. This could account for a 15 per cent drop in GDP. To this must be added the impact of a 34 per cent cut in investment, which could reduce GDP by 13 per cent. These domestic factors would seem more than adequate on their own to account for the drop in output. There could have been a build-up of stocks of unsold goods, but the official statistics show nothing dramatic.

The real complication is that the two sources of depression are not be completely independent, and that could justify, at the absolute maximum, attributing half of the fall in output to external factors. The point is that only half of the drop in real wages can be directly explained by the wage control system. The rest was due to the financial crisis in enterprises. Some of this can be explained by the drop in payments from the former CMEA countries, although a less restrictive monetary policy would have enabled enterprises to pay higher wages thereby reducing the severity of the depression.

Turnaround in 1992?

Three further points can be considered to help complete the macroeconomic picture after January 1991. The first is to extend the account into the second year after the 'shock'. It then becomes clear that there were differences between Polish, Czech and Slovak experiences. Figures for 1992 show a further substantial fall in economic activity, but only because the main drop came late in 1991. By the new year, output had stabilised after a fall in output somewhat less than that experienced in Poland. Moreover, unemployment actually declined from a peak level of 550,585 — equivalent to 7.1 per cent of the total labour force — in January 1992.

Up until then the overall level of unemployment had followed more or less exactly the Polish experience, rising consistently more slowly than the drop in output. Differences between the Czech and Slovak republics appeared in mid-1990, with unemployment peaking at 4.3 per cent and 12.7 per cent respectively in January 1992. There were also considerable variations within the Czech republic, with Prague experiencing minimal unemployment, and actually absorbing labour from neighbouring towns. High unemployment was a feature largely of small rural towns.

Some suspicion surrounds this apparent fall in unemployment as 450,000 people had disappeared from the statistics (P.Miller, *HN* 13 May 1992). They had presumably either given up hope of working or were working abroad or in the black economy. Nevertheless, the break in the upward trend seems undeniable and can be partly attributed to government job-creation and job-preservation measures, possibly cutting 1.5 percentage points off the figure. More significantly, it was seen as a sign to some extent of success in economic transformation, but to some extent as a sign of its postponement. The latter point applies to the large state enterprises. Having achieved the relatively painless loss of foreign workers and prisoners (around 60,000 in 1989) and shed some labour by voluntary redundancy, they were hesitating before large-scale reorganisation. Trends here were very similar between the Czech and Slovak republics.

The positive element was the growth in employment in firms employing under 100 and this also explains around a quarter of the Czech–Slovak divergence. These firms took on 250,000 employees during 1991 in the Czech republic, but only 30,000 in Slovakia. The most likely source of demand for this employment expansion was tourism which brought in an estimated $825 million in 1991, compared with $310 million in 1990. Most of this was spent in Prague and is equivalent to half a million jobs at the average industrial wage. 1992 saw still more tourists.

Other factors contributing to higher unemployment in Slovakia include a lower take-up of job-creation and job-subsidy schemes and less opportunity for working abroad, but the impact of those was small. More important may have been the position of the Romani minority, members of which suffer considerable antipathy and discrimination and have generally taken irregular employment in the least skilled and most insecure jobs. To judge from official figures, almost all are unemployed, accounting for 30 per cent of the unemployment in Eastern Slovakia (Tesařová, 1992, p.322).

The second point to complete the picture is the apparent success in foreign trade and payments. Despite fears of a huge imbalance, 1991 ended with a trade deficit of only $450 million and a balance of payments surplus of $360 million. $1.9 billion from the IMF and other international agencies bolstered convertible currency reserves while gross debt increased only by $1.3 billion to $9.4 billion. Debt servicing in 1991 still took only 18.4 per cent of hard currency export earnings.

Good results were helped by the estimated surplus of $515 million on tourism and by $200 million from Czechoslovaks working abroad. They were also a consequence of the low level of domestic demand leading to a 21.9 per cent fall in imports while exports were down only 6.1 per cent. There was, of course, a sharp drop in trade with the former CMEA countries, but exports to the European Community grew by an impressive 23.1 per cent.

Overall, however, there was a shift towards exporting less rather than more sophisticated products. One dramatic exception was the motor car industry, discussed in Chapter 11, but the share of machinery fell from 39.2 per cent in 1990 to only 28 per cent. The structure of imports was similarly unfavourable, with machinery falling from 37.1 per cent to 27.8 per cent, consistent with a minimal level of domestic investment and modernisation. 1992 saw a continuing fall in machinery exports and only a small recovery in machinery imports.

This, however, was a more favourable outcome than in Poland in that there was no pressure for a further devaluation. There is a serious danger that any real recovery in consumer demand will lead to higher spending on imported consumer goods. The trade balance did show signs of worsening during 1992. Nevertheless, there were signs of a switch back to buying domestically produced goods, especially cars. Thanks also to the contributions from tourism and foreign investment, the international sector has not become another constraint on public spending or a threat to internal stability. Nevertheless, opening the economy has, as its critics predicted, brought no automatic restructuring. The shift back towards exporting more basic goods carries all the disadvantages outlined by Komárek in the 1980s.

Thus a favourable Agreement of Association was signed with the European Community in December 1991, allowing a ten-year transition period to complete trade liberalisation and possible community membership. Seventy per cent of exports are allowed unrestricted access to EC markets while only 20–25 per cent of imports are freed at once. Nevertheless, implicit controls continue on precisely those least processed products in which international competition is most severe. By June 1992, despite a voluntary agreement to restrict the growth of steel exports to 15 per cent, Czechoslovakia was being accused of dumping by several EC member states.

If international relations can be judged a partial success, then the state budget, the third element for a more complete assessment of 'shock therapy', is a less satisfactory story. The hope for 1991 of an Kčs 8 billion surplus, equivalent to 0.8 per cent of GDP, failed because of revenues 5 per cent below the planned level alongside expenditure marginally above target. At first, with enterprises' profits riding high on the basis of price rises, the budget seemed on course for a massive surplus. As in Poland, decisions were taken in the summer to cut taxes to stimulate demand. The macroeconomic effect was minimal but the budget surplus disappeared in the closing months of the year.

The main disappointments were in turnover tax, falling short by 13 per cent, profits tax, 5 per cent below target, and the pay-roll tax, 12 per cent short. Together these provided 74 per cent of revenues, compared with a planned 80 per cent. The main reason behind this disappointment was, of course, the depressed state of the economy. Klaus tried, unconvincingly, to blame the high spending of the Czech and Slovak governments, but they could hardly have altered their spending plans at the last minute. Moreover, that would have meant breaking commitments on the indexation of various incomes. Nevertheless, the budget for 1992 contained substantial cuts in entitlements to state benefits, although early results suggest a possible deficit for each of the Czech, Slovak and federal governments.

It can be added that, with demand depressed so far below the level of potential output, the budget deficit has not led and need not lead to inflation. In fact, one of the factors stemming price increases was the decision to continue subsidies on electricity, public transport and some other basics, at least until after the 1992 elections. A realistic assessment was probably provided by a deputy minister in the Czech government (Kupka, 1992, p.310), generally supportive of the reform strategy. Maintaining spending probably helped prevent a further drop in real output, he concluded, while the deficit was 'an acceptable price' for an attempt to maintain social peace, to bring about economic recovery and to maintain 'a certain relationship to the Slovak republic'.

10. The Battle for New Policies

As in Poland, the failure of 'shock therapy' to bring rapid success had a major impact on the developing political structure. However, instead of apathy, instability and fragmentation, Czechoslovak political life began to polarise along much clearer lines that bore some relationship to a 'left' versus 'right' division. The driving force in this was Václav Klaus. He dropped his former image as a specialist economist and took up the mantle of a clearly right-wing politician with a firm conception for the future of the Civic Forum. He argued for essentially three changes to the broad movement which still lacked clearly defined structures.

The first was to be a total commitment to his conception of economic reform. He even blamed the looseness of the Civic Forum structures for allowing discussions to cause 'unnecessary' delays. The second change was to be a more definite opposition to socialism 'in all its forms'. This tied in with calls for a tougher purge of former officials of the Communist system and led into Klaus's call for a comprehensive 'debolshevisation' of society. The relevance of this to economic reform was unclear, as former Communists were not a significant barrier to change. They often possessed useful expertise and sometimes entrepreneurial ability. Nevertheless, Klaus gave the impression of a clear link between his economic programme and the strongest possible rejection of all aspects of the Communist past. It was a position that had popular appeal, but it also had implications for economic policy, as became clear in debates over the return of previously nationalised property. The third change was to be the conversion of Civic Forum into a properly organised political party. Taken together, this programme won the epithet of 'Thatcherite Leninism'.

By the spring of 1991 Civic Forum had split into a number of clearly defined groupings. Klaus led the Civic Democratic Party. Those wanting to continue the broad and tolerant traditions of the old body formed the Civic Movement: although commanding less popular support this was better represented than Klaus's party in the federal and Czech governments. Some other Civic Forum MPs, led by Valtr Komárek, declared allegiance to a newly revived Social Democratic Party. Others joined the small, neo-liberal Civic Democratic Alliance. Led by Vladimír Dlouhý, its policies were similar to those of Klaus, but it was less prone to anti-Communist demagogy and attracted those intellectuals who accused Klaus of an arrogant and intolerant style.

By the summer of 1991 critics of the government's economic policy were reemerging, developing the ideas they had put forward in the debate of September 1990 and finding a home in the new political structure. The Czech Communists, regarded as pariahs by all other parties, presented an alternative based on a much slower transition, similar to the self-management-based reforms discussed in Chapter 2 (Z.Hába, *RP*, 4 June 1991, and M.Benčík and M.Grebeníček, *HN*, 13 May 1991).

A group around Milan Matějka of Prague's High School of Economics teamed up with a coalition based on the newly formed Farmers' Party. Arguing that the government's strategy would lead into ever deeper depression, they called for reflation, a substantial revaluation of the Czechoslovak Crown and protectionism, alongside selective help to enterprises and an export-promotion policy. Komárek put a similar view, inaccurately adding that his research institute had worked out an adequate and far less painful reform scenario in 1989 (*RP*, 16 July 1991).

This had little impact on the government. Klaus made every effort to suggest that the only alternatives were his strategy and central planning. Komárek's criticisms were 'an attempt at a return to before November 17' — meaning before the 'velvet revolution' of 1989 — and the Social Democrats were condemned as the main threat to democracy at the Civic Democratic Party's conference on 6 October 1991.

Despite these attempts to denigrate all opposing views, a real debate over economic policy did take place within the corridors of power primarily between members of the Civic Democratic Party and members of the Civic Movement who could not be tarred with the Communist or even socialist brush. Among the latter, the most important figure was the Czech Minister of Industry Jan Vrba. He was not for a general reflation, fully accepting the need to start with restraint to overcome the alleged inflationary overhang. He saw the need, however, for an industrial policy and for a more systematically interventionist approach in agriculture, energy, export promotion and the environment.

By the spring of 1992 he had taken up views similar to those of the more sophisticated critics of the Balcerowicz programme in Poland. Restrictive policy had 'over-shot', he argued, and had brought no automatic restructuring. If anything, desirable structural changes were being reversed. Firms could not invest and modernise and voucher privatisation would bring no obvious benefits: he was more interested in preparing a list of 50 enterprises for direct sale to the best available foreign investor. He saw no recovery without state intervention and that implied dropping the insistence on a balanced budget (*LN*, 18 April 1992).

Despite occasional references to a new priority of countering depression, the supporters of the Klaus strategy typically responded that the depression was due largely to external factors and that a restrictive policy was still correct (e.g. K.Dyba, *LN*, 18 April 1992). Generally speaking that view prevailed, but modifications were forced in various sectors, particularly where protests from below strengthened the hand of individuals like Vrba who occupied positions of some power. The outcome was a kind of compromise in which neo-liberal or monetarist policies were adjusted and modified, but no full alternative could be developed.

Agriculture: The Fiercest Battle

Czechoslovak agriculture before 1989 was based on 1,660 large-scale cooperatives with 681,000 employees and 245 state farms employing 175,000. It was frequently portrayed as a relative success story. The key objective had been net self-sufficiency in food production and this had broadly been achieved by the end of the 1980s. Moreover, earnings in agriculture were roughly 8 per cent above the industrial average and food consumption was comparable to the levels of Western Europe.

Self-sufficiency and reliability of domestic supplies had their disadvantages. Costs per unit were estimated to be roughly 80 per cent above the West German level (Burianová, 1989). Possible reasons included a low level of internal and international specialisation, the need to use marginal land to maximise output, restrictions on the import of sophisticated machinery, pesticides and fertilisers, and the low quality of inputs provided by domestic industry. It was not clear that large-scale farming itself was the problem. Although nobody publicly opposed giving a chance to private farming, there were voices suggesting that the existing structure of agriculture could provide a basis for the future, within the context of reform throughout the rest of the economy. It certainly had to be the basis for feeding the population over the next few years.

In fact, agriculture was hit by changes both earlier and harder than other sectors. Conflict was also fiercer, revolving around three inter-related issues. The first was the effect of price changes, the second was the nature of reform in the system of land ownership, and the third related to assessments of agricultural cooperatives' past achievements

The first price changes in July 1990 led to an immediate fall in meat and milk consumption. The worst hit was beef with purchases dropping 10 per cent. Farmers were quick to protest, calling for subsidies to support exports and domestic sales. Bohumil Kubát, the Czech Minister of Agriculture after June 1990, was particularly unsympathetic. His view was consistently that price liberalisation and privatisation would solve all problems. Then the threat of unsold cows being dumped in Wenceslas Square in Prague brought a partial change of heart from the government and beef was exported in exchange for goods in short supply, including some very welcome motor cars from the Soviet Union. The reform programme adopted in September 1990 even contained a commitment to a price support policy, but nothing immediate was done.

The price liberalisation of January 1991 brought a further drop in food sales. Overall, output fell by 9 per cent in 1991. Meat purchases from farmers dropped by 1.2 per cent in 1990 and then by a further 22.5 per cent in the first seven months of 1991. There was some recovery after changes in government policy, referred to below, but the drop for the whole year was still 16 per cent. Moreover, the rise in food prices brought minimal benefits to Czech farmers while food processing enterprises, able to exploit surpluses to force down the price paid to farms, doubled their profits. The situation was slightly different in Slovakia where a price-support policy operated to raise slightly the price received by farmers: losses were therefore shared between farms and food processing firms.

Overall, 63 per cent of Czech and 90 per cent of Slovak cooperative farms and 87 per cent of all state farms suffered losses in 1991. The respective average earnings rose in money terms by 1.5 per cent and 3.8 per cent suggesting a very substantial fall in real incomes. Not surprisingly, farmers were far from happy, demanding Kubát's resignation and calling for subsidies for exports, a price-support policy guaranteeing their normal former level of output and a clear government programme for the future of agriculture. A mounting wave of protests was set to culminate in the blocking of all main roads on 11 July.

The atmosphere was de-fused when the federal Minister for the Economy Vladimír Dlouhý announced on 1 July that a body really would be set up to support prices. On 18 July he addressed a rally of farmers in Prague and apologised for mistakes in agricultural policy. Further demonstrations at the end of October, in which cattle were escorted into central Prague, forced the three governments to work quickly to formulate their policies.

The outcome was a compromise which could not fully satisfy the agricultural community. A price-support agency appeared and spent Kčs 8 billion in 1991 subsidising the export of 35 per cent of beef production, 10 per cent of wheat output and various other items. Its aim, however, was to guarantee sales at only around 65 per cent of the 1990 level. Trade barriers were reintroduced on almost all agricultural products: the highest level was 80 per cent for certain kinds of sugar. The aim was to compensate for subsidies to agriculture in other countries and to protect production judged to have real prospects. This proved not to be enough to prevent an escalation of losses in 1992, and cuts in the use of inputs contributed, along with unfavourable weather conditions, to an estimated 15 per cent fall in the grain harvest.

The freeing of market forces has brought rapid decline with minimal restructuring towards greater efficiency. 110,000 people left farming in 1991 and the forecast for 1992 was that another 70,000 would go: that would account for nearly a quarter of the previous farming workforce. The danger was that the price changes would have led simply to a lower level of food consumption, lower employment in agriculture and high rural unemployment. The Czech and Slovak governments were therefore under pressure to provide programmes for rural restructuring, meaning help for farms to adapt and help for new economic activities. In Slovakia the proposal was to spend Kčs 8.2 billion in 1992, but the Czech government was more cautious about naming a figure.

These battles over agricultural policy were further embittered by the course of proposals for transforming the ownership system in cooperatives. The legal position was that land was still the property of its owners from the days before collectivisation, but various additional regulations had separated formal ownership from all other rights. The case for change was overwhelming from the point of view of compensating for the injustices of the collectivisation process in the 1950s when strong pressure had been applied to join cooperatives (Myant, 1989a). It was also a prerequisite for the emergence of private farming and a precondition for the successful participation of cooperatives in a market system. Without clarity on who their owners were, there would be no means to prevent managers from using existing assets for their own personal enrichment, following the example of Poland's *nomenklatura* companies.

May 1990 saw the first significant amendment with a law allowing the 'owner' to regain use provided this did not disrupt a cooperative's operations. If the original land could not be returned, then an alternative had to be offered. The impact of this change was minimal and it was anyway seen as no more than a stop-gap measure. The general direction of government thinking in early 1990 suggested that a full transformation to market conditions would be achieved on the basis of two legal measures. One would return ownership to former, i.e. in legal terms existing, owners or their heirs, while a completely separate law would convert existing cooperatives into shareholder cooperatives. Three factors changed this. These were the appointment of Kubát as Czech Minister of Agriculture after the June 1990 elections, pressure from some farmers, and the political atmosphere heading towards an ever more forceful rejection of the past.

An assembly in Slaný on 14 July 1990 of 375 farmers aiming to set up their own farms complained that many obstacles persisted despite the new law. It supported a letter to Havel calling for a radical reform based on privatisation or reprivatisation. The need was said to be 'to reject in total the laws originating during the past regime'. There was apparently no point 'in further correcting of something fundamentally beyond repair'. Minister Kubát added his signature to this (*LD*, 16 July 1990). He then encouraged and supported the development of an alternative to the federal government's proposal which became known as the 3-Ts' proposal after Týl, Tlustý and Tomášek, its sponsor in parliament his two expert advisers. Political support was very wide including especially Civic Forum's agricultural section, the Czech Ministry of Agriculture and the Christian Democrat coalition. The essential idea was to return all land to former owners and also to give them the rest of the cooperatives' property in proportion to their former land holdings. It would mean a windfall gain to an estimated four million people, 25 per cent of the population, few of whom still worked in or cared about agriculture, while half the existing workforce would be left with nothing, despite having devoted effort to building up cooperative farms.

Proponents frequently claimed to be for 'a new kind of cooperative' and Kubát rejected a return to individual farming as 'a step backwards' (*LN*, 11 April 1991). Others, however, were more forthright: Tlustý presented individual ownership as the key to higher productivity elsewhere (*SS*, 16 November 1990). Opponents were quick to condemn the proposal as a step towards 'the complete destruction of cooperatives' (A.Adámková, *HN*, 29 November 1990). That certainly would have been its most obvious logic, but much of the motivation was simply a desire to condemn and bury the Communist past in its totality without regard to economic consequences.

The law finally passed in May 1991 was a compromise between the 3-Ts' and the federal government's thinking. All owners at the time of collectivisation had until 31 December 1992 to reclaim their land, subject to an upper limit of 50 hectares, but other property could be returned only on the basis of a court decision. Following an amendment passed in February 1992, any limit to land holdings was removed so that even the former aristocracy could reclaim its property.

Despite the modifications from the 3-Ts' version František Trnka, the leader of the Farmers' Party, still condemned the law as an effort to break up cooperatives thereby threatening chaos in food production. He later claimed to have evidence of Czech government officials tempting farmers to leave cooperatives with promises of money and other advantages (*RP*, 19 March 1992). The Czech Ministry of Agriculture responded with accusations that many cooperative managements were blocking attempts by former owners to reclaim their property. A proposal came before the Czech parliament in November 1992 for such activity to be punished with substantial fines.

An accompanying law on cooperatives was passed in December 1991, allotting the property according to land ownership and years of past labour. Scope was allowed for conversion into a variety of legal forms and general assemblies in 80 per cent of cooperative farms decided during 1992 to become shareholding cooperatives; another 10 per cent chose other legal forms that retained the existing organisational structure while 10 per cent opted for division into smaller cooperatives.

It remains to be seen whether the cooperatives can survive these legal changes. Opinion polls, however, consistently confirm very little interest in private farming. It is made unattractive by the low level of demand and the lack of easy credit. Moreover, ambiguities in the land ownership law made the return of property a very slow process (Horkel et al., 1992). By mid-1992 20,000 Czechs had announced the aim of returning to family farming on 4.4 per cent of the agricultural land.

Despite this slow development of alternative forms of agriculture, accusations that the Czech Ministry of Agriculture was intent on destroying cooperative farming were encouraged by a bitter dispute centring on the Slušovice cooperative in South Moravia. With over 5,000 members, it had been the most successful of a group of large cooperatives that had become wealthy by diversifying beyond agriculture (Myant, 1989a, Čuba and Divila, 1989, and Vácha, 1988). It had used the relative freedom from central controls allowed for cooperatives to provide an enormous range of products and services, including even micro-computers. Reinvestment of profits from all these activities into agriculture had led to productivity levels higher than the average for any Western European country, even though the land was judged to be relatively poor.

Its success drew comparisons with the 'excellent firms' of US management literature (Peters and Waterman, 1982). It too had a charismatically autocratic chairman and tough internal discipline, but a regime that allowed high earnings and job security for those who conformed. It was a system that created strong loyalty and a sense of involvement in the ambitious project of becoming an 'exemplary' agricultural enterprise.

Slušovice enjoyed some protection from the local party hierarchy, but the authorities in Prague seem to have viewed its entrepreneurial style with the utmost suspicion throughout the 1970s and most of the 1980s. Its behaviour certainly was radically different from that of the typical state enterprise under central planning. At the very end of the 1980s, and albeit somewhat tentatively, it was being paraded as an example for others to follow. This seems to have aroused considerable antipathy and jealousy in more traditional enterprises: there was an extraordinary eagerness to believe that the successes were somehow phoney, or the result of official patronage. Nothing substantial to support those suspicions has come to light.

After November 1989 Slušovice has been less successful. Apart from the problems affecting all of agriculture, its non-agricultural activities were hit especially hard by the freeing of imports. It was also caught with considerable debts from recent investments. There were suggestions that the losses were part of an 'organised catastrophe', in which property had been shifted into newly formed companies enriching selected former employees while the cooperative carried the debt. This remains to be proven.

These economic problems received maximum publicity amid a hail of general criticism. The chairman, František Čuba, came into immediate conflict with the Civic Forum organisation when, true to his managerial style, he dismissed internal critics as 'disrupters', insisting that 'democracy ends at the gates of the enterprise' (*SS*, 3 January 1990). Accusations followed of a reign of terror under 'Čuba's secret police' (*LD*, 24 August 1990). One leading former dissident employee portrayed Slušovice as 'a surviving model of totalitarianism, which prevents the free development of the personality' (S.Devátý, quoted in J.Truneček, *HN*, 1990, No.44, p.8). Other former dissidents came forward to defend Slušovice, suggesting that its political record in the past had been better than that of most enterprises (*RP*, 2 May 1991).

Nevertheless, much of the press took up accusations of 'an ever more powerful mafia growing ... also into the security police' (*LD*, 24 August 1990). Even President Havel referred in a major speech on 21 August 1990 to 'dark Slušovice fibres' and Čuba resigned the next day 'under the de facto diktat of the President' (*RP*, 3 September 1990). A string of legal disputes followed as the cooperative subdivided into seven main units. Ever more extraordinary claims and counter-claims continued to surface with Kubát seemingly regarding it as a top priority to prove that Slušovice was essentially a criminal organisation. Čuba, however, led the majority who kept their faith in him into a new cooperative, named DAK MOVA Slušovice. Registration was refused in the Czech republic, but was accepted in Slovakia where the cooperative had some branches. To Čuba this whole bizarre story had one simple explanation: behind it all lay a desire to bury the Slušovice experience and to prove that 'everything that was done in this republic before the November revolution was completely bad' (*RP*, 2 May 1991).

In his view, there was an alternative way forward for agriculture, based on share-owning cooperatives with considerable internal flexibility. Specific activities could be leased to individuals or work groups with the possibility of privatisation in the future. The ultimate structure of agriculture would be determined in time by the market. In the meantime, individual farming might develop under the initial patronage and protection of large cooperatives. It would mean a continuation and development of the ideas developing before November 1989. Similar views were put by Trnka of the Farmers' Party (e.g. *RP*, 14 September 1990), himself a former Slušovice employee. Any such alternative was given much less chance by the campaign against Slušovice.

Towards an Industrial Policy

Industrial policy was another area of sharp conflict with the outcome again a compromise between different conceptions. Industrial enterprises were in considerable difficulties already in 1990, due to falling demand from the former CMEA countries, but they entered 1991 in a very poor state of preparation for the shocks that lay ahead. The typical attitude was a mixture of helplessness and complacency. They were unaware of the need for major changes in behaviour, convinced that they could carry on roughly as before with the help of state subsidies and in any case unsure of how they could improve their position for the future. Only a very small minority were proposing significant changes in technology or product ranges.

There were, however, two areas of change. The first was a thirst to find foreign partners. Hopes were generally naive: a foreign link-up was often seen as a means to survive without undertaking major restructuring, but establishing contacts did represent a useful start. The second change was in dividing existing enterprises into subsidiaries under the overall control of a holding company. These sub-units were generally based on existing product ranges, so that there was no implied de-monopolisation. Nevertheless, this was a helpful step towards encouraging foreign partners while maintaining as much as possible from the past (Havlín et al., 1990). It could therefore be claimed that some preparations had been made before the shock of January 1991.

In early 1991, however, enterprises were hit by a financial catastrophe. One partial cause was the drop in demand, but that only began to show itself after April when the average profit rate fell from the January peak of 26.3 per cent to 8 per cent for the latter half of the year. Three other factors, none of which can be related in any way to an enterprise's long-term business prospects, were even more important.

The first was the legacy of past debts, which suddenly carried an interest rate of 24 per cent instead of the previous 8 per cent. Moreover, in marked contrast to the practice under central planning, banks were refusing further loans to potentially insolvent enterprises. The second was the failure of foreign customers, in the former CMEA or in developing countries, to pay their bills. The original exports had been encouraged by the government in the past, but the exporting enterprises now found that nobody would cover them for the resulting losses. The third factor related to the financing of stocks. The background was a change in rules in the early 1980s in which the state cut the turnover funds from enterprises and instead allowed them to finance short-term stock-holding by credits with minimal rates of interest and no set repayment dates. This caused some problems for enterprises in the latter 1980s if they were saddled with stocks of unsaleable goods, but their survival was not threatened. After January 1991, however, these credits suddenly became 'real' and carried the 24 per cent rate of interest.

Under the weight of these three factors many enterprises, especially in the steel, engineering and electronics industries, simply stopped paying their bills. This had occurred during the 1980s whenever the government attempted to impose a tighter monetary policy. Investigations had always confirmed that the origins of bad debt were a small number of large and powerful enterprises. The problem was then multiplied as their suppliers in turn became insolvent and failed to pay bills.

The assumption during preparations for reform before 1990 was that the banking system would somehow be able to carry this burden by granting extra credits to key enterprises within some form of financial restructuring. This, however, was to prove a naive assumption as banks acquired greater independence and began to behave according to a commercial logic. There was some help from foreign investors — Volkswagen paid off the debts of the Škoda car manufacturer — but the debt crisis was also a discouragement to foreign investment. The obvious solution of writing off all past debts was dismissed as potentially inflationary.

The volume of 'payment arrears', a euphemism introduced by the IMF, grew steadily through 1990, reaching Kčs 47.1 billion — 6 per cent of annual value-added — in December. It then escalated in the new year to hit Kčs 147.2 billion in September 1991 — possibly passing Kčs 300 billion before the end of 1992 — affecting 43 per cent of economic units. It was estimated that Kčs 36 billion were due to primary insolvency, another Kčs 29 billion to unpaid bills from abroad while the rest was the result of firms passing on bad debt (Veselý, 1992). In a genuine market system, the problem would be resolved by bankruptcies. That would have been politically unacceptable, economically pointless and, finally, impossible in view of the absence of an adequate legal framework.

The problem would have been even greater but for a partial resolution forced by protests from enterprises. An assembly of workers at the Zetor tractor factory in December 1990 in Brno threatened to block the main Prague to Bratislava motorway and even to invade the federal Ministry of Finance after banks refused to grant further credits. The immediate problem was the postponement of Kčs 500 million in debt repayments from Iraq. Zetor, however, had assured hard currency markets for 80 per cent of its output and, within a generally uncompetitive economy, must be judged one of the enterprises with the best prospects. Klaus wisely gave in, after meeting a delegation from the factory, and found the necessary funds.

Mid-February produced an even more explosive situation in the giant ČKD engineering combine in Prague. Future prospects were not good, as 70 per cent of past exports had been directed to the Soviet market and alternatives had yet to be found. A beginning had, however, been made with subdivision of the combine and a search for foreign partners to help in restructuring. Before these efforts could bear any fruit, bad debts led to a suspension of wage payments.

After an angry protest by employees, unions and management joined forces to confront bank representatives. Warning of the danger of ending up a nation of 'street traders, bar men and souvenir sellers', they forced 'a draw' in which funds were made available to prevent complete financial collapse. A few weeks later Klaus persuaded the existing banks to contribute funds to a new 'Consolidation Bank' which would offer eight-year loans at 13 per cent interest to finance stockholding (Nefová, 1992). It was a compromise that could not prevent the growth in bad debt, and did not ward off financial crises in a number of major enterprises. It did, however, postpone the kind of catastrophe experienced by Ursus in Poland. Moreover, the general message for enterprises such as ČKD was that they could still expect the government to help them survive. It was therefore worth trying to find new markets and foreign partners (J.Klíma, *HN*, 24 June 1992).

The Czech Ministry of Industry wanted a more pro-active approach. Rather than just emergency help to the likes of Zetor, Vrba began looking at the idea of deciding which should be helped and which should be 'left to fall' (P.Husák, *LN*, 28 February 1991). The idea was welcomed by the Union of Industry of the Czech Republic, which had sent a petition to the government in mid-February warning that industry was on the point of 'collapse'. 'A selective approach is essential', insisted its president, Hynek Hanák of the Tatra lorry manufacturer in Kopřivnice. 'Theoretically all can have a chance, but only the viable ones with prospects can really hope to survive' (*LN*, 28 February 1991).

There was an opposing view from some managements. A few claimed to have been able to adapt fairly well to the new conditions, finding new products to replace, for example, orders from the military.

Journalists who were looking for such responses could find directors
who regarded the Union of Industry as 'members of the old regime, at
least in their way of thinking' (K.Kříž, *LN*, 13 May 1991), or as 'a
pressure group ... wanting to force the government into a softening of
monetary policy and into increasing subsidies and intervention in
enterprises' (J.Franěk, *LN*, 7 March 1991). Instead, it was suggested,
enterprises should stop looking to outside agents and help themselves
to solve the debt problem.

Such voices came only from a very small minority who had
maintained and developed international contacts over a number of
years or who had by good fortune avoided the debt problem. They
were undoubtedly right that many inefficient firms saw an industrial
policy as a means to restore the easy conditions of the past. Hanák, of
course, was not openly advocating this. The assumption implicit in this
criticism was that powerful enterprises could always manipulate
decisions in the state apparatus.

There was strong opposition to any selective help from within the
federal government and especially from Klaus's federal Ministry of
Finance, but the State Bank joined with others in favouring the writing
off of at least a part of the estimated Kčs 150 billion owed by
enterprises to banks since before November 1989. After fierce
disagreements, a compromise was reached: Kčs 50 billion was made
available in December 1991 and January 1992, to be covered later by
returns from privatisation, to boost the banks' asset base and to help
reduce the burden of enterprise debts. The banks were given the main
role in selecting which enterprises were to be helped and their criterion
was the plausibility of future business plans. Among those included
were Zetor, a major exporter already in 1991, and ČKD, which
claimed to be making real progress towards finding new markets and
laying the basis for joint ventures. It did seem that some of the most
notorious 'dinosaurs' might be able to survive.

Vrba had ideas for going further, but could not win approval for a
scheme costing another Kčs 50 to 60 billion to finance measures to
make existing enterprises more attractive to potential foreign partners.
It was dismissed on grounds of cost and as a continuation of the state
dirigisme of the past.

Even when backed by international expertise, the Czech Ministry of
Industry had a tough battle to reverse the logic of neo-liberal thinking.

Thus a major study in 1992 carried out by the Sema Group and Roland Berger — French and German consultancy firms — proposed a reduction of steel output across the federation from 15.5 million tons in 1989 and 11.68 million tons in 1991 to around 9 million tons in the year 2000. Employment would drop from 153,000 to 45,000 on the basis of an expensive modernisation programme. It was clearly recognised that no new foreign owner would come forward to finance this. The Czech Ministry of Industry proposed to withdraw steel from current privatisation plans and to undertake rationalisation under state ownership. The Czech Ministry for Privatisation could see no reason for making an exception to its position of finding private owners as quickly as possible and no final decision could be taken during 1992.

There was more success in the formulation of an export promotion policy. The government's implicit assumption had been that devaluation alone would encourage exports. In fact, as critics had forecast, it helped only those sectors that produced the least processed products which tended to be sold for immediate payment. Problems were immense especially for the machinery industry, which had to grant credits but could not charge a foreign buyer the domestic interest rate. It was finally agreed in February 1992 to set up an agency, hopefully to become self-financing but with an initial capital to Kčs 1.7 billion, to offer export credit guarantees and to cover the difference between domestic and international interest rates. Its impact is yet to be felt.

Slovakia's Specificity

The development of economic policy followed a substantially different course in Slovakia. The existence of the Czech and Slovak governments, sometimes duplicating the role of the federal government, was a potentially complicating factor in much of policy formulation. In practice, however, the greater problem was that political life in the Czech and Slovak republics developed along substantially different lines with the leading Slovaks in the federal government, such as Prime Minster Marian Čalfa and Minister for Strategic Planning Pavel Hoffmann, tending to take a similar view to their Czech colleagues.

The dominant movement in Slovak politics in 1990 was Public Against Violence, the sister organisation to the Czech Civic Forum.

After the 1990 elections it gave the Slovak prime ministership to the charismatic but erratic Vladimír Mečiar. He won immense popularity in Slovakia — and unpopularity among Czechs — during tough negotiations with federal ministers which were perceived at home as an attempt to win the best possible deal for Slovakia. During these conflicts, however, other leading Public Against Violence figures lost confidence in Mečiar's confrontational style. In April 1991 he was removed from his post and replaced by a Christian Democrat. That, however, marked no end to conflict with the federal government and Mečiar quickly set up the Movement for a Democratic Slovakia which rapidly moved ahead in all Slovak opinion ratings.

Two factors can explain the background to Slovak political developments. The first, as revealed by opinion polls, was a rapid and dramatic growth in national self-confidence. Slovaks had felt themselves the junior partner in the federation and now hoped that freedom from Communism would also mean freedom from Czech condescension. There was, however, no obvious means to give expression to this new-found self-confidence as the overwhelming majority opposed outright separation. The result was a string of conflicts with the federal and Czech governments over largely symbolic issues.

These continued even after Mečiar's removal, but he gave the conflict a new twist with the idea of a declaration of Slovak sovereignty, after which an internationally recognised Slovakia could renegotiate a confederal relationship with a Czech republic. It could have been an ingenious means to satisfy Slovak aspirations while retaining some form of Czechoslovak state. Czech politicians, however, generally had no sympathy for what they saw as a dangerous step leading inevitably to the break-up of Czechoslovakia.

The second factor was a strong Slovak desire to find an economic policy that recognised their alleged specificity. The practical meaning of this was very unclear. In one view, in which Slovakia was to take full control over its economic destiny, there would even be separate fiscal and monetary policies, with a separate Slovak National Bank. Despite accusations before his removal, successors to Mečiar's ministers found no evidence of preparations for such a major break with federal policies and his movement has consistently denied any desire to retreat from the platform of 'radical economic reform' (e.g. M.Kontra, *HN*, 10 June 1991). At the time of the 1992 general election

Mečiar was making it clear that he was not contemplating anything that would be incompatible with a united Czechoslovak economy.

Generally, however, Slovak economic thinking had a consistently more interventionist flavour even after Mečiar's removal. The small differences over agriculture have already been mentioned. The distinction is more clearly illustrated by the energy programmes published by the Czech and Slovak governments in May 1992. The former, formulated by Karel Dyba, the Czech Minister for Economic Policy and Development and an ally of Klaus, emphasised the removal of state subsidies and the partial privatisation of electricity generation after which it was assumed that competition would develop. It made no reference to future investment, played down the costs of future programmes, such as disposal of nuclear waste, and assumed that current capacity would be more than adequate.

The Slovak government, however, noted the likely need for future investment, even if there were to be a structural shift towards less energy-intensive sectors, and implied that most of the cost would have to be covered by the state. To some extent the differences reflected different starting points. Slovakia did suffer from an energy deficit, 'importing' coal and electricity from the Czech republic. There was, however, plenty of scope for a more interventionist policy in the Czech republic, and some privatisation under Slovak conditions need not have been incompatible with the general energy strategy. There clearly was some difference of philosophy between the two republics.

Nevertheless, and despite the attempts of various Slovak economists to argue to the contrary, the case for recognising a 'specific' Slovak economic problem, justifying full local control over economic processes, is not particularly strong. It has been developed by a number of Slovak economists over many years, but not much of the detail has been published. The clearest case against was put in a report commissioned by the federal government in 1991 (Čapek et al., 1991). Five points can be mentioned as possible indications of specificity.

The first of these relates to the level of industrialisation. The evidence here is that the difference is not very great: Slovakia's national income per head was around 70 per cent of the Czech level in 1948 but up to 94 per cent by 1989. On some indicators of economic performance Slovakia was slightly ahead.

The second point is that Slovakia may have a bias towards the basic and heavy industries that dominated in post-war industrialisation and towards exporting to the former Soviet Union. These factors would at least point to a more painful process of restructuring and integration into a Western European economy. Official statistics, however, suggest trivial differences in sectoral or export structures. The most striking feature about the Czech and Slovak economies is their similarity, although the latter is somewhat less dependent on exports and more dependent on sales into the other part of the federation.

The third point is that Slovakia may have a bias towards branch factories, producing components for Czech enterprises. Several such cases can be quoted, but a clear bias cannot be proven. Moreover, this point is partially contradicted by a fourth argument, which suggests that Slovakia has a bias towards the production of internationally uncompetitive finished products in small, isolated towns which in turn are based upon that single employer. This was one of the features of post-war economic development and is particularly true of the consumer electronics industry which has suffered a catastrophe after the drop in domestic demand, a fall in exports to the former CMEA and the arrival of higher quality imports. The social consequences for the communities concerned may be worse than those associated with the 'branch factory syndrome' of some regions in Western Europe (Myant, 1992). Again, there are cases in Slovakia which fit this theory, but there are also many in the Czech republic.

The fourth argument is that Slovakia had a greater share of armaments production. This clearly is true (M.Ježek, 1991, and Outrata, 1991). Armaments accounted for 3 per cent of Czechoslovak industrial output in the peak year of 1987 and 60 per cent of that was concentrated into Slovakia, and above all into the heavy engineering works around Martin in the Váh valley of Western Slovakia. 70 per cent of output had been for export, putting Czechoslovakia in seventh place among world arms exporters. The potential for future sales after the end of the cold war was obviously very uncertain. Moreover, President Havel quickly committed himself to ending arms exports as a humanitarian gesture. Following federal government decisions, the plan was to reduce output to 15 per cent of its peak level by 1992 within which Slovakia was to have only a 40 per cent share. Around 58,000 jobs could be expected to disappear.

Faced with this prospect Mečiar, after a visit to the Soviet Union in March 1991, implausibly reassured a rally in Martin that he could find markets for the Soviet-designed Czechoslovak tanks. There were also known to be willing buyers in the Middle East and critics of federal policy noted that other major arms exporters could step in to fill the gap left by Czechoslovakia's withdrawal. The federal authorities did moderate their stance, allowing the continuation of some exports, but the issue had been portrayed as one in which a Slovak government had to fight against federal indifference or naivety. After Mečiar's removal in April 1991, short protest strikes were staged in armaments factories and several other threatened enterprises, despite opposition to participation from the 'non-political' trade unions.

Even this bias towards military production does not provide a strong case for an altogether specific economic policy. Federal ministers, and especially Vladimír Dlouhý, frequently pointed out that there were regions within both republics that were suffering. The solution was to devise a regional policy, or policies, that could help the worst affected. In fact, of course, not very much was done owing to the unwillingness to make funds available.

Nevertheless, the issue of arms conversion was taken more seriously than most at the federal level: Kčs 1.5 billion in subsidies were granted in 1989 and 1990. The heavy engineering works in Martin, with plans to link up with various Western European firms, received the most assistance. Under continuing Slovak pressure, the federal government decided in May 1991 to give grants of up to 30 per cent of investment costs to support conversion programmes, and approved schemes for another Kčs 1.5 billion during that year. Again, the largest single commitment was to Martin (Vráblik and Kocevová, 1992).

An explanation is therefore needed for Slovakia's search for a specific economic policy. To some extent it was a natural extension of political feelings into economic thinking, and that may have been the dominant factor. It also reflected a different historical experience. Slovakia had done relatively well under central planning and while isolated from the Western European economies. There was therefore far less basis for blanket criticisms of state intervention (Čapek et al., 1991). Indeed, opinion polls revealed consistent differences in the perception of economic developments. Sixty five per cent of Slovaks in the spring of 1992 believed that the economy was going in the wrong direction and 31 per cent favoured a return to what had existed before November 1989. Among Czechs, to whom the economic reform was a source of optimism, the equivalent figures were 38 per cent and 16 per cent.

To this, however, must be added the fifth possible argument for specificity which has not as yet been emphasised by Slovak economists. Although the effects of 'shock therapy' were pretty similar in the two republics, geographical and other factors gave Slovakia less chance of benefiting from the opening of links with Western Europe. Specificity was therefore not so much a question of existing structure as of future prospects. That does provide a case for an even more interventionist approach, to improve the infrastructure and to make Slovak enterprises more attractive to foreign partners, but association with, and possibly help from, the potentially more successful Czech economy would obviously be an advantage rather than a disadvantage.

Unfortunately, this now looks less likely to happen. Exasperation from the Czech side led in the autumn of 1991 to tough negotiations over the budget for 1992. With strong pressure for cuts wherever possible, the Czech government insisted on an end to subsidies for Slovakia. The most careful estimates suggested that the transfer of income from the Czech republic to Slovakia during the 1980s had still been equivalent to nearly 10 per cent of the latter's Net Material Product (Křovák and Zamrazilová, 1990) and part of this was accounted for by a greater contribution per head for Slovakia from the federal budget. The calculations are not simple and some Slovak economists have even suggested that the Czech side could have been the net gainer because taxes on wage bills and profits of Slovak subsidiaries of Czech-based enterprises were paid into the Czech budget.

Nevertheless, attempts to take account of as many factors as possible consistently point to Slovakia benefiting from the federation. Czech ministers took the view that that was no longer acceptable in view of the public statements by leading Slovak politicians. Voices were even raised suggesting that separation might be inevitable and that it would be better to get the agony over quickly. No major political force on either side was advocating full separation, but mutual misunderstandings and some policy differences were exacerbating conflicts. Moreover, nobody with real influence on either side seemed able to understand how they were offending their partner in the federation.

11. The Rush to Privatise

Czechoslovakia started on the road to a market economy with a minimal private sector. The main nationalisation law, passed in 1945, brought 61 per cent of industrial employees into the state sector. Legal and economic changes followed by various forms of political intimidation effectively eliminated the private sector in the rest of industry and in trade and distribution during the 1950s. Legal private sector employment fell to a low point of under 20,000 in the early 1980s. The beginnings of modest reform allowed some recovery to 91,000 registered businesses in 1989, but most of the individuals were undertaking private activity in addition to a full-time job.

An explosion of private activity was expected in 1990 as formal legal restrictions were relaxed. By the end of 1991 there were 1,340,000 registered private enterprises. Fully 70 per cent, however, were either only at the stage of preparing for activity or were subsidiary activities for someone in full-time employment. There were some reasonably sized firms, but most of those already active were still very small. The private sector as a whole employed 1,159,000, 16 per cent of all employment, and accounted for an estimated 9.3 per cent of value-added. Unrecorded private activity was not believed to be particularly substantial (J.Jílek, *HN*, 10 July 1992). The private sector clearly is an area of new growth, but it has not compensated for the decline in activity elsewhere and especially not in Slovakia which accounts for only 23 per cent of all private businesses.

Barriers to the growth of private enterprise were brought firmly to the public's attention as early as the first assembly of the Association of Czechoslovak Entrepreneurs in April 1990. Claiming 75,000 members, although most of these were people *wanting* to set up businesses (*LD*, 12 April 1990), this new body complained at the continuing absence of genuine equality of conditions and at a tax system that they felt discriminated against them. Even a new law of 1 May 1990, passed under Komárek's authority with the aim of liberalising conditions, still left private firms at the mercy of monopoly suppliers, unable to get foreign currency and with limited access to premises. These complaints continue to be heard. Indeed, the potential benefits of reforms are partially cancelled out by the restrictive monetary policy making banks especially reluctant to lend without adequate collateral (Konečná, 1992).

The logical way to accelerate the emergence of a substantial private sector was privatisation. Nobody objected openly to the principle of 'small' privatisation, which would make available small units such as shops and workshops to potential entrepreneurs. If anything, the government's usual critics complained throughout the early part of 1990 that not enough was being done while ministers preferred to waffle about their hopes for the total privatisation of all economic activity in one act.

Throughout the debates over privatisation, three broad positions can be identified. In one view, supported especially by Václav Klaus, the aim was simply to achieve private ownership as rapidly as possible. Tomáš Ježek, his friend from the Institute of Forecasting and Civic Democratic Alliance founder member who became the Czech Minister for Privatisation after the June 1990 elections, spoke of completing the whole process in two or three years. After that he looked forward to retiring into a university professorship (Ježek, 1990).

The main alternative view, which can be associated with Vrba's approach to industrial policy, linked privatisation to a general restructuring of the economy. It was a possible means to the end of bringing in new management abilities and expertise and new investment and technology. In this view, the form of private ownership and the identity of the private owner could be crucially important. This pointed towards a controlled process of privatisation with some active participation by the state.

A third approach put the primacy on political or moral considerations, emphasising the righting of the alleged wrongs of the Communist past. That meant favouring the return of previously nationalised property. Along with the other two conceptions, it did have an impact on the formulation and implementation of policies. The final outcome was a compromise in which the advocates of the neo-liberal approach, benefiting from domination of the federal Ministry of Finance and the Czech Ministry for Privatisation, carried the most obvious weight.

Returning to Former Owners

Demands for the return of former businesses were based on three arguments. The first was the obvious moral one. The second was that many small businessmen claimed genuinely to want to go back to their former activities and could presumably do the job well. The third was the possibility that simply taking some property out of the state's hands would make it easier for other small businesses to find premises. The Czechoslovak Association of Entrepreneurs therefore took the case of property taken over in the 1959-65 period to the Supreme Court and were reassured that it had probably been confiscated 'illegally'. They wrote to Havel on this basis, also incidentally attacking Klaus's preoccupation with 'big' privatisation (*LD*, 27 July 1990 and 1 September 1990).

Ježek, 21 days after setting up his ministry, had a draft law ready. Slightly over 70,000 properties, mostly small shops, pubs and restaurants, could be returned on proof of ownership to all those still resident in the country who claimed within six months. Worried that going further could create scope for endless legal haggles, Ježek hoped for no more than a few further tidying-up measures after which restitution would be definitively ended.

Political pressures, however, began to take a different course. Calls were made for the return of *all* property nationalised after 1948 and the federal government accepted this on the grounds that, in the words of Deputy Prime Minister Pavel Rychetský of the Civic Movement, 'it is morally the right thing to do'. Some wanted to go even further, arguing for the return of everything nationalised after 1945. They could point to the fact that compensation was mentioned in all nationalisation laws but never actually paid.

There were two powerful arguments against too sweeping a restitution programme. The first was its legal implications, possibly threatening the constitutional legitimacy of all post-war changes including the confiscation of property of the former German minority after 1945. The second objection related to its impracticability. A petition was presented on 13 February 1991 from leading economists opposing 'the attempts to broaden the extent of restitution either of physical assets or by financial compensation'. The former method, it claimed, would be very slow and complicated, delaying economic reform, while the latter could not be afforded on any significant scale. The petition was signed by leading researchers and government ministers: the only names conspicuous by their absence were those of Klaus and his close adviser Dušan Tříska. The former had privately agreed strongly with the sentiment but was constrained by his ambitions as a right-wing politician.

There were a few voices querying the moral justifiability of the idea. Vladimír Mečiar complained in a television broadcast on 17 February 1991 that restitution meant one section of the population paying out of their own pockets for mistakes that they had not committed. It seemed to him that the heirs of former owners were a no more deserving cause than, for example, teachers who were being asked to accept pay restraint.

Nevertheless, the government's compromise version, covering all property of individuals nationalised under post–February 1948 legislation, was accepted by parliament on 21 February. The estimated value was Kčs 300 billion with the possibility of 800,000 cases, although the actual number of claims appears to have been much lower. Compensation was to be purely financial, based upon 'big' privatisation, with scope for physical restitution if the owner was prepared to pay the increased value. Extreme optimists thought all legal haggles could be settled within five years.

No country ever before has embarked on such a substantial programme of returning property, especially after so long a period. In practice, however, the volume is small in relation to the total privatisation programme and there is no sign yet of its creating great fortunes or causing discontent from those left out. The need for privatisation proposals from individual enterprises to cover the return of some property did marginally complicate big privatisation, as discussed below, but other complications proved so much greater than expected that the delay from this alone was not significant. The only serious negative consequence — and this too should not be exaggerated — has been the uncertainty over ownership frightening away foreign investors. One case has arisen of a firm sold to a major Western company subsequently being claimed by a former owner.

'Small' Privatisation

Even before restitution had been broadened, preparations were under way for 'small' privatisation. As Ježek explained his idea, based on the realisation only in September 1990 that everything could not be privatised quickly under one scheme (*SS*, 4 October 1990), the key distinguishing feature was to be the method used; public auction, rather than the size of unit. This, however, effectively restricted applicability to physical assets rather than ongoing businesses carrying debts and contracts for the future. It was clear from the start that shops and other service outlets would be the most appropriate candidates.

The union representing shopworkers objected to the first draft of the law, fearing the disruption of working conditions on the arrival of a new and unknown owner and warning that the auctions could become a means of 'washing dirty money'. Black-marketeers and former corrupt officials, the people likely to have the most savings, could find a legitimate home for their wealth. Short warning strikes were staged on 25 and 26 September with calls for employees to be given an advantage with interest-free loans up to the total price of the property and demanding further rules to ensure that shops and businesses were committed to continuing with their past activity. A joint meeting of the Czech, Slovak and federal governments very narrowly rejected this view.

The law finally passed on 25 October gave no preference for employees. As several critics later pointed out (Turek, 1991, and Kožušník, 1991), many of the problems that were to arise with small privatisation could have been avoided by developing the shopworkers' ideas with privatisation based at least in part on loans or leasing deals to existing employees. That, however, would have been a slower process, taking the initiative away from the government, while the neo-liberal advocates of auctions believed it necessary to find as quickly as possible 'owners, who will be responsible for their economic activity' (D.Tříska, *HN*, 10 October 1990). The consistent claim was that 'if enterprises remain under the control of their managers and employees, their behaviour will not change substantially' (R.Holmann, *LN*, 11 September 1991).

Nevertheless, only Czechoslovak citizens could take part in the first round of auctions — others were allowed to buy later if a minimum price had not been reached – and there was a two-year wait before property could be sold abroad. Change of use was allowed, apart from some restrictions on former food shops. The revenue received was to be kept by the government for some unspecified future use. The immediate net effect was therefore to be strongly deflationary, absorbing in Ježek's view up to one-eighth of personal savings.

The first auctions were held amid considerable publicity at the end of January 1991. Progress was much slower than initially hoped but, by May 1992, 17,500 Czech and 8,500 Slovak properties had been transferred to private control accounting for nearly all of those judged to be eligible. In practice, as ownership of buildings was yet to be clarified, the sale was typically of a two-year lease. A later amendment extended this to five years. Only 25 per cent of auctions led to a full transfer of ownership.

It quickly became clear that the process was more complicated than anticipated. Existing managements naturally disliked the uncertainty of an auction while larger organisations and local authorities had no desire to lose without compensation units they owned. They all found various means to cause delays. Moreover, not all new owners could fulfil their financial obligations and 13 per cent of auctioned property was returned to the state almost at once. This and various other complications could lead simply to the closure of a previously functioning enterprise. Not surprisingly, then, small privatisation was somewhat chaotic, but the real controversies revolved around three key issues.

The first was the question of who the buyers really were. Some were undoubtedly front-men for foreigners who would reveal themselves in time. Others were believed to be coming with 'dirty money' acquired domestically, while there were even suggestions that international crime syndicates could be finding a safe haven for their gains in small privatisation.

Estimates of the extent of these phenomena are extremely vague. The Czech savings bank reported giving credits on only 4,000 objects totalling Kčs 4.28 billion, compared with a total of Kčs 22.5 billion paid at auctions. There was little impact on personal savings, or on money in circulation. Although estimates are necessarily vague, one Czech government minister guessed that around 50 per cent of funds came from abroad (V.Štěpová, *Práce*, 2 April 1992). In Slovakia there was less evidence either of foreign or of 'dirty' money, with 70 per cent of buyers relying on loans. The Investment Bank alone granted credits equivalent to nearly half the Kčs 11.5 billion paid.

A second problem related to corruption in the conduct of the auctions. 'Dutch' auctions were allowed if no interest was expressed at the reservation price. Fifteen per cent of Czech and 20 per cent of Slovak auctions ended by this means, even including some obviously attractive properties. Following reports of an atmosphere of intimidation at many auctions, with firearms visible in some cases (K.Janková, *Práce*, 1 November 1991), it was widely assumed that some potential buyers were taking steps to 'dissuade' others from participating.

The third major area of controversy concerned the need to ensure the survival of an adequate distribution and service network. The Czech and Slovak Ministers for Privatisation, committed to the philosophy of the free market, were confident that the structure of internal trade outlets would quickly adapt to the pattern of consumer demand. The Ministries of Internal Trade, backed by some local administrations, accumulated evidence showing that a range of basic consumer goods and services had disappeared from shops in some areas. It seemed that the 'monopoly' of a handful of state enterprises could be transformed by the auction process into a monopoly of 'a couple of mafias' (V.Štěpová, *Práce,* 16 March 1992).

The alternative, as put by Czech Minister of Internal Trade Vlasta Štěpová, was to create a reliable distribution network based on joint stock companies and joint ventures with foreign firms. She, and her Slovak counterpart, both sought to emulate the Western European norm in which most sales are through multi-outlet retailers. In Slovakia this philosophy led to the selection of 100 food shops and 46 shoe outlets which were to be offered for foreign partners. In the Czech case it led to sharp and public conflicts with Tomáš Ježek. He blocked Štěpová's plans, seeing in them a means for existing managements to escape the dangers from a new and unknown owner. Moreover, the best shops in particular would thereby be prevented from falling into the hands of potential domestic entrepreneurs. Ježek argued that genuinely committed foreign firms could be offered new sites to build on and did not need to be given even easier access to the domestic market (*Práce*, 14 May 1991). His argument will appear weak if a large proportion of the property auctioned has fallen into foreign hands in an uncontrolled process at effectively give-away prices.

These difficulties were not enough to discredit small privatisation, but rough surveys of opinions show mixed feelings (*HN*, 20 May 1992). Some newly privatised small businesses were seen to be providing very attractive services with much longer opening hours. Employees, however, noted a clear worsening of conditions (*Sondy*, 1992, No.11, p.3, and 25-6, p.5). Moreover, private shops dependent on the domestic distribution system could not provide a significantly better range of products than their predecessors. They sometimes charged lower prices, but improvements in shop window displays were possible only with imported goods, which much of the population had no intention of buying, or very specific products such as bread that could be made on site.

'Big' Privatisation

The complications surrounding 'big' privatisation, it was naively hoped, would be mastered 'more easily than with small privatisation' (D.Tříska, *HN*, 5 September 1991). This was based on faith in the voucher method. Orthodox methods, it was accepted, would be very slow. Getting each company into good shape before coming to the market 'would mean a consulting agency for each one' (D.Tříska, *Financial Times*, 1 June 1990), while the small volume of personal savings ruled out speedy sales of shares. Ježek quoted a friend's estimate that selling shares would achieve full privatisation after 612 years: 'perhaps he got it wrong', Ježek quipped (1990, p.1), 'and it would only take 537 years'.

In September 1991 Klaus (*LN*, 2 September 1991) tried to add even more arguments suggesting that the voucher method could help break the barriers experienced in small privatisation. There would be none of the opposition from managements, employees or customers to the hiving off of parts of an existing enterprise. Existing firms would simply be transferred to private ownership unchanged. The process would tread on no toes and provoke no conflicts.

The great unanswered question related to developments after privatisation. The general belief had to be that 'any "restructuring" of an enterprise will be carried out more efficiently by owners and certainly not by the state' (I.Svítek, *LN*, 3 April 1991). Presumably Tříska believed that they would not even need to delay while employing a consulting agency. Another of Klaus's advisers, however, openly followed through the logic of the neo-liberal approach and painted a picture of a massive restructuring process in which people, land and capital employed in the 'wrong' places making the 'wrong' things would be released. This would enable a completely new organisational structure to arise from the ruins of the old system (R.Holmann, *LN*, 30 January 1992). Klaus himself, perhaps with more than half an eye to the June 1992 elections, was happy to avoid such speculation.

In practice, however, difficulties were to prove far more serious than with small privatisation. The essential problem was that the first conceptions of privatisation mentioned at the start of the chapter were combined. Privatisation by voucher had had to face opposition and scepticism on many sides. The Slovak government even worked out a different scheme based on public participation in a large holding company which would allow the gradual emergence of a regulated capital market. This and other forms of opposition were only allayed by substantial changes to the original voucher idea.

The enabling law passed on 26 February 1991 contained two significant concessions. The first was a stipulation that vouchers would have to be bought, although for a very low price finally set at Kčs 1,000, a quarter of the monthly industrial wage. This might have avoided the danger of the maximum dispersion of ownership among individuals with no interest in becoming 'active' shareholders, but it also broke the principle that everyone had the right to a share in the national wealth.

The second and more important concession was the acceptance that vouchers would be used alongside other forms of privatisation within schemes worked out by the enterprises themselves and approved by the responsible ministry, meaning the Czech or Slovak Ministry of industry, agriculture or internal trade. An additional provision enabled others to submit alternative projects. This was often done by units within an organisation proposing their own separation. The possible privatisation methods included sale by auction, by public competition or to a chosen purchaser, and transfer to a new owner without sale. The organisation could be kept as a whole or subdivided. It, or parts, could be converted into a joint stock company with shares sold domestically or to a foreign firm or made available through the voucher method. Any combination of these three was also possible. No indication was made of any general preference for one method rather than another.

This vagueness gave government officials both the scope and the responsibility to make judgements on alternative forms of privatisation and Ježek, although initially one of the great enthusiasts for the voucher method, began to formulate aims that went beyond simply establishing private ownership. On one occasion he suggested the four potentially conflicting objectives of involving foreign capital, compensating former owners, selling directly to new entrepreneurs and enabling domestic citizens to become shareholders (Bautzová, 1992). He could have added more, but that would have implied an even more complex task for his ministry.

Moreover, in line with the original voucher philosophy, the individual privatisation proposals contained details relevant only to the question of ownership: no business plan was required. The chosen timescale also made wider considerations impossible. A list for a first wave — 1,436 Czech and 573 Slovak enterprises accounting for 12 per cent of Czech and 10 per cent of Slovak total fixed assets — was to be ready by the end of October with transfer to private ownership complete after another five months. A list for a second wave was to be ready by May 1992. The need for this haste led to a string of problems and conflicts associated with the formulation of privatisation plans, the registration of the public to participate in voucher privatisation and the final balancing of supply and demand for shares for individual firms.

Enterprises' Privatisation Plans

Allowing enterprises to formulate their own plans meant that specific conditions and needs could be taken into account. Moreover, it allowed for relatively open discussion, involving government officials, management and unions representing the workforce. Generally existing managements could dominate the process, but they had to be realistic about what could be achieved in this 'privatisation game'. Direct sale to themselves at a nominal price might be the ideal, but was obviously likely to arouse government suspicion. Incorporation into a powerful foreign firm was also often desired, but could face strong opposition, as explained below.

Managements' preferences were therefore often a careful combination of what they would like tempered by what they thought would be acceptable. There were also enormous individual variations, but there was a tendency towards broadly three elements. The first was a desire to retain the existing organisational structure, which would avoid uncomfortable changes, protect monopoly positions and probably win approval. The second was a preference for foreign participation as a source of capital. The third was a willingness to tolerate the voucher method, believed to be favoured by the privatisation ministries. Some voucher privatisation gave a proposal a greater chance of acceptability while it was positively preferred when no additional capital was required.

With the passage of time managements came to see ever more advantages for themselves in the voucher method. In one prominent case, the Tatra lorry manufacturer in Kopřivnice, 97 per cent privatisation by vouchers was favoured as a means to thwart plans from the Czech Ministry of Industry for a partial foreign takeover. More generally, managements expected it to bring them more independence (V.Havlín and J.Mihola, *HN*, 31 January 1992). They had no fear of neo-liberal predictions that new private owners 'will be much harder in their demands and will succeed in bringing order' (R.Češka, *Práce*, 20 June 1991). A leading figure in the Czech Union of Industry dismissed the controlling influence of shareholders by describing a likely general assembly as 'something like a trade union meeting' (B.Ošťádal, *HN*, 24 September 1991).

Once approved by the responsible ministries, privatisation plans were passed to the respective privatisation ministries. Officials in Ježek's ministry stuck to the normal public position that state officials cannot be trusted to make unbiased judgements. When rival proposals were submitted, however, they had to make choices and found themselves breaking neo-liberal taboos and trying to find the form of ownership that could give the best chance of business success. To some extent they relied on the recommendation from the Ministry of Industry which knew more about individual managements' competence. Sometimes, however, that advice was rejected and sometimes the

Ministry of Industry forwarded several proposals for the same enterprise.

In so far as there were general preferences, those who could present a well-documented proposal tended to inspire confidence. With so little other information available, officials could interpret the lack of obvious errors as an indication of business competence. More specifically, in line with the usual neo-liberal view, there was a liking for auctions especially for smaller units. Not surprisingly, incumbent managements absolutely detested that idea, and some were able to persuade officials that they had the ability and expertise to run the enterprise best and should allow a direct sale.

Officials had some preference for the voucher method, at least so as to ensure that enough shares could be on offer to satisfy likely demand. They also had an understandable prejudice in favour of demonopolisation, but that was a very delicate issue. Especially when direct sales of parts of a larger unit were proposed, it was suspected that managements could have slipped in forms of reorganisation that hived off under their own ownership key profitable parts. The *nomenklatura* privatisation experienced in Poland could be implemented within an even safer legal framework.

The obvious losers in this would be the employees of the remaining sections of the parent enterprise, and trade union organisations were warning most strongly against it. Preferences for employees in share purchases had, however, been restricted in the law to a maximum of 10 per cent, reflecting the belief that they were the last people likely to be responsible owners, and the ministries for privatisation had no policy of consulting employees' representatives. Nevertheless, even government officials were worried that some major scandals surrounding privatisation could do them immense harm and complained repeatedly that every conceivable means of lobbying was being used to influence their decisions. The oft-recited principle that privatisation must be open and subject to public control could not be maintained if officials had no time to check the proposals.

These wider considerations soon left Ježek collapsing under the volume of work. The timescale was making it impossible even to check that projects submitted complied with the most basic legal requirements: many in fact contained elementary errors and obvious omissions and few were finally approved without some adjustments.

The problem was less severe in Slovakia where there were fewer really desirable enterprises — average profitability of those on offer was half the Czech level — and on average only two proposals for each. Ježek, however, had to handle 11,155 proposals relating to 1,436 enterprises. His ministry had a total of 70 employees, including all grades, meaning possibly 20 minutes on each project many of which were around 40 pages long. A number of students were drafted in to help but the task was still unmanageable.

Ježek therefore proposed in November 1991 a few months' delay, but did not call for a complete reformulation of the whole conception of big privatisation. Klaus, seemingly impervious to all the arguments, was totally opposed to any delay at all. He eagerly pointed out that sticking to the voucher method alone would have avoided the difficulties behind the calls for delay and would have kept the 'helpful advisers' out of the ministry's building (*LN*, 12 May 1992). The relationship between the two became extremely bitter. Ježek accused Klaus of turning a blind eye to the impossibility of the timescale and of all economic realities in a bid to improve his electoral chances. Delay would indeed have been politically harmful to Klaus who did not want to fight the elections in June 1992 with an economic record of failure. He was backed by Ivan Mikloš, the Slovak Minister for Privatisation, who was already largely isolated within his own government. He too was keen to make as much progress as possible before the elections which, it was already clear, could lead to a swing to the left in Slovak politics.

The conflict was resolved in December 1991 with a compromise which delayed the deadline for approving projects until March, the date originally set for completing the first privatisation wave. This, however, bred further problems. The disruption to the timescale meant that citizens were expected to buy their voucher books before they knew what shares would be on offer. Although this clearly conflicted with the terms of the original law, both Klaus and Ježek were united in dismissing it as a trivial objection.

By the time of the June election, proposals were approved for the creation of 2,795 private enterprises. This included all of those involving privatisation by voucher. The remainder, mostly smaller firms accounting for 38 per cent of the total value of assets allotted to the first wave, were to be examined at a more leisurely pace with decisions hopefully by the end of the year. There appear to have been clear differences in the method chosen depending on the size of the unit. Ten per cent of proposals were for privatisation by public auction, and that was approved for 8 per cent of enterprises covering 0.4 per cent of the total capital. The controversial method of direct sale was proposed in 45 per cent of cases, and approved for 19 per cent of units accounting for over 3 per cent of total capital. Forty per cent of projects approved, accounting for over 90 per cent by asset value, were for privatisation as a joint stock company and 53 per cent of their shares were to be offered for vouchers. The remainder were for compensating former owners, or for sale to a named foreign partner, to employees or to management. Less complete figures, covering the period up to November 1992, suggest similar proportions for the main methods of privatisation.

Problems with Vouchers

Problems with the approval of projects were matched by a string of difficulties on the registration side for vouchers. At first public interest seemed to be low. Opinion surveys in November 1991 suggested that only 38 per cent viewed voucher privatisation favourably and only 25 per cent planned to participate. Registrations were in line with this, still not reaching one million in early January 1992. Although this was a high enough level to allow the scheme to go ahead, it was a potential political embarrassment to Klaus.

Then the situation was transformed by the intervention of investment funds through which, according to the original law, citizens could invest their vouchers. It had been assumed that their role would be rather small and, beyond the need for formal approval from the relevant privatisation ministry, legal controls on their operations were minimal. By the late autumn some were adopting aggressive sales techniques. The most important pace setter was Harvard Capital and Consulting, headed by the one-time émigré to the USA Viktor Kožený. He set a target of controlling 400,000 voucher books, and 22,000 agents were paid Kčs 300 for each one they could acquire. As an additional attraction, investors were offered a guarantee of Kčs 10,350 a year after shares had been issued if they wished to withdraw from the fund. This compared very favourably with the Kčs 1,000 cost of the voucher book.

Questions were asked about Koženy's resources with the implication that he might have hidden foreign backing to be able to make such a generous promise. He denied this, and other funds felt able to upstage his offer. The public suddenly realised that voucher privatisation was an incredibly easy way to acquire wealth and they rushed to register. By the closing date in March 8,562,421 had signed on, three-quarters of the adult population. In all 436 funds took part in privatisation, controlling over 70 per cent of the voucher points.

A string of minor scandals were not allowed to delay the process. In late January over one million undistributed voucher books disappeared. The suspicion was that a fund had stolen them. It could then hope to offer registration to members of the public who agreed to assign it their voucher points. Klaus rejected any thoughts of further delay and issued replacement registration cards within 48 hours. Further controversy was aroused by the appearance of the names of prominent state officials on the supervisory boards of funds, despite a federal government decision prohibiting this. The privatisation ministries regarded this as a trivial problem. Ježek was not even impressed by the information that funds were falsely claiming prominent people on their boards, although the quality of those individuals was one of his main criteria for allowing a fund permission to operate. He evidently had neither the time nor the will to keep a close check.

He did, however, formulate some basic rules to prevent complete domination by one fund and to ensure that each fund had a reasonable spread in its portfolio. In the end, the public chose to invest in what appeared to be the most reliable funds: 35 per cent of voucher points went into the six biggest, with the Czech Savings Bank's fund controlling over 12 per cent; Harvard ended up in sixth place. The fate of smaller funds, with the need to cover substantial overheads before enterprises start paying dividends, is very uncertain. Many can be expected to collapse quickly, or to merge with others.

A final complication concerned the exchange of vouchers for shares. The voucher method requires the simultaneous sale of shares in a very large number of enterprises so that buyers have a genuine choice and so that relative valuations can be determined. The simplest option would have been to allow demand alone to set share prices. This, however, would have led to extremely uneven and unpredictable returns to individuals for their voucher points.

Shares were therefore offered at set prices based on the book value of enterprises' assets. These, derived from historical cost of investment minus an arbitrary depreciation allowance, need bear little relationship to any market valuation. Only those looking for foreign participation needed to attempt the latter which for all but the most promising firms was likely to be well below the book value. An exact balance between supply and demand for shares in any individual enterprise would have been extremely unlikely even with a more realistic valuation, and provision was therefore made for an unspecified number of further iterations. Shares in enterprises over- or under-subscribed by more than a small amount would be offered again at a revised price.

When supply and demand were balanced up in June 1992, only 48 Czech joint stock companies could be declared sold in total, although 30 per cent of all shares had been disposed of. Successive iterations gradually used up the public's voucher points as relative prices moved closer to likely share valuations based on prospective future dividends. After four rounds 21 per cent of shares will still on offer and only 251 enterprises had been sold in full. The federal government then decided to allow one last round in December after which the remaining voucher points would have no value and the remaining shares would be sold to the public.

It will be some time before a full assessment can be made of privatisation by voucher. An adequate legal framework, clarifying the rights of shareholders and setting out rules for trading in shares, is not yet in place. The necessary legislation was postponed throughout 1992 and was finally scheduled for parliamentary approval in early 1993. It may suffer further delay. As Tomáš Ježek has lamented, without this 'absolutely final step', the public cannot receive their shares and the privatisation process cannot be completed (*RP*, 10 October 1992).

The real open questions, however, relate to the likelihood of 'active' owners emerging and to the possibility of creating stable and effective management structures. There is a glimmer of hope on the first of these. Investment funds have been more successful than individuals in using up their voucher points and some have pursued a conscious strategy of concentrating on particular sectors. The rules allow each one to acquire up to 20 per cent of the shares in an enterprise. Small coalitions of funds could dominate parts of the economy giving them the potential power to initiate substantial restructuring in enterprises or across whole sectors.

Few have yet declared their strategies, and many may be happy to remain relatively passive owners interested only in share dealing. That would be in line with most international experience of institutional investors. Several, however, including Viktor Kožen's Harvard, have stressed a determination to be more actively involved and quickly established contact with the managements of firms in which they had a substantial shareholding. The Czech government has tried to encourage funds to get together and select a single representative who could take on the power of a general assembly of shareholders.

Irrespective of how far funds do find the means to become effective 'active' owners, the immediate impact of voucher privatisation on enterprise managements has been to discourage forms of behaviour appropriate to a market economy (Turek, 1992). During privatisation itself there has been no incentive for managements to identify their interests with the long-term prosperity of the enterprise. Their concern has rather been to seek the form of reorganisation that could give the best prospects for themselves. That could, for example, mean seeking the lowest possible valuation for an enterprise so as to make more likely a direct sale to the existing management on very favourable terms. Thus investment, modernisation, the development of enterprising ideas for the future, or simply arguing for a high valuation could all be considered counter-productive for an ambitious manager.

Allowing managements to formulate their own privatisation plans has reinforced those modes of thought and behaviour geared towards getting the best possible terms from a central authority. That, of course, is precisely what happened under central planning. The effective paralysis of decision-making relating to enterprises' long-term development has been so widespread as to lead to the general use of the term 'pre-privatisation agony'. There is no reason why new modes of behaviour should emerge immediately after privatisation has been completed but, as the next section shows, the prospects are substantially better where enterprises have been sold, in part or in total, to successful foreign firms.

Selling the Family Silver?

The issue of foreign participation in privatisation was probably the most important single factor in shifting thinking away from a pure application of neo-liberal theory. While voucher privatisation proved a much slower and more complicated process than hoped, foreign investment was already having a direct impact on some parts of the economy by 1991. It was always an emotional and often a controversial issue. President Havel warned frequently of the dangers of selling the 'family silver' to foreigners while others, as has been argued, saw external investment as the key to economic recovery.

Klaus could sometimes be seen encouraging foreign investment, but his public statements for domestic consumption carried a different emphasis. He portrayed property that went into joint ventures with foreign capital as 'lost to privatisation' (Kuehnl and Obrman, 1990). In September 1991, when struggling to defend his conception of the maximum emphasis on voucher privatisation, he pointed to the high costs involved in attracting foreign firms and suggested that they might on balance have brought no benefit (*LN*, 2 September 1991).

Ježek, however, was prepared to use his powers under the privatisation laws to sell some enterprises directly to foreign owners before the voucher process could begin. Vrba, of course, was an enthusiast for foreign participation, as were many enterprise managements. In fact, by early 1992 the focus of discussion had shifted to a self-critical examination of why so little foreign capital had been attracted.

There were still attempts to generate scepticism about individual cases with the argument usually being that the Czechoslovak firm was one of the better ones and had good prospects on its own. This sort of dispute was probably inevitable as only those with some prospects could attract any foreign interest. There have also been accusations of attempted corruption, and the workload of the privatisation ministries may have enabled some unfortunate decisions to be taken.

There are cases where scepticism about foreign ownership has been very widespread and these, as Ježek has pointed out, relate largely to the firms that are in greatest demand. Some of the most public privatisation battles have been over proposals for those firms in very traditional sectors of Czech industry — there is little equivalent in

Slovakia — that really are internationally competitive. These include glassware and china manufacturers and a number of breweries.

Foreign firms could often win allies in the existing management structures who would present rival privatisation bids. A plausible argument could always be made that the foreign link would open up new prospects of a world market. There were, however, also fears that the foreigners might simply want to close down a rival with great potential once Czechoslovakia reentered the world market. The main argument, however, was one of national pride. The most emotion, not surprisingly, was aroused by breweries, with employees at Pilsner Urquell preparing to strike in April 1992 when they thought that a 'laughable' firm — the second biggest brewer in Holland — might acquire a share in ownership in their 'world famous' enterprise.

For most of Czechoslovak industry, however, foreign participation must offer the best prospect for improving international competitiveness and a continual effort was made, starting with Komárek, to 'drag' multi-national companies into the country. The first basis was the law on joint ventures as revised in 1989, but results were rather unimpressive. The number of firms founded on this basis passed 1,000 in early 1991 and was estimated at approximately 3,000 by the end of that year. Of these, however, only 12 per cent were recorded in the company register, without which they could not commence trading. Most were very small, often amounting to little more than partnerships between close relatives, one of whom had emigrated some years before. A small number of 'big' joint ventures, with a founding capital of over Kčs 1 million, accounted for over 95 per cent of the total capital assets. They were responsible for slightly over 3 per cent of industrial output in the first half of 1992.

The vision of foreign firms coming to gain the advantages of a relatively cheap skilled labour force in the centre of Europe thereby improving their own competitive position and helping to modernise Czechoslovak manufacturing industry looked a forlorn hope. They were put off partly by the familiar bureaucratic obstacles of having to make contact with unfamiliar official bodies. The main disincentives, however, were the deep historical problems of the low level of technology and the newer problem of uncertainty of markets for Czechoslovak enterprises.

The autumn of 1990 and early 1991 saw a number of major breakthroughs. A few of the very best firms were persuaded to invest in Czechoslovakia with the prospect of taking profits back only after several years. The most important case, and by far the biggest private investment in Eastern Europe, was the purchase by Volkswagen of 31 per cent of the shares, set to rise later to 70 per cent, in the Škoda car manufacturer. The deal was broadly agreed in December 1990 and the new firm, formally a joint venture, started operating on 1 April 1991. The deal has special significance for three reasons. The first was its background in a Czechoslovak search for a sensible strategy for the motor industry; the second was the means of taking the decision; and the third was the subsequent impact of the new firm on the Czechoslovak economy.

It had been taken for granted since the early 1950s that, as an industrial economy, Czechoslovakia should manufacture its own cars under their traditional name. Unfortunately, the scale of production of around 180,000 since the mid-1970s was very low when compared with the major world producers. Investment and development costs for the new Škoda Favorit, launched in 1989, were therefore immense when set against likely sales revenues. It was clear that a similar modernisation could not be repeated in the near future to keep up with changing world standards. Some critics had anyway consistently doubted the wisdom of a small country trying to maintain an independent motor industry, but hopes of rising living standards suggested growing demand for cars. One option was to switch to specialising in high volume production of some components while importing finished vehicles. The example cited was Austria, but it was clearly very risky to assume that Czechoslovakia could find a similar niche for itself. The alternative was to seek links with a foreign partner in the hope of finding investment to raise capacity to a target of 350,000 within ten years.

These thoughts had been circulating in the late 1980s. During 1990 the decision was taken in the Czech government to seek a partner. Twenty four major world producers were considered and the options were soon reduced to two, Volkswagen and a Renault–Volvo consortium. It was quite clear that Volkswagen's offer was by far the best. It intended to build a new engine factory with an annual capacity of 500,000 by 1995: this was exactly what Škoda lacked. It planned to raise output to 400,000 by 1997 with improvements to the existing Favorit after which a jointly designed product would be launched. The Škoda name would be retained and there was a commitment to keep roughly the existing level of 22,000 employees. Volkswagen was promising a total commitment of $6.6 billion and, as it had previously bought its way into and modernised the Spanish car manufacturer SEAT, there seemed every reason to take the promise seriously. Nothing since has served to weaken the impression that Volkswagen is committed to Czechoslovakia and that, unlike domestic enterprises, it has a long-term vision for expansion and development.

Thus, although the negotiations could not be conducted in public, the choice was made on the basis of widely known criteria. Indeed, at one point employees threatened to strike if the Renault—Volvo offer were accepted as they saw it as a threat to their job security. The issue in selecting foreign buyers generally was not one of selling the firm for the best price possible. 'Asset strippers' were firmly warned off with the government making clear its determination to arrange 'beauty contests' to select the partners most likely to offer investment, modernisation and job security. The fact that these criteria were stated so clearly and so persistently, including from the Czech Ministry for Privatisation, suggests a clear awareness of what industry really needed. Foreign participation, or even outright sale to a foreign partner, became the preferred option for most managements. It was also a favoured arrangement for employees, with union organisations often noting the constructive approach to industrial relations of multinational companies.

At first VW—Škoda seemed to be doing very well. Exports in the first half of 1991 were higher than in any preceding complete year. Component suppliers, amounting to 237 Czechoslovak firms, faced a manageable situation as the deal had provided funds to pay off the car manufacturer's bad debts. They were now also under some pressure to improve their performance to reach more exacting standards as there was no longer any certainty that their products would be accepted. There seemed a real chance that the Volkswagen deal could bring some recovery for the economy as a whole while also putting pressure on enterprises throughout industry even before their privatisation. This had been one of the ideas behind the strategy of offering carefully selected enterprises for sale.

There were, however, two important lessons that became clear over the following months. The first was that even a new owner cannot work miracles. Reports suggested a very gradual improvement in quality standards, but that could not save the manufacturer from collapsing demand. Exports, at 130,000 vehicles, were roughly twice the previous best figure, with a major expansion into Eastern Germany. Nevertheless, domestic sales almost ended in March 1991, totalling 42,400 for the year, of which around 13,000 were exported privately by individuals profiting from price relativities.

On top of collapsing consumer demand domestic sales were hit by imports of an estimated 105,000 cheap used cars. A planned expansion to 205,000 vehicles for the year had to be reduced to 170,000. The message was clear. Foreign ownership offered no immediate solution. Nevertheless, it did give long-term prospects for an enterprise which was previously heavily in debt and could therefore have been declared bankrupt.

The second lesson was that attracting foreign capital required some interventionist measures. Thus a letter to Volkswagen from the Czech Prime Minister Petr Pithart, dated 31 March 1991 but published only several months later, revealed a Czech government commitment to investment in telecommunications for the Mladá Boleslav plant. It had also agreed to allow easy import of equipment and components while giving protection against car imports when necessary. It promised various financial concessions and even agreed that Volkswagen would not be punished under new anti-monopoly laws. Klaus was right in asserting that there were costs in attracting foreign capital.

In October 1991 the federal government responded to the firm's difficulties with a reduction in taxes on new cars — the turnover tax fell through the year from 40 per cent to 20 per cent — and the imposition of a special duty on used car imports. Domestic sales, possibly also stimulated by the realisation that export success was an indication of the car's quality, picked up from the start of 1992, even leading to domestic shortages. Output for the year as a whole is likely to have been around 200,000 vehicles, an all-time record.

Škoda can therefore be seen as the leading force in the beginnings of a recovery of large-scale manufacturing industry. It alone accounted for over 2 per cent of industrial output, considerably more if component suppliers are included, and it provided around 2 per cent of total export revenue. It brought new management methods into the engineering industry and also contributed to the development of industrial relations.

The labour force was certainly not passive, and protests were staged in November 1991 when depressed demand led to labour force reductions. They ended, however, in agreement for a 7 per cent wage increase which left Škoda workers earning nearly 25 per cent more than the industrial average. An attempt to introduce Saturday shifts in mid-1992, to cope with higher demand, was possible only after a 10 per cent wage rise had been granted. In contrast to the position in other foreign-owned firms, unions did not regard Škoda as a model employer, but these were very different conflicts from those gripping Polish industry, or indeed declining sectors in Czechoslovakia. Although it should not be forgotten that living standards had fallen there too, the issue in Škoda was the employees' desire to share in some of the gains expected from the transition to the market. This was one case where there clearly was hope for the future.

It must, however, be emphasised that Škoda was a very special case. It represents the largest single investment by an outsider in Eastern Europe. Of the $700 million shown up in the capital account for 1991, half was accounted for by Volkswagen. It is the major reason for 'transport equipment' making up 66 per cent of direct investment and it partly explains German domination, making up 73 per cent of direct investment. It even explains much of the geographical bias in foreign investment towards the Czech rather than the Slovak republic. Once it is excluded Slovakia appears to have enjoyed slightly more foreign investment per head.

For much of industry the Czech and Slovak governments' approaches to foreign investment have been similar to the Volkswagen case. Every effort has been made to play off potential investors against one another to achieve the most favourable terms with the firm most likely to contribute to the long-term prosperity of the Czechoslovak economy. With business plans and the precise identity of the owner the central issue, this is obviously governed by a totally different logic from that applied in big privatisation generally.

It has, however, been impossible to repeat the success of the Škoda—Volkswagen deal throughout all sectors of industry. One suggested explanation is the atmosphere of political uncertainty while another is the failure of governments to adopt a systematic enough approach to attracting capital: agencies at the Czech and Slovak levels were established with only 7 and 15 inexperienced officials respectively (Z.Drábek, *LN*, 1 April 1992). This need not be decisive as individual enterprises have undoubtedly made enormous efforts. The great advantage for Škoda was that it already enjoyed a totally dominant position in Czechoslovak car production. There was therefore no need for any awkward reorganisation and Volkswagen could be tempted by the prospect of stepping into the shoes of an existing monopoly. Other successes have generally also been with reasonably successful established firms.

Much of manufacturing, however, is characterised either by excessive concentration or by irrational fragmentation. The former case includes the giant heavy engineering combines of ČKD and Škoda-Plzeň, hit hard by the collapse of traditional markets and the burden of past debts. Škoda's negotiations with such credible potential partners as Siemens and Westinghouse were complicated by attempts to preserve as much as possible of the employment levels of the whole combine and its future was still very uncertain in the autumn of 1992.

The consequences of fragmentation are illustrated by the case of goods vehicle production, split between three enterprises, none with an annual output capacity as high as 20,000. A study by the Czech Ministry of Industry in 1990 concluded that the only real hope for survival was by merger into one firm, also incorporating a small manufacturer of buses, followed by a link with a major world lorry producer. Unfortunately, mutual jealousies ruled out merger, or even cooperation with the same potential partner. Tatra-Kopřivnice in particular, claiming a world reputation with its vehicles for rough terrain, insisted on retaining a separate identity. Although deals have been agreed with Mercedes-Benz, Renault and Iveco, none are quite as clear and as obviously beneficial as the Škoda–Volkswagen arrangement. Rather than becoming a major component in a multi-national's European plans, Czech subsidiaries may be small and easily dispensable peripheral ventures. This fragmented approach may therefore have led to a less secure outcome than if the sector had been subjected to vigorous reorganisation prior to privatisation.

The first wave of big privatisation will substantially increase foreign participation in Czech and Slovak industry and shift the balance somewhat away from the German domination that has caused some unease in the Czech government. Voucher privatisation may also allow in more foreign capital, although the benefits of that route are very uncertain. Opinion polls suggest that few Czechoslovak citizens are intending to sell their shares at once. The strong position of investment funds may also keep much of industry under domestic control. Nevertheless, the difference between the market value of shares and the price paid via vouchers is likely to be enormous for those firms regarded as the Czech 'family silver'. The voucher method, apart from the risks of inflationary pressures and its unclear relevance to the necessary industrial regeneration, may ultimately lead to a highly undesirable ownership structure.

PART IV

Conclusion

Jan Olszewski Dec 91
Christian Demo leader promised
to respond to criticisms from
Industry, Agriculture + lay basis
for eco recovery.

12. Successes and Disappointments

Poland's Last Chance?

By mid-1992 it was very clear that the chosen strategy for transition to a market system in Poland and Czechoslovakia had encountered serious problems. Poland had been the first to face serious problems. For several months after the parliamentary elections of October 1991 it proved impossible to create a stable coalition government out of the diverse mass of political groupings. A government was formed under Jan Olszewski in December 1991, with backing from various Christian Democrat groups. It promised to respond to criticisms from industry, agriculture and other sectors and to lay the basis for economic recovery. It failed to gain parliamentary backing for its budget proposals and collapsed amid bitter conflicts with Wałęsa.

The 'last chance' to avoid Wałęsa himself trying to assume the post of prime minister was represented by the government which received parliamentary approval in July 1992 under Hanna Suchocka of the Democratic Union. It won further backing from the Liberal Democratic Congress, various Christian Democrat groups and even, albeit with strong reservations over its programme, from Solidarity of Labour. At last the core of Mazowiecki's supporters from the first Solidarity government in 1989 were in a coalition — albeit an unstable one with a very precarious parliamentary majority — with some of Wałęsa's supporters.

The government's programmatic statement referred to the aim of a 'social market' policy. The choice of, and statements by, prominent ministers suggested that there had been a shift of thinking. There was no place for Balcerowicz who left office with the fall of the Bielecki government and had become something of an ogre figure in parts of the press. Lewandowski, who never quite reconciled himself to his earlier loss of ministerial office, was back in charge of privatisation, but it was accepted that greater emphasis would be placed on forms of ownership that involved employee participation. This was seen as a means of reducing social conflicts.

Kuroń was back at the Ministry of Labour advocating a stronger emphasis on the social element throughout all aspects of government policy. No longer was this just a supplement to head off social discontent. The core was to be a system of three 'pacts', with trade unions, farmers and employers, on how to restructure the economy. Kuroń seemed to have learnt that it was impossible to create a modern capitalist economy first and only later return to being a Social Democrat, concerned with social issues and strategies for state intervention.

Such thinking in 1989 might have led to a different strategy from the start. However, by mid-1992 no government could expect such popularity as Mazowiecki's had enjoyed in its early days and that limited Suchocka's room for manoeuvre. The Solidarity union, itself facing a financial catastrophe and with a membership reduced to around 1.8 million, seemed to be moving more clearly into opposition. Ideologically it appeared to be moving to the right, with demands for a firmer purge of former Communists, while its social militancy could be seen as a shift to the left.

At its congress in June 1992, it bid a sad farewell to the 'myth' of Wałęsa, now seen as having betrayed the hopes of the Polish working people. In the words of Solidarity chairman Marian Krzaklewski,'we didn't sit in prison for this union so that today we wouldn't be able to afford a tram ticket or food for our children' (Wilczak, 1992, p.5). Wałęsa replied in kind, choosing interviews with several Western European papers to condemn the Solidarity delegates and workers in major industries who had previously brought him to high office as 'nothing but children, well educated in Communist thinking'.

Disillusionment among the industrial workforce stimulated a wave of strikes throughout the late summer of 1992. Solidarity's position was threatened by the more militant Solidarity 80. This union organisation won legal recognition only in September 1991 and was led by Solidarity activists from the 1980s who had never reconciled themselves to the Round Table or to supporting subsequent governments that had compromised with the old Communist authorities. Its 'wandering pickets' gained prestige easily and helped initiate strikes in coal mines throughout August. The key demands included higher wages, an end to the *popiwek* and the writing off of enterprises' past debts. There were also calls for delay over the conversion of mines into state-owned joint stock companies until the other issues could be resolved.

Protests spread throughout manufacturing. The highest profile example was in Ursus where employees dismissed the restructuring programme, based on the government study of September 1991, as no more than a plan for redundancies offering no hope for the long-term future. They had watched a worsening financial crisis as only 4,000 tractors were sold in the first seven months of the year. They demanded government help and claimed that this had been an implicit promise if, as had happened, they accepted the need for cuts in employment. There had certainly been no such commitment in public.

The Solidarity organisation held a ballot in Ursus and won 80 per cent support for strike action, which began on 24 August. The detailed demands included the writing off of past debts, the granting of easier credit terms to farmers and a reduction in the 'dividend' tax obligations. There was also opposition to any sale of the enterprise to foreigners who, it was assumed, would want only to close it down. Privatisation, it was argued, should take a form allowing employee participation. A final demand was for a wage increase with the level at the time around 94 per cent of the industrial average. They were building towards an alternative economic programme which differed markedly from the approach that had dominated while Balcerowicz had been Minister of Finance. Further elements were added by the Solidarity organisation for the Warsaw Region which began organising for a street demonstration uniting protests from various factories. They demanded the formulation of active policies for countering unemployment, a restoration of unemployment benefits for those without work for over 12 months and the formulation of a comprehensive strategy for economic development.

Despite accusations that many of the strikes were the result of political manipulation, the government was willing to hold discussions with strike leaders. On 2 September agreement was reached with representatives from Ursus on a programme for 'accelerated' restructuring in a form that took account of the employees' demands. A joint team from unions and management was given four weeks to work out a programme avoiding redundancies. This would open the way for division into several companies, some under full employee ownership, which would begin life with no debts from the past.

The Suchocka government then gave life to its general commitment to a new approach by developing the Ursus agreement into a more dramatic initiative that helped bring the strike wave to an end at least for a time. The 'debt' to state enterprises would finally be 'repaid' with a relaxation of the *popiwek*, steps to resolve the problem of past debts and a statutory 10 per cent of shares for free distribution to employees at zero charge in privatisation schemes. In exchange, partnerships of unions and managements were to be given three months to work out proposals for their enterprises' future. If privatisation was involved, then the Ministry for Privatisation would have to give approval. Plans for restructuring would have to be approved by the Ministry of Industry and Trade while a write-off of debts would require consent from the Ministry of Finance.

Critics — even including some within the government coalition — have been quick to dismiss the 'Enterprise Pact' as another pointless exercise (e.g. *ŻG*, 1992, No.41, p.6 or Frasyniuk, 1992). Before long it had become clear that there were major ambiguities as to what the government was offering. It was unclear whether it would coordinate its approach with ideas for structural policy or for selective help to those enterprises with the best prospects. Some critics therefore suggested that the 'pact' should be seen as a means to dodge the question of whether to adopt an interventionist or a non-interventionist industrial policy. There were no clear criteria for which forms of organisation would be preferred within possible privatisation schemes and neither was it clear how reorganisation would be harmonised with Lewandowski's revived programme for general privatisation. In addition to these objections, critics could point out the unrealistically short timescale. The whole initiative could appear as a desperate government bid to prolong its life expectancy by creating the impression of decisiveness. It is a familiar story from Poland's recent past. A confident and stable government could have allowed more time for serious proposals to be presented and considered.

With so many ambiguities and no specification of proposed costs to the state budget, it is also difficult to see why enterprises should not feel encouraged to put the maximum demands leading to a deadlock and still greater bitterness towards the government. Some optimists, however, have suggested that the 'pact' could be the first swallow before the summer. The government has finally acknowledged that economic recovery depends on the creation of an active partnership.

Success depends partly on winning acceptance that demands must be moderated and that in turn depends on agreement, especially with union organisations, for a 'social contract'. 'Lines of communication' need to be created between society and government around a commitment to broad common objectives. In a strange repeat of the experience before 1989, and unlike the situation in Czechoslovakia, Polish governments have appeared to be 'hermetically sealed from society' (P.Rojek, *ŻG*, 1992, No.36, p.3), except when forced to communicate under pressure of a real crisis.

Unfortunately, the road to a stable 'social contract' would be extremely bumpy. It depends first of all on a government appearing permanent and enjoying the support of Wałęsa as well as a stable majority in parliament. Workers in Ursus and elsewhere might try to win a better deal as soon as a new government is appointed, just as they tried in August 1992 to improve on the terms they had accepted in the autumn of 1991.

Agreement also depends on unions which are divided between three main centres, with 12 smaller groupings. They compete with each other in their militancy and the leaderships do not fully control lower levels. It is hard to see them coming together around one broad policy approach. Even if they could, a 'social contract' would still probably depend on the government changing its policies along the lines demanded in the workers' protests of mid-1992, and that would appear to conflict with the aim of restricting the budget deficit and remaining on good terms with the IMF. As a number of commentators were suggesting, the idea might be both too late, the feeling of social unity of late 1989 having been dissipated, and too early. Maybe only when the situation finally becomes utterly hopeless, so it has been suggested, will the different parties finally have no choice but to get together.

Czechoslovakia Nears its End

Czechoslovakia may appear to have avoided some of Poland's difficulties, but the slide towards separation into independent Czech and Slovak states during the autumn of 1992 is at least in part a consequence of the federal government's economic strategy. There was 85 per cent participation in the parliamentary elections of June 1992 and fragmentation into an excessive number of groupings was avoided by a rule denying representation to any that received under 5 per cent of the votes in either republic. Nevertheless, the results were very different between the Czech and Slovak republics and it would have taken considerable will and political skill to create a stable federal government with a coherent policy. Unfortunately, the dominant groupings and personalities on both sides preferred to turn a blind eye to the costs of separation.

Václav Klaus's Civic Democratic Party won 30 per cent of the votes for the Czech parliament and 34 per cent of Czech votes for the federal parliament. Having abandoned hopes for the federation, he took the post of Czech Prime Minister and, together with other right-wing parties, was able to form a stable government. Its programme was for 'successfully completing the transformation into the standard market economy which has proven itself throughout the world'. The process was to be accelerated, with the past tempo characterised as 'the lowest limit' of the acceptable. Casting doubts on any elements of the past strategy was condemned as leading to 'a return to *dirigiste* interventions by the state' with catastrophic consequences for the whole economy.

Despite this rhetoric, ministerial appointments need not point to any dramatic policy change. The Civic Movement lost all parliamentary representation, its careful attempts to find a middle ground having failed to win votes from either supporters or opponents of the government's economic strategy. Jan Vrba was removed from the Ministry of Industry. This may mean a setback for attempts to evolve pragmatic corrections to the non-interventionist approach but his replacement, the former federal Minister of the Economy Vladimír Dlouhý, has often been flexible in the past. His standing as a former federal minister and his respect throughout the Czech government may even make it easier for him to develop elements of an industrial policy.

Indeed, events during the autumn of 1992 left little doubt that the Czech government was still fully aware of the need to maintain social peace and of the benefits of intervening to prevent the sort of catastrophe that had engulfed Ursus. One indication was a decision in

October 1992 to put off for six months the operation of a law that would have exposed insolvent state-owned enterprises to bankruptcy. State Bank director Josef Tošovský argued during September that the government should take advantage of the post-election situation to press ahead and allow the potentially unpopular liquidation of a number of enterprises that had become a permanent drain on banks' ability to give credits. Klaus, however, feared that this would lead to a chain of bankruptcies with serious social consequences while parts of existing firms could be sold off at minimal prices. Dlouhý warned of possible economic instability at a delicate time in the privatisation process and indicated that, although he was not yet proposing another major write-off, he was actively looking for means to resolve the problems of enterprise debt (*HN*, 12 October 1992).

A further indication of the Czech government's approach was its reaction to a crisis in the Škoda–Plzeň heavy engineering combine. The management announced in September that, following the failure of the state railways to pay for locomotives that Škoda had built, it was unable even to pay employees' wages and lay-offs would begin in October. The Czech government discussed the crisis as a priority issue and moved quickly to replace the existing management. A new director was instructed to begin the reorganisation of the enterprise and short-term financial help was made available. A privatisation scheme was hastily formulated, in a form that won trade union approval, and financial arrangements were found to get round the debt problem. This will not save all the jobs in the combine and may turn out not to have been the best solution. Nevertheless, it demonstrated the willingness and ability of Vladimír Dlouhý to take some responsibility for the survival and restructuring of one of the country's biggest enterprises.

Privatisation policy has also undergone modification, but it is again unclear whether this will lead to an acceleration of changes. Tomáš Ježek was removed from the Ministry for Privatisation and, although his replacement was a fellow member of the Civic Democratic Alliance, policies were soon shifting in the direction desired by Klaus. Under new guidelines, direct sales were downgraded in favour of competitive bids or auctions. New rules meant that all privatisation projects could be challenged from outside the Ministry for Privatisation and would then have to be checked and approved through a series of committees with the authority ultimately resting in the whole Czech government. The aim of both changes was to cut out scope for corruption, but the latter change pointed to a much slower process of project approval. Had this been adopted from the start, the first wave of voucher privatisation might have suffered much greater delays and Klaus might not be sitting in the prime minister's chair.

The Movement for a Democratic Slovakia of Vladimír Mečiar won 37 per cent of the votes for the Slovak parliament and 34 per cent of Slovak votes for the federal parliament. Together with the Slovak Nationalists, it soon had an absolute majority in the Slovak parliament. Mečiar became Prime Minister and his government's economic programme was superficially very different from that of the Czech government, referring to the aim of 'a market economy with a social and ecological dimension' and setting the principal objective as preventing the collapse of the Slovak economy.

There was, however, a commitment to continue with the past reform strategy. Changes to privatisation policy were very similar to those implemented in the Czech republic: the Movement for a Democratic Slovakia, like Klaus, had been highly critical of direct sales before the elections. There was a general commitment to maintain harmony with the Czech republic over fiscal and monetary policies and a recognition that hopes for a more interventionist policy depended on the state budget.

The Slovak government's programme was less coherent than the Czech equivalent, containing inconsistencies and sections that seemed to contradict one another. It was, however, not clear that agreement on a common federal policy would be impossible. Contrary to some accusations to the contrary, Mečiar was not aiming for a return to the socialist past. There was a lot of truth in his frequent claim that he did not have a clearly defined political position in the traditional sense.

Nevertheless, and despite clear evidence from opinion polls in both republics that only a small minority wanted separation, the Civic Democratic Party quickly came to the view that separation, giving it full freedom to continue uncompromisingly with the chosen reform strategy, was the best option. Estimates of the costs are necessarily highly speculative. The most careful study produced a forecast of a small but significant drop in output in the Czech republic and a more substantial fall in Slovakia causing unemployment to rise rapidly in both republics during 1993 (I.Šujan, *HN*, 18 August 1992 and 24

November 1992). Estimates from researchers working for the trade unions pointed to a more substantial drop in output, leading to 10 per cent Czech and possibly 25 per cent Slovak unemployment (*HN*, 30 July 1992).

Both partners will suffer from a weakening of links between the two closely integrated economies if, as seems likely, Slovakia is forced to devalue making impossible the maintenance of a fixed exchange rate between the two. They will both lose from a likely diplomatic weakening in dealings on the international stage, for example with the European Community. The road to separation has been started without any certainty that existing international agreements with the federal republic will all be transferred to the two successor states.

Foreign investment will be harmed by the narrowing of markets and from uncertainty over economic and political developments. This could also hit tourism. The Czech republic stands to lose the most from these factors and one of Vrba's last warnings before leaving office was that practically all agreements being negotiated with foreign firms were either being cancelled or were meeting with worried looks from the Western side. This followed a considerable success with agreements in the first quarter of 1992 for an inflow of $592 million, finally putting Czechoslovakia ahead of all other Eastern European countries in attracting foreign investment.

These costs have been ignored or downplayed by political leaders on both sides. The key Czech claim was that agreements reached at least in outline prior to separation should ensure that economic processes and policies can continue broadly as before, thereby minimising the disruption and costs. If this confidence were justified, then it ought also to have been possible to reach agreement without the risks involved in separation. The truth is that leading Civic Democratic Party politicians rather liked the idea of getting rid of the troublesome Slovaks and looked forward to greater credibility in the mainstream of European life as an independent state.

The likely break-up of Czechoslovakia is not the result of economic policies alone. Political and social factors led Slovak politicians into their demands for a confederation which the Czech side has felt able to refuse. Nevertheless, economic factors have contributed substantially. The chosen economic strategy brought enough signs of growth to the Czech republic to help the election of a right-wing government while it seemed to promise nothing but higher unemployment to Slovakia. Nevertheless, by ignoring the possible costs of separation, the Czech government has risked leading its own country into a deeper depression and slower recovery process than was necessary.

Has the Strategy Worked?

There clearly were important differences between the course of events in Poland and Czechoslovakia. Nevertheless, the comparison between the two makes some generalisation possible about the effects of the chosen strategy. The differences and similarities can be followed around the three key policy issues of price liberalisation, trade liberalisation and convertibility, and privatisation. In the first two cases the policies pursued were very similar while substantial differences emerged over privatisation.

Price liberalisation was linked with a highly restrictive macroeconomic policy aimed at the rapid stifling of inflation and the imposition of hard budget constraints on enterprises. The assumption was that prices would rise rapidly for a brief period after which they would stabilise and then fall, heralding a rapid return to economic growth. In both countries, however, prices rose higher than forecast and, far from falling over the following months, were still rising throughout 1992. The restriction of demand led instead to a sharp fall in output.

Figures indicate significant differences in the scale of inflation with Poland still experiencing price rises of around 50 per cent in 1992, contributing to a 1,750 per cent increase over the 1989 level. In Czechoslovakia 1992 still saw inflation of around 10 per cent and the price level in December of that year was roughly 85 per cent higher than in 1989.

The persistence of price increases cannot be seen as a purely temporary phenomenon which will disappear once inflation has somehow been 'squeezed out' of the system. It also stems from the non-interventionist strategy for transition to the market, which has contributed to rising food prices and continuing social conflict. Both of these are more clearly visible in Poland, which is of course experiencing a higher inflation rate. Purchase prices of basic agricultural products were rising in 1992 at a much faster rate consumer goods prices as a whole. The cause, of course, was the collapse of agricultural output.

In Czechoslovakia the situation has been less clearcut with the government, throughout the autumn of 1992, refusing to accept that the decline of agriculture was a source of inflation. Food prices did rise more rapidly than the average during 1992 and agricultural output fell — probably by around 10 per cent from the 1991 level — but surpluses were still being bought up by the price support agency. In fact, noting rising meat prices, the government threatened to reintroduce price controls and took steps during November under anti-monopoly regulations to penalise meat processing enterprises. It even suggested — in a highly unusual step that might usefully have been applied in other sectors — that privatisation proposals should incorporate specific steps to promote greater competition.

Figures also indicate some differences in the signs of possible economic recovery. The scale of the initial drop in industrial output was remarkably similar in the two countries with output reaching its lowest level around the end of 1991 at 40 per cent and 34 per cent below the 1989 levels in Poland and Czechoslovakia respectively. Poland then probably recorded marginally over zero growth in 1992 with unemployment stabilised at around 13 per cent: it has generally been falling in the big cities but has continued to rise in smaller industrial towns. There is no guarantee against a further downturn in the future because of the decline in agriculture, the strong propensity to buy imports as opposed to domestically-made goods and the continuing crisis in the state-owned enterprises.

Czechoslovakia in 1992 saw a clear recover with Czech retail trade growing by 25 per cent during the first nine months. This helped reduce the Czech unemployment level to a mere 2.5 per cent at the end of October. The geographical pattern, as in Poland, showed job creation especially in big cities alongside continuing job losses in some of the more isolated and smaller towns. Industrial output fell by roughly 10 per cent in 1992 compared with the level for 1991 as a whole but, as explained above in Chapter 9, the level was actually rising after December 1991. Nevertheless, recovery is still threatened by the continuing financial crisis in state enterprises and by the problems associated with separation. Unemployment can therefore be expected to rise again but, thanks to new growth from outside the traditional industries, the danger of a serious deepening of the depression is smaller than in Poland. Slovakia's economic progress, however, appears to have been very similar to that in Poland. Retail trade grew by only 2 per cent in 1992 and unemployment, albeit falling very slowly, was still at 10.4 per cent in October.

Although there are differences between Poland, Slovakia and the Czech republic, the general conclusion must be that price liberalisation accompanied by macroeconomic restriction has not been an unqualified success. In fact, in some respects it has served to slow the possible pace of transition to a modern market economy. The most striking example relates to the financial crisis in state enterprises. Far form facilitating adaptation to new forms of behaviour appropriate to a market system, this has led them to ignore financial discipline as they have run into debt with eachother, making nonsense of talk of establishing hard budget constraints. Moreover, banks have been persuaded to become involved in granting credits to powerful enterprises, restricting their ability to help the new private enterprises.

In view of these disappointments it is worth considering three possible alternatives to the strategy adopted. The first relates to a more controlled process of price liberalisation. A comparison between Poland and Czechoslovakia does suggest a case for forms of intervention to speed up adjustment to the equilibrium level or to prevent excessive fluctuations. Consideration could also have been given to a policy to reduce monopoly power and for more controls on the prices of selected basic goods. Full liberalisation might therefore have been allowed to take somewhat longer than initially planned, but the case for ending the central regulation of prices early in any transition strategy is very strong.

The second alternative relates to the possibility of accompanying price liberalisation with less restrictive fiscal and monetary policies. It was a particularly strange assumption that the growth in the money supply should be kept in line with the growth of national income at a time of massive systemic changes when the role of money was undergoing a fundamental transformation. A less restrictive macroeconomic policy would have prevented so dramatic a fall in output and would also have given more encouragement to the growth of new private enterprises. The costs could have included a higher rate of inflation and a higher level of imports. This alternative could therefore have required a different policy in relation to trade liberalisation.

The third possible alternative would have been to accompany price liberalisation with more conscious and systematic intervention especially in agriculture and with measures to cushion some enterprises against financial catastrophe. The case for an active industrial policy from the start must be overwhelming as governments have felt compelled to take steps in a piecemeal and pragmatic way in both countries. A more coherent policy could have followed a selective approach — along the lines of Šulc's 'big package' — while it could also have embodied the much simpler step of writing off all past enterprise debts. This last option has even been advocated from outside Eastern Europe (e.g. Begg and Portes, 1992).

The second key policy issue was trade liberalisation and partial convertibility; again, Poland and Czechoslovakia have pursued similar strategies. The arguments for the approach adopted are clear. Trade liberalisation should bring competitive pressures to bear on domestic enterprises, lead to the rapid imposition of world price relativities and, if the exchange rate can be held firm, set a limit to overall price increases. The strategy was derived from the standard IMF package as applied in Latin America, but its relevance was challenged from the start. The most obvious source of doubt stems from the observation that the strategy was not adopted in, or recommended from, those countries that have successfully joined the most advanced economies since World War II. Japan, for example, did not move immediately to trade liberalisation and convertibility, preferring to take time to prepare gradually for those steps.

This, then, was one of the most controversial issues in the debates in Czechoslovakia in 1990. There was, however, never any disagreement over the ultimate objective. The dispute was purely over the speed with which it could be achieved. The danger with a 'premature' opening of the economy, so critics claimed (e.g. Pick, 1992), is that the exchange rate had to be set at so low a level as to give a substantial initial boost to inflation. As argued in Chapters 4 and 9, the measures adopted to check these price rises were the major cause of the collapse in industrial output and of the financial crisis in state enterprises.

Thus far from encouraging a desirable restructuring within enterprises or to more modern sectors, the policy of rapid trade liberalisation and internal currency convertibility, so it has been argued, has left much of the two countries' economies paralysed by the effects of a deep depression. Both were left with no means other than devaluation or domestic demand restraint to hold back imports of high quality consumer goods. There is therefore a lasting danger either of a permanent depression or of a downward slide in currency levels giving powerful further boosts to inflation.

There is still a threat of future balance of payments crises and this can be expected to increase when, or if, demand picks up. The problem is much more serious in Poland where it is amplified by the burden of past international debt. The Czech republic, however, may have better prospects thanks to the growth in tourism. Convertibility may have helped stimulate this and, it may even have increased the revenue received inside Czechoslovakia. The point is that the black market in foreign currency has been substantially reduced forcing tourists to pay considerably more in convertible currency for Czechoslovak goods than was the case before November 1989. In this specific case convertibility could have been a spur rather than an obstacle to restructuring of the economy towards sectors with growth potential.

Nevertheless, as in the case of price liberalisation, there are strong grounds for considering alternatives. The strategy initially was simply for a steady liberalisation of trade and abandonment of any forms of state intervention. In both Czechoslovakia and Poland the need has been accepted for the belated formulation of export-promotion policies and for the reimposition of some import restrictions. That could be taken as indicating an implicit acceptance that the liberalisation policy did 'over shoot.'

There has even been a belated realisation that other countries, despite verbal commitments to free trade, are perfectly capable of protecting their own producers. The belief that all positive changes must lead towards greater liberalisation has, it has been suggested, led to the acceptance of unnecessarily unfavourable terms for trade with the European Community. An obvious option would therefore have been to liberalise more slowly while arguing forcefully with international partners that the transition to a modern market economy was bound to be a slow and complex process during which there would be an overwhelming case for continuing with selective or general restrictions on imports. That, of course, would have risked protecting the inefficient and encouraging pressures from lobby groups, but that could be judged a necessary cost in view of the problems caused by the over-hasty liberalisation.

The final key policy issue was privatisation where the policies adopted have differed substantially between Czechoslovakia and Poland. To some extent this reflects differing starting points, with the initially much smaller private sector in Czechoslovakia, but it also reflects differences in the countries' political structures. Thus the federal government in Czechoslovakia pressed ahead with the voucher idea while the Polish governments dithered, proving incapable of taking any decisive economic policy steps after January 1990. It is, of course, an open question whether the determined action in Czechoslovakia will prove to have been an advantage, enabling a thriving private sector to emerge, or whether it will ultimately be judged a serious error.

There were plenty of alternatives to the policies adopted three of which seem particularly worthy of consideration. The first relates to the possible links between privatisation and the restructuring of enterprises. A frequent proposal was for greater emphasis on 'commercialisation' under state, or possibly mixed, ownership. Supporters of this option frequently foresaw a transitional stage before enterprises gained the full independence associated with privatisation. During this period an active government could have intervened to reduce monopoly power, impose managements where appropriate and to help in the search for foreign partners. This, rather than privatisation alone, could have been the central element in microeconomic policy.

The obvious objection is that, in view of the weakness and inexperience in market practices of the officials in the central administration, this could have degenerated into offering protection to those with the most political power. That is a powerful argument, but it is not clear that the danger can be averted either by Lewandowski's scheme in Poland or by voucher privatisation in Czechoslovakia. The case for an all-powerful central body may be weak, but the argument for formulating and acting on sectoral strategies — as exist for example for the Czechoslovak steel industry — may be very strong. That would mean accepting a slower pace of privatisation than has been planned in Czechoslovakia, but it might yield superior results in the end.

The second possibility is that property could have been, and still could be, sold to the public rather than distributed for vouchers. Polish experience suggests that the scope for this is limited in the case of joint stock companies. 'Small' privatisation in Czechoslovakia points to serious risks even for the case of small businesses. To some extent the situation could be helped by an expansionary macroeconomic policy, leading to an expansion in savings potential and enabling banks to grant more loans at reasonable interest rates. A more ambitious step would be the construction of a scheme for credits on very specific terms for the sole purpose of buying productive assets (Turek, 1992).

That could have significantly different implications from the voucher privatisation in Czechoslovakia. If shares are to be sold, then managements would have an immediate incentive, even prior to privatisation, to maximise share values by working to enhance enterprises' long-term business prospects. There would also be less chance of privatisation providing a further stimulus to inflation. There could also be consequences for the outcome of the auctions in Czechoslovakia's 'small' privatisation as domestic bidders, even when lacking foreign backing, would have had a better chance of participating. The idea of privatisation credits has been propounded in very general terms in Poland by Wałęsa, but has yet to be elaborated as a serious alternative to existing policies.

The third possibility relates to the role of employees both before and after privatisation. The dominant view in both countries has been that their powers should be minimised. The reasoning behind this relates to past experience, when self-management contributed very little, to more recent Polish experience of the Bermuda Triangle and to the standard neo-liberal view that employees cannot be a force for economic rationality in business decisions.

There are, however, grounds for doubting the strength of these points. At least in the period after the collapse of Communist power, when the controls from central planning effectively ceased to operate, employees may be the group which can identify most closely with the long-term interests of their enterprise. They have no easy escape into *nomenklatura* companies or into direct sales of a profitable part of a large enterprise. Moreover, in view of the problems in finding 'active' owners from any other source, they might be able to play a crucial role in controlling managements before a full legal framework could take shape. Indeed, the suggestion that some development of self-management could be considered specifically for the transition period has come from some who fully accept an orthodox market economy as the objective (e.g. Gruszecki, 1990). There is, of course a powerful counter-argument as employees are likely to resist restructuring that involves substantial redundancies. Nevertheless, there might be a way to involve employees as a controlling force on certain management decisions and as a participant in evolving long-term programmes for enterprises' futures. The implication is that Poland's Enterprise Pact might — depending on how the ambiguities referred to earlier are sorted out — have considerable potential.

Towards Political Fragmentation?

Two clear conclusions stand out from the preceding discussion of the strategies adopted in Poland and Czechoslovakia. The first is that there was no shortage of alternatives. The second is that, although there are striking similarities between the two countries, Czechoslovakia seems to have doing somewhat better than Poland. The fundamental explanation for this, as has been indicated at several points already, lies not in differences in the policies pursued but in the initial starting positions. Czechoslovakia, and especially the Czech republic, has been blessed with a greater potential for tourism and a better chance of linking its existing firms with established Western corporations. The reason for the latter stems partly from a stronger industrial base, partly from a better infrastructure and partly just from an excellent geographical location, extremely close to the industrial centres of Germany. These fortuitous factors have helped counter some of the negative effects of the economic strategy which have been more clearly dominant in Poland and Slovakia.

This relative economic success has in turn contributed to political stability, but the relationship between economic and political developments is difficult to disentangle. A simplistic implicit assumption was that protests at the social consequences of economic changes might force delays to the process of transition. In reality, political and social reactions have been more varied and complex, including apathy and division as much as outright militancy. The forms of response are dependent on past traditions and deep-rooted attitudes.

In the Czech republic, thanks to its more favourable economic situation and to some government efforts to soften the social impact of changes so as to avoid some of the worst absurdities afflicting Polish industry, large sections of the population have so far continued to keep faith with the process of economic transformation. This is not true in Slovakia. Even there, however, despite substantial disillusionment, there has not been a massive upsurge of industrial militancy. Moreover, the high participation in the 1992 elections shows a continuing faith that politicians do have something to offer. Perhaps the population could still retain some confidence and optimism through the belief that new policies and a better deal for Slovakia would lead to better times in the future.

The Czechoslovak picture, then, is one of two populations that could still see hope for the future but only by rejecting eachother. The result was the ultimately unstoppable drift towards separation. Although this will have negative economic consequences, the new Czech and Slovak republics should have effective governments capable of formulating and implementing policies. In Poland, however, economic disappointments contributed to a degeneration into a more general apathy, fragmentation and disillusionment which left governments too unstable to impose their will.

Apart from the course of economic developments themselves — and that is probably the most important single causal factor — the events outlined in the preceding chapters suggest that four further factors may have contributed to Poland's slide towards paralysis. The first, and probably least significant, is the failure to hold a public debate and to approve the economic programme through a freely elected parliament. This may have made it harder to claim such widespread legitimacy for policies that were inevitably leading to cuts in living standards. A second factor is the relatively uncompromising implementation of the strategy. Polish governments, aware only of their country's past survival through chaos and sharp political and social polarisation, may have been less worried to see major enterprises drifting into financial catastrophe. They may therefore have seen less need than the outwardly unyielding Klaus to make quiet compromises. The significance of this factor should not be exaggerated as the apparently firmer commitment to the *laissez faire* approach in Poland may simply reflect the inability of governments to take firm action.

A third factor is the nature of the anti-Communist opposition, combining spontaneous industrial militancy with organised groupings that were old and experienced enough to have developed their own splits and jealousies. The fourth factor was the past experience of reform attempts which may have engendered cynicism towards politicians promising improvements but delivering nothing: the break between the Communist and 'post-Communist' periods could therefore have been less clear than in Czechoslovakia, allowing some of the cynicism of the past to be carried forward.

The influence of these past traditions can be seen coming together in Wałęsa's campaign for the presidency, and then in his conduct when in office. He was very much a product of Poland's history of opposition to Communist power, and drew support from the disillusionment with the Balcerowicz programme. Unlike Václav Havel in Czechoslovakia, he made no effort to become a stabilising element and continued to behave as if he were still in opposition. Unlike Klaus, he came with no coherent strategy, but he behaved as if he had the right to set the direction for political life. He thereby restricted the ability of the Bielecki and Olszewski governments to implement, or in many cases even to formulate, policies.

Why Did They Go Wrong?

There were, then, differences between the two countries both in the details of economic developments and in the precise effects of economic difficulties on the evolving political structures. Nevertheless, as the preceding chapters have indicated, there was an essential similarity which can be traced ultimately to a faulty conception of how the transition to the market could best be achieved. The fundamental mistake was that the strategies were too narrowly conceived. They were based on economic thinking alone and within economic terms on ideas derived partly form the standard IMF stabilisation package and partly from neo-liberal thinking.

The psychological attractions in adopting this approach are clear. Klaus, for example, could enjoy greatly enhanced credibility as a politician by claiming to know in advance how the transition to an advanced market economy could best be achieved. At a more general level, the IMF view blended in exceptionally well with well-developed theories that attributed the inefficiencies of central planning to shortage or excess demand. However, the evidence from research in earlier decades, and from consumer behaviour after price liberalisation, suggests that it is the wrong starting point for understanding the old system's ills. The problem was rather one of a quite distinct economic system which gave rise to inflexibility and isolation from international contacts leading into general stagnation. Attempts to reduce the causes of this to terms familiar in orthodox economic theory are not convincing.

The attractions of the neo-liberal theoretical framework are also easy to understand in view of its ability to provide a powerful critique of central planning. Explicit adoption of the framework was not universal among those actively forming policies. However, the principle that nothing could be achieved without market prices and private ownership did have very wide currency. The theoretical framework that can give the most coherence to those general ideas is that provided by Hayek, Mises and, to a lesser extent, the property rights school. Unfortunately, these provide an incomplete vision of a modern market economy.

The practical effect of adopting this theoretical perspective was to simplify the transition process, leading to an unfortunate ordering of some individual steps while other important elements in the transition were ignored altogether. The need for the creation of an appropriate legal framework, for a new administrative machinery or for an effective apparatus to facilitate the introduction of a new tax system were all subordinated to economic measures in the narrowest sense. The case for reorganisation to break up monopolies or for an active state role in the economy generally were ignored until pressures forced their gradual and often very partial reincorporation. Pressures for state involvement and for a recognition of the 'social' element were typically seen only as a constraint that might slow the pace of transition.

Neo-liberal thinking not only justified ignoring the economic arguments for state intervention, it also justified those steps that have hampered the emergence of a modern market system. As has been argued especially by Zdislav Šulc, the highly restrictive macroeconomic policies, allegedly aimed at creating tight financial discipline, did not create the normal environment for an enterprise in a market economy. Above all, they prevented money from playing its normal role. Enterprises, although nominally freed from rigid state control, could not raise the finance they needed to implement independently-taken decisions. Moreover, banks, which should be free to choose to whom they can lend, were often faced with no alternative but to continue supporting enterprises that were effectively bankrupt.

Neo-liberal thinking also helped reinforce a fundamental misunderstanding of how the modern corporation operates. Share ownership is not essentially a means of controlling potentially inefficient managers. The origins and predominance of the joint stock company with limited liability relate rather to an easy means of raising finance. As Schumpeter argued, the key to the growth of capitalism is the use of credit to free ambitious entrepreneurs from tight financial constraints. The chosen macroeconomic policies, and possibly also privatisation by voucher, make this very difficult.

Once the neo-liberal framework is dropped, it is possible to create the basis for a comprehensive alternative that could have been adopted from the start. Many of the steps taken would, of course, still have a place. They would, however, have been supplemented by a range of further measures. Even after the damage done by the adoption of a faulty strategy from the start, there is still scope for making corrections. It is, for example, never too late to write off the debts built up by enterprises under central planning.

Perhaps the most remarkable failing of the strategies for economic transformation adopted in Poland and Czechoslovakia is that, by picking up ready-made theories, they were based on an implicit denial of the most striking feature of what was taking place. Both countries were travelling into uncharted territory and therefore could not reasonably start from the assumption that any hastily formulated strategy derived from one existing theoretical framework must necessarily be the right one. Indeed, even past attempts at reform under socialism could be taken as evidence that hopes for rapid results from an essentially simple and narrowly economic strategy were invariably disappointed. The case by the end of 1992 was quite overwhelming for a more open approach, with a willingness to reassess the strategy in the light of the disappointments after the first stage of what will undoubtedly be a long and complex process with an uncertain end result. Unfortunately, the realisation of this is strongest in Poland, where the situation appears to be so desperate as to severely constrain the policy options.

References

Alchian, A.A. and H.Demsetz (1972), 'Production, information costs, and economic organization', *American Economic Review*, **62**.

Alchian, A.A. and S.Woodward (1988), 'The firm is dead: long live the firm', *Journal of Economic Literature*, **26**.

Baczyński, J. (1991), 'Rachunek krzywd', *Polityka*, No.9, p.1.

Baka, W. (1989), 'Pacta sunt servanda', *Polityka*, No.14, p.3.

Balcerowicz, E. (1990), 'Reforma samorządowa na Węgrzech 1984-1987', in A.Topiński (ed.), *Zmiany systemowe w krajach socjalistycznych*, Warsaw: Ossolineum.

Balcerowicz, L. (1989), *Systemy gospodarcze: Elementy analizy porównowaczej*, Warsaw: Szkoła Główna Planowania i Statystyki.

Balcerowicz, L. (1991), 'Komora wysokich ciśnień', *Zarządzanie*, No.6-7.

Baran, P. and P.Sweezy (1966), *Monopoly Capital*, New York: Monthly Review Press.

Barzel, Y. (1989), *Economic Analysis of Property Rights*, Cambridge: Cambridge University Press.

Bautzová, L. (1992), 'První vlna to zlomí a druhá dorazí', *Ekonom*, No.10.

Begg, D. and R.Portes (1992), *Enterprise Debt and Economic Transformation: Financial Restructuring of the State Sector in Central and Eastern Europe*, London: Centre for Economic Policy Research.

Belka, M., A.Krajewska, S.Krajewski and B.Pinto (1992a), 'Dlaczego spada rentowność', *ŻG*, No.11.

Belka, M., A.Krajewska, S.Krajewski and B.Pinto (1992b), 'Polityka zatrudnienia', *ŻG*, No.13.

Belka, M., A.Krajewska, S.Krajewski and B.Pinto (1992c), 'Pragnienia i rzeczywistość', *ŻG*, No.15.

Berend, I.T. (1990), *The Hungarian Economic Reforms 1953-1988*, Cambridge: Cambridge University Press.

Berg, A. and J.Sachs (1992), 'Structural adjustment and international trade in Eastern Europe: the case of Poland', *Economic Policy*, **14**.

Berle, A. and G.C.Means (1968), *The Modern Corporation and Private Property*, New York: Harcourt, Brace & World, Inc.

Bienkowski, A., M.Greta, W.Lyczek and W.Puliński (1990), 'Rolnictwo w procesie urynkowania gospodarki', *GN*, No.9.

Błaszczyk, B. (1983), 'Uspołecznienie planowania społeczno-gospodarczego', in W.Morawski (ed.), *Demokracja i gospodarka*, Warsaw: Uniwersytet Warszawski Instytut Socjologii.

Bočinská, E., J.Straka and E.Šíp (1992), 'Postačuje současná právní úprava ochrany soutěžního prostředí?', *NH*, No.6.

Brach, B. (1990), 'Czy koniec rynku producenta?', *ŻG*, No.2.

Bugaj, R. (1989), 'Lenin w likwidacji', *Polityka*, No.2.

Bugaj, R. (1991), 'Póki nie jest za późno', *Polityka*, No.30.

Burianová, K. (1989), 'Nepříliš lichotivé srovnání', *HN*, No.5.

Caban, W. (1990), 'Zachowania przedsiębiorstw w pierwszych miesiącach 1990 roku', *GN*, No.9.

Caban, W. (1991), 'Przedsiębiorstwa państwowe w procesie urynkowienia gospodarki', *GN*, No.4.

Čapek, A., et al. (1991), *Varianty vývoje česko-slovenských vztahů, jejich ekonomické implikace*, Prague: Ekonomický ústav Československé akademie věd.

Chandler, A., Jr. (1977), *The Visible Hand: The Managerial Revolution in American Business*, Cambridge, Massachusetts: Harvard University Press.

Chandler, A., Jr. (1990), *Scale and Scope: The Dynamics of Industrial Capitalism*, Cambridge, Massachusetts: Belknap Press.

Chiplin, B., J.Coyne and L.Sirc (1977), *Can Workers Manage?* London: The Institute of Economic Affairs.

Chmiel, J. (1991), 'Płacowa topografia', *ŻG*, No.14.

Comisso, E.T. (1979), *Workers' Control Under Plan and Market*, New Haven: Yale University Press.

Čuba, F. and E.Divila (1989), *Cesty k prosperitě*, Prague: Svoboda.

Czíra, L. and M.Munková (1989), 'Rozvoj samosprávy v štátnych podnikoch', *HN*, No.33.

Dąbrowski, J., M.Federowicz and A.Levitas (1990), *Zachowania przedsiębiorstw państwowych*, Warsaw: NSZZ "Solidarność" Region Mazowsze.

Dąbrowski, J., M.Federowicz and A.Levitas (1991a), 'Stosunki przemysłowe', *ŻG*, No.11.

Dąbrowski, J., M.Federowicz and A.Levitas (1991b), 'Sytuacja finansowa firm państwowych w roku 1990', *Zazrądzanie*, No.6-7.

Dąbrowski, M. (1990a), *Reforma Rynek Samorząd*, Warsaw: Państwowe Wydawnictwo Ekonomiczne.

Dąbrowski, M. (1990b), 'Wdrażanie II etapu reformy gospodarczej a nadzwyczajne uprawnienia dla rządu', in M.Kozak (ed.), *Z analizy procesów reformy gospodarczej w latach 1987-1988*, Warsaw: Ossolineum.

Dąbrowski, M. (1991), 'Stracone półrocze', *Polityka*, No.2.

Dąbrowski, M. and B.Błaszczyk (1991), 'Krok w nieznana', *Polityka*, No.28.

Demsetz, H. (1988), *Ownership, Control and the Firm*, Vol.2, Oxford: Basil Blackwell.

Dittert, J. and M.Kolanda (1989), 'Spíše starost než chlouba', *HN*, No.35.

Downs, A. (1967), *Inside Bureaucracy*, Boston: Little, Brown & Co.

Drezga, D. (1983), *Radnici govore o samoupravljanju*, Zagreb: Globus.

Dryll, I. (1989a), 'Czy kopalnia może być nasza?', *ŻG*, No.26.

Dryll, I. (1989b), 'Bitwa o samorząd', *ŻG*, No.42.

Dryll, I. (1990a), '"Lekki" dramat', *ŻG*, No.19.

Dryll, I. (1990b), 'Solidarność pełna niewiadomych', *ŻG*, No.21.

Dryll, I. (1990c), 'Jeden "Ursus" jeden koń', *ŻG*, No.25.

Dryll, I. (1990d), 'Polska jest zdenerwowana', *ŻG*, No.28.

Dryll, I. (1990e), 'Spór o Rakowskiego', *ŻG*, No.31.

Dryll, I. (1990f), 'Jak górnik z górnikiem', *ŻG*, No.45.

Dryll, I. (1990g), '"Lekki" lider czarney listej', *ŻG*, No. 47.

Dryll, I. (1991a), '"Popiwek" u premiera', *ŻG*, No.7.

Dryll, I. (1991b), 'Antyinflacyjny bastion', *ŻG*, No.9.

Dryll, I. (1991c), '"Patefony" strajkują', *ŻG*, No.28.

Dyba, K. and J.Charap (1990), 'Krok k ozdravení koruny', *HN*, No.34.

Dyker, D. (1990), *Yugoslavia: Socialism, Development and Debt*, London: Routledge.

Ellman, M. (1989), *Socialist Planning*, 2nd edn, Cambridge: Cambridge University Press.

Engels, F. (1969), *Anti-Dühring*, Moscow: Progress Publishers.

Estrin, S. (1983), *Self-Management: Economic Theory and Yugoslav Practice*, Cambridge: Cambridge University Press.

Farkas, R.P. (1975), *Yugoslav Economic Development and Political Change*, New York: Praeger.

Frasyniuk, W. (1992), 'Stanąć na obu nogach', *ŻG*, No.43.

Fronczak, K. (1990), 'Wariant Krakowskie', *ŻG*, No.51-52.

FSÚ (Federální statistický úřad), *Statistická ročenka ČSSR* and *Statistická ročenka ČSFR*, various issues.

Garliński, G. (1992), 'Bariery i oczekiwania', *ŻG*, No.27.

Gliński, B., S.Kuziński and Z.Traczyk (1989), *Centrum w procesie zmian*, Warsaw: Zakład Nauk Zarządzania PAN.

Goldmann, J. (1985), *Strategie ekonomického růstu*, Prague: Academia.

Gomułka, S. (1991a), 'Najpierw szok potem wspinaczka', *Polityka*, No.18.

Gomułka, S. (1991b), 'Twórcza destrukcja', *ŻG*, No.18.

Górski, M. and D.Jaszczyński (1991), 'Makroekonomiczne uwarunkowania i skutki polityki stabilizacyjnej w Polsce', in G.Kołodko (ed.), *Polityka Finansowa Stabilizacja Transformacja*, Warsaw: Instytut Finasów.

Granick, D. (1975), *Enterprise Guidance in Eastern Europe*, Princeton: Princeton University Press.

Graniewska, D. (1991), 'Bezrobotni są wśród nas', *ŻG*, No.45.

Gruszecki, T. (1990), *Prywatyzacja. Stan wyjściowy i analiza programu rządowego*, Warsaw: Stefan Batory Foundation Central and East European Study Programme.

Grzegorczyk, W. (1989), 'Przyczyny rozwoju i skutki występowania gospodarki ukrytej w Polsce', *Handel Wewnętrzny*, No.3-6.

Grzegorzewski, Z. (1992), 'Ucieczka do ... prywatyzacji', *ŻG*, No.5.

GUS (Główny urząd statystyczny), *Rocznik statystyczny*, various issues.

Havlík, P. (1992), 'Srovnání hrubého domácího produktu mezi Východem a Západem: problémy a výsledky', *NH*, No.3.

Havlín, V., J.Chlumský and J.Mihola (1990), 'Váhání, opatrnost, nepřipravenost?', *HN*, No.45.

Hayek, F.A. (1935), *Collectivist Economic Planning*, London: Routledge and Kegan Paul.

Hayek, F.A. (1944), *The Road to Serfdom*, London: G.Routledge and Sons.

Hayek, F.A. (1949), *Individualism and Economic Order*, London: Routledge and Kegan Paul.

Hayek, F.A. (1960), *The Constitution of Liberty*, London: Routledge.

Hejnák, M. and J.Křovák (1991), 'Liberalizace cen a vývoj cenových struktur', *Politická ekonomie*, **39**.

Horkel, V. et al. (1992), 'Současný stav a podpora soukromého podnikání v ČSFR', *NH*, No.6.

Hrnčíř, M. (1990), 'Alternativní přístupy k přestavbě hospodářského mechanismu', *Politická ekonomie*, **38**.

Jarosz, M. (1988), *Samorządność pracownicza: Aspiracje i rzeczywistość*, Warsaw: Książka i Wiedza.

Jarosz, M. (1991), 'Bezrobocie — szkody i pożytki', *Polityka*, No.11.

Ježek, M. (1991), 'Konverze zbrojní výroby', *NH*, No.8.

Ježek, T. (1990), 'Privatizaci chci skončit do tří let', *HN*, No.45.

Jezierski, A. and B.Petz (1988), *Historia gospodarcza Polski ludowej 1944-1985*, Warsaw: Państwowe Wydawnictwo Naukowe.

Jezierski, H. (1989), 'Ratunek dla "Lenina"', *Polityka*, No.24.

Jeziorański, T. (1989), 'Zasadnicze pytania', *ŻG*, No.42.

Jeziorański, T. (1990), 'Bez wyobraźni', *ŻG*, No.1.

Jeziorański, T. and R.Bugaj (1989), 'Ostrożnie z inflacją', *ŻG*, No.13.

Józefiak, C. (1984), 'Tradycyjny system planowania centralnego i kierunki jego ewolucji', in J.Mujżel and S.Jakubowicz (eds), *Funkcjonowanie gospodarki polskiej Doswiadczenia, problemy, tendencje*, Warsaw: Państwowe Wydawnictwo Ekonomiczne.

Kaldor, N. (1985), *Economics without Equilibrium*, Cardiff: Cardiff Press.

Kalecki, M .(1964), *Z Zagadnień gospodarczo-społecznych Polski Ludowej*, Warsaw: Państwowe Wydawnictwo Naukowe.

Kalinová, L. et al. (1990), *Základní rysy přechodu k tržní ekonomice*, Prague: Vysolá škola ekonomická.

Kamušić, M. (1970), in M.J.Broekmeyer (ed.), *Yugoslav Workers' Self-Management*, Dordrecht: D.Reidel Publishing Co.

Káňa, M. (1990), 'Méňě než velí rozum', *HN*, No.16.

Kánský, J., V.Glaser and J.Ungermann (1989), 'Změna dosavadních trendů je nutná', *HN*, No.21.

Karcz, K. (1991), 'O cenach', *ŻG*, No.8.

Karpińska-Mizielińska, W. (1991), 'Przekształcenia własnościowe', *ŻG*, No.24, supplement.

Karpiński, A. (1986), *40 lat planowania w Polsce: problemy, ludzie, refleksje*, Warsaw: Państwowe Wydawnictwo Ekonomiczne.

Kavčič, B. (1972), *Sodobni sociološki problemi samoupravljanja v podjetjih*, Ljubljana: ČZP.

Kędzior, Z. (1991), 'Kondycja gospodarstw domowych', *ŻG*, No.26.

Klacek, J. et al. (1989), *Nerovnováha, inflace a antiinflačni politika*, Prague: Ekonomický ústav Československé akademie věd.

Klacek, J. et al. (1991), *Economic Reform in Czechoslovakia: Current Evaluation*, Prague: Ekonomický ústav Československé akademie věd.

Klaus, V. (1989), *Socialist Economies, Economic Reforms and Economists*, Prague, Prognostický ústav Československé akademie věd.

Klaus, V. (1990), 'Cíle a postupy finanční politiky v roce 1991', *HN*, No.51.

Klaus, V. and V.Rudlovčák (1989), 'Spotřebitelský trh, úspory, chování spotřebitelů a změny vyvolané začínající přestavbou hospodářského mechanismu', typescript, Prague: Prognostický ústav Československé akademie věd.

Klaus, V. and D.Tříska (1988), 'Ekonomické centrum, přestavba a rovnováha', *Politická ekonomie*, **36**.

Kleer, J. (1992), 'Jak nas widzą', *Polityka*, No.17.

Klvačová, E. (1990a), 'Strukturální politika', in V.Izák et al., *Poznámky k ekonomické reformě*, Prague: Ekonomický ústav Československé akademie věd.

Klvačová, E. (1990b), 'Meze možnosti a úskálí zásahů státu', *HN*, No.47.

Kolanda, M. (1984), 'K problémům exportních výkonů podnikové sféry čs. zpracovatelského průmyslu', *Politická ekonomie*, **32**.

Kolanda, M. (1989), 'Strategie rozvoje strojírenského a elektrotechnického průmyslu', *Politická ekonomie*, **37**.

Kolář, J. (1992), 'Mezinárodní srovnání parity kupní síly Kčs u životních nákladů a možnosti aplikace výsledků', *Statistika*, No.7.

Kołodko, G. (1989), *Kryzys Dostosowanie Rozwój*, Warsaw: Państwowe Wydawnictwo Ekonomiczne.

Kołodko, G. (1990), *Inflacja Reforma Stabilizacja*, Warsaw: Studencka Oficyna Wydawnicza ZSP.

Kołodko, G. (1991a), 'Po roku i po szoku', *ŻG*, No.2.

Kołodko, G. (1991b), 'Inflacja i stabilizacja', in G.Kołodko (ed.), *Polityka Finansowa Stabilizacja Transformacja*, Warsaw: Instytut Finansów.

Komárek, V. (1990), 'Alternativní scénáře reformy', *HN*, No.5.

Komárek, V. et al. (1990), *Prognóza a program*, Prague: Academia.

Konečná, M. (1992), 'Bariéry rozvoje', *Ekonom*, No.22.

Kornai, J. (1980), *The Economics of Shortage*, Vol.A, Amsterdam: North Holland.

Kornai, J. (1982), *Growth, Shortage and Efficiency*, Oxford: Basil Blackwell.

Kornai, J. (1990a), *Vision and Reality, Market and State: Contradictions and Dilemmas Revisited*, Budapest: Corvina.

Kornai, J. (1990b), *The Road to a Free Economy*, New York: W.W.Norton.

Korošić, M. (1983), *Ekonomske nejednakosti u jugoslavenskoj privredi*, Zagreb: Sveučilišna naklada Liber.

Kotulan, A. (1990), 'Ceny a daně', in V.Izák et al., *Poznámky k ekonomické reformě*, Prague: Ekonomický ústav Československé akademie věd.

Kouba, K. (1989), 'Economic reform: supply and demand pricing', Paper to IEA conference *Market Forces in Planned Economies*, Moscow, March.

Kowalik, T. (1991), 'W kierunku gospodarki mieszanej', in E.Domańska (ed.), *Pamięci Edwarda Lipińskiego szkice ekonomiczne*, Warsaw: Państwowe Wydawnictwo Ekonomiczne.

Kowalska, M. (1991), 'Słowa kontra słowa', *ŻG*, No.7.

Kozak, M. (1989), *Demokracja związkowa*, Warsaw: Państwowe Wydawnictwo Ekonomiczne.

Kozek, W. (1989), *Reformy gospodarcze a społeczeństwo*, Warsaw: Wydawnictwo Uniwersytetu Warszawskiego.

Kožušník, Č. (1991), 'Strategie privatizace', in V.Komárek (ed.), *Problémy přechodu k demokracii a k tržní ekonomice*, Prague: Prognostický ústav Československé akademie věd.

Krajewski, S. (1985), *Procesy innowacyjne w przemyśle*, Warsaw: Książka i Wiedza.

Kramer, J. (1991a), 'Normalne reakcje', *ŻG*, No.8.

Kramer, J. (1991b), 'Między stabilizacją i destabilizacją', *ŻG*, No.26.

Krejčí, J. (1972), *Social Changes and Stratification in Postwar Czechoslovakia*, London: Macmillan.

Křovák, J. and E.Zamrazilová (1990), 'Analýza přesunu národního důchodu meze republikami', *Politická ekonomie*, **38**.

Kuehnl, K. and J.Obrman (1990), 'Interview with Finance Minister Václav Klaus', *Radio Free Europe Report on Eastern Europe*, 21 September.

Kupka, V. (1992), 'Transformace české ekonomiky Zamyšlení nad zprávou za rok 1991', *Finance a úvěr*, **42**.

Kupka, V. and M.Špak (1987), 'Prognostické práce a strategie čs. rozvoje', *PH*, No.12.

Kuroń, J. (1991), *Moja Zupa*, Warsaw: Polska Oficyna Wydawnicza BGW.

Kurowski, S. and M.Przygodski (1991), 'Program ożywienia', *ŻG*, No.27.

Łaski, K. and J.Zięba (1989), 'Porównanie gospodarki Polski i Hiszpanii', *ŻG*, No.15.

Leopold, A. (1990), 'Założenia polityki rolnej na najblisze lata', *GN*, No.6.

Leopold, A. (1991), 'Porządkowanie rolnictwa', *ŻG*, No.46.

Lewandowski, J. (1991), 'Sztuka tego co możliwe', *ŻG*, No.29.

Lewandowski, J. and J.Szomburg (1990), 'Dekalog prywatyzacji', *TS*, No.45, supplement.

Lipowski, A. (1990), 'Równoważenie gospodarki', in M.Kozak (ed.), *Z analizy procesów reformy gospodarczej w latach 1987-1988*, Warsaw: Ossolineum.

Lipton, D. and J.Sachs (1990), 'Creating a market economy in Eastern Europe: The case of Poland', *Brookings Papers on Economic Activity*, 1.

Maj, H. (1990), 'Hamowanie inflacji', *ŻG*, No.40.

Maj, H. (1991a), 'Do wymiany', *ŻG*, No.14.

Maj, H. (1991b), 'Czterotakt Balcerowicza', *ŻG*, No.17.

Maj, H. (1991c), 'Proces dostosowań mikroekonomicznych', in G.Kołodko (ed.), *Polityka Finansowa Stabilizacja Transformacja*, Warsaw: Instytut Finansów.

Masłyk-Musiał, E. and J.Panków (1990), *Ministerstwa w reformie gospodarczej*, Wrocław: Ossolineum.

Matějka, M. (1990), 'Ekonomika nelze vidět černobíle', *HN*, No.7.

Mencinger, J. (1992), 'From a capitalist to a capitalist economy', in J.Simmie and J.Dekleva (eds), *Yugoslavia in Turmoil: After Self-Management*, London: Pinter.

Mieszczankowski, M. (1988), 'Spuścizna drugiego etapu', *ŻG*, No.47.

Mieszczankowski, M. and L.Pawlicki (1989), 'Kto w Polsce dużo zarabia', *ŻG*, No.19.

Mihailović, K. (1981), *Ekonomska stvarnost Jugoslavije*, Belgrade: Ekonomika.

Mikołajczyk, Z. (1989), 'Niewiadomo układu docelowego', *ŻG*, No.2 & 3.

Mises, L. von (1936), *Socialism: An Economic and Sociological Analysis*, London: Cape.

Mises, L. von (1949), *Human Action: A Treatise on Economics*, London: W.Hodge.

Mlčoch, L. (1990), 'Syntéza deskriptivních analýz tradičního modelu II', *Politická ekonomie*, **38**.

Młynarczyk, W. (1991), 'Zamierzenia produkcyjne rolników', *GN*, No.16.

Modzelewski, K. (1991), 'Francuskie ciastko', *ŻG*, No.42.

Mujżel, J. (1990), 'Instytucje i narzędzia polityki społeczno-gospodarczey na progu II etapu reformy', in M.Kozak (ed.), *Z analizy procesów reformy gospodarczej w latach 1987-1988*, Warsaw: Ossolineum.

Mujżel, J. (1991), 'Propozycja dla rządu', *ŻG*, No.25.

Myant, M. (1981), *Socialism and Democracy in Czechoslovakia 1945-1948*, Cambridge: Cambridge University Press.

Myant, M. (1982), *Poland: A Crisis for Socialism*, London: Lawrence & Wishart.

Myant, M. (1989a), *The Czechoslovak Economy 1948-1988: The Battle for Economic Reform*, Cambridge: Cambridge University Press.

Myant, M. (1989b), 'Poland — the permanent crisis?', in R.Clarke (ed.), *Poland: The Economy in the 1980s*, Harlow: Longman.

Myant, M. (1992), 'Centre—periphery relations in Czechoslovakia', *The Journal of Interdisciplinary Economics*, **4**.

Nachtigal, V. (1991), 'K reálnosti temp československých makroagregátů', *Politická ekonomie*, **39**.

NEDO (National Economic Development Office) (1976), *A Study of the UK Nationalised Industries*, London: HMSO.

Nefová, E. (1992), 'Platební neschopnost podniků, zásoby a úvěry', *NH*, No.2.

Niskanen, W.A. (1971), *Bureaucracy and Representative Government*, Chicago: Aldine-Atherton.

Nove, A. (1991), *The Economics of Feasible Socialism Revisited*, London: Harper Collins.

Nowak, K. (1992), 'Kto handluje ten żyje?', *Polityka*, No.2.

Obradović, J. and W.Dunn (eds)(1978), *Workers' Self-Management and Organizational Power in Yugoslavia*, Pittsburg: University of Pittsburg.

Okun, A. (1981), *Prices and Quantities: A Macroeconomic Analysis*, Oxford: Basil Blackwell.

Olšovský, R. (1992), 'Vývoj platební bilance ČSFR v roce 1991', *Finance a úvěr*, **42**.

Outrata, R. (1991), 'Základné národohospodárske východiská stratégie priemyselnej politiky v SR', *NH*, No.4.

Pajestka, J. (1981), *Polski kryzys lat 1980-1981*, Warsaw: Książka i Wiedza.

Peters, T. and R.Waterman (1982), *In Search of Excellence*, New York: Harper & Row.

Pick, M. (1990), 'Cesta ke směnitelnosti', *HN*, No.24.

Pick, M. (1992), 'Alternativy hospodářské politiky', *NH*, No.2.

Poprzeczko, J. (1991), 'Przeciw utopii liberalnej', *Polityka*, No.6.

Pościk, B. (1991), 'W "lekkim" po roku szoku', *ŻG*, No.30.

Prašnikar, J. (1983-4), 'The Yugoslav self-managed firm and its behaviour', *Eastern European Economics*, Winter.

Rakowski, M. (1991), *Jak się to stało*, Warsaw: Polska Oficyna Wydawnicza.

Rosati, D. (1990), 'Pytania bez odpowiedzi', *ŻG*, No.37.

Rosati, D. (1991), 'W podwójnym Nelsonie', *ŻG*, No.18.

Sadowska-Cieślak,E. and J.Olszewski (1991), 'Niech mówią liczby', *ŻG*, No.30.

Sanford, G. and M.Myant (1991), 'Poland', in S.White (ed.), *Handbook of Reconstruction in Eastern Europe and the Soviet Union*, Harlow: Longman.

Schumpeter, J. (1953), *Capitalism, Socialism and Democracy*, London: Allen & Unwin.

Schumpeter, J. (1954), *History of Economic Analysis*, London: Oxford University Press.

Šifter, I. (1978), *Direktor iskustvo i praksa*, Belgrade: Privredni Pr egled.

Šíp, E. (1992), 'Ceny spotřebitelského trhu − úvahy a předpovědi', *Finance a úvěr*, **41**.

Sirc, L. (1979), *The Yugoslav Economy under Self-Management*, London: Macmillan.

Śmiłowski, E. (1991), 'Niepokój o przyszłość', *Polityka*, No.4.

Smuga, T. (1991), 'Zatrudnienie', *ŻG*, No.24, supplement.

Sochor, L. (1984), *Contribution to the Analysis of the Conservative Features of the Ideology of 'Real Socialism'*, Cologne: Index.

Sonntag, K. (1991), 'Mieć by dać', *Polityka*, No.17.

Štěpánek, V. (1989), *Společné podniky v socialistických zemích*, Prague: Ekonomický ústav Československé akademie věd.

Šujan, I. (1990), 'Československá ekonomika na rázcestiach − je reálny návrat medzi vyspelé krajiny?', *NH*, No.2.

Šulc, Z. (1990a), *Jak se zrodil západoněmecký 'hospodářský zázrak'*, Prague: Práce.

Šulc, Z. (1990b), 'Snaha rozdávat nikam nevede', *HN*, No.18.

Šulc, Z. (1990c), 'Vůz nelze zapřahat před koně', *HN*, No.12.

Szomburg, J. (1990), 'Prywatyzacja recesja restrukturyzacja', *ŻG*, No.45.

Tański, A. (1991), 'Koło zamachowe?', *Polityka*, No.37.

Tarnowski, P. and R.Bugaj (1989), 'W pół drogi', *Polityka*, No.15.

Teichová, A. (1988), *The Czechoslovak Economy 1918-1980*, London: Routledge.

Tesařová, D. (1992), 'Nezaměstnanost v ČSFR', *Statistika*, No.7.

Tomal, D. (1989), 'Lenin w likwidacji', *Polityka*, No.2.

Turek, O. (1989), 'Podklad pro "říjnový" materiál PgÚ − úsek rozvíjení reformy', typescript, Prague: Prognostický ústav Československé akademie věd.

Turek, O. (1990), 'O reformě pragmaticky', *HN*, No.16.

Turek, O. (1991), 'Koncepce transformace: v čem podpořit, v čem korigovat', in V.Komárek (ed.), *Problémy přechodu k demokracii a k tržní ekonomice*, Prague: Prognostický ústav Československé akademie věd.

Turek, O. (1992), *Zamyšlení nad strategií transformace*, Prague: Prpgnostický ústav Československé akademie věd.

Tyson, L. (1980), *The Yugoslav System and its Performance in the 1970s*, Berkeley: University of California.

Vácha, S. (1988), *Jak řídí Slušovice*, Prague: Novinář.

Veselý, Z. (1992), 'Platební neschopnost v roce 1991', *Finance a úvěr*, 42.

Vickers, J. and G.Yarrow (1988), *Privatization: An Economic Analysis*, Cambridge, Massachusetts: MIT Press.

Vintrová, R. (1992), 'Možnosti oživení', *Ekonom*, No.17.

Vít, J. (1990), 'Dolar za 24 korun?', *Profit*, No.5.

Vít, J. (1992), 'Cíle a nástroje měnové politiky v roce 1992', *Finance a úvěr*, **42**.

Vráblík, J. and M.Kocevová (1992), 'Konverze zbrojní výroby', *NH*, No.6.

Wilczak, J. (1992), 'Pożegnanie z mitem', *ŻG*, No.25.

Winiecki, J. (1991), 'Zbyt powolna zmiana systemu', *GN*, No.3.

World Bank (1988), *Polska: reforma, dostosowanie i wzrost*, Warsaw: Wydawnictwo Interpress.

Wróbel, E. (1991), 'Uroki kapitalizmu', *ŻG*, No.51-2.

Záhorka, J. (1991), 'K problémům regulace trhu zemědělských výrobků', *Finance a úvěr*, **41**.

Zarzecki, J. (1990), 'Mechanizacja a proces koncentracji w rolnictwie chłopskim', *Wieś i rolnictwo*, **68**.

Index